Created and Directed by Hans Höfer

INSIGHT GUIDES

SARDINIA

Edited by Joachim Chwaszcza
Photography by Joachim Chwaszcza, Franco Stephano
Ruiu, Rainer Pauli and others
Managing Editor: Joachim Beust

Translated by Jane Michael-Rushmer

APA PUBLICATIONS

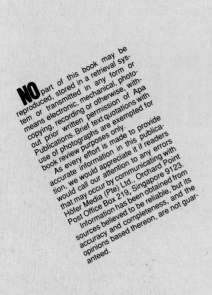
SARDINIA

First Edition
© 1991 APA PUBLICATIONS (HK) LTD
All Rights Reserved
Printed in Singapore by Höfer Press Pte. Ltd

ABOUT THIS BOOK

I t isn't all that long ago that Sardinia was disparagingly referred to as "India in the middle of Europe". One former Italian viceroy was less than complimentary about the island's inhabitants: "The vices to which these people are most commonly inclined are theft, murder and deception".

Insight Guide: Sardinia, combining penetrating prose with stunning photography, aims to paint a rather more objective picture of the island and its people. The philosophy guiding the Insight series has been that, in a crowded publishing market, too many guidebooks content themselves with anodyne prose and picture-postcard photography. Yet why should a country's warts be omitted? They can often be as interesting as beauty spots and usually make the destination more enticing to the adventurous traveller.

In Sardinia, however, the beauty spots predominate: splendid seaside resorts such as Porto Rotondo or Porto Cervo on the Costa Smeralda coexist with such places as Orgosolo, once the stronghold of Sardinian bandits. Monuments in stone to the ancient Nuraghe culture bow before today's steel creations of the petrochemical industry. The sandy shores of the coast give way to the rugged, barren hills and mountains of the interior. Traditional folk festivals compete with the sounds of the disco on the beach.

The people, too, are nothing if not distinctive. John Warre Tyndale, in his three-volume *Island of Sardinia*, published in London in 1849, wrote: "It may be said of the Sardes in general that they are honourable, liberal, and given to hospitality, retaining most of the qualities of a simple and unsophisticated life, and, as Plutarch observes of Aratus and men of similar dispositions, 'Virtue in them is the produce of nature, unassisted by science, like the fruits of the forest, which come without the least cultivation'." In more recent times, Peter Nichols wrote in his 1973 book *Italia, Italia*: "To be in central Sardinia is to live among people who have rejected every element of what is proudly called European civilisation: the Phoenicians were there and the Romans and the Byzantines, and the Genoese and the Spaniards and the Piedmontese and now the Italians, and it is as though they had never been. They have all been rejected."

The Writers

The task of producing the book was entrusted to project editor **Joachim Chwaszcza**, a Munich-based freelance writer and photographer who in this volume puts the same kind of emphasis on relevant and accurate information as he did for three other titles brought out recently by Apa Publications – *City Guide: Prague*, *Insight Guide: Yemen* and *Pocket Guide: Sardinia*.

Chwaszcza's first task was to locate authors who would combine the in-depth knowledge and first-class writing abilities demanded by Insight Guides. He turned first to **Dr Rainer Pauli**, who works in the field of systems engineering at Munich's Technical University. The author of a comprehensive guide to Sardinia's art and cultural heritage, Dr Pauli is widely recognised as an authority on the island. He contributed chapters on the island's history and on subjects as diverse as language, the Shepherd's Knife and the Cork Oak, and also provided a number of photographs of his "second home".

Chwaszcza

Pauli

Massaiu

Merlin-Massaiu

Wofftraud de Concini lives, writes and translates in Trento in northern Italy, and has written extensively about Sardinia. As well as contributing to the History section of the book, she wrote the chapters on Sassari and the area from Alghero to Oristano.

Among the Sardinian contributors, mention should first be made of **Mario Massaiu**. Born in Oliena, he attained his doctorate in comparative studies of literature in Milan. Massaiu is not only an expert on the works of Sardinia's best-known writer Grazia Deledda, about whom he wrote a feature for this book, but he also knows his native region of Barbaggia like the back of his hand. A correspondent for a number of Italian newspapers, he was awarded the coveted prize for literature *Premio Grazia Deledda* in 1971. His work in this book ranges from chapters on history and features on banditry and murals to Places chapters on Cagliari, the area from Cagliari to Olbia, and the Barbagia.

His wife **Clotilde Merlin-Massaiu**, who has collaborated with him on a number of books, contributed the article on caves and cavers to *Insight Guide: Sardinia*.

Antonio Bassu lives in Nuoro, where he works as a journalist for the newspaper *Nuova Sardegna*. He also works in television and as recently made a name for himself as an author. He wrote this book's chapter on food and drink.

Leandro Muoni, president of the Associazione Nuovi Scrittori Sardi, wrote about Sardinian folklore.

Cora Fischer, one of Germany's best-known "society" journalists, wrote the chapter on the high-society playground of the Costa Smeralda, an area she has monitored for many years.

The Photographers

Insight Guide: Sardinia maintains the same high standard of photography for which Apa guides have become renowned. **Franco Stephano Ruiu**, from Nuoro, has been photographing festivals and village life in his native country for many years. **Jörg Reuther**, a regular contributor to Insight Guides, provided many of the best shots.

Thanks are due to ESIT and **Signori Marongiu** and **Nardi** in Cagliari for their support and assistance in the creation of the book. **Stefano Albertini** and **Martina Kiderle** translated the Sardinian authors' texts. The translator responsible for the English edition of the book was **Jane Michael-Rushmer**.

Muoni   *Bassu*   *Reuther*

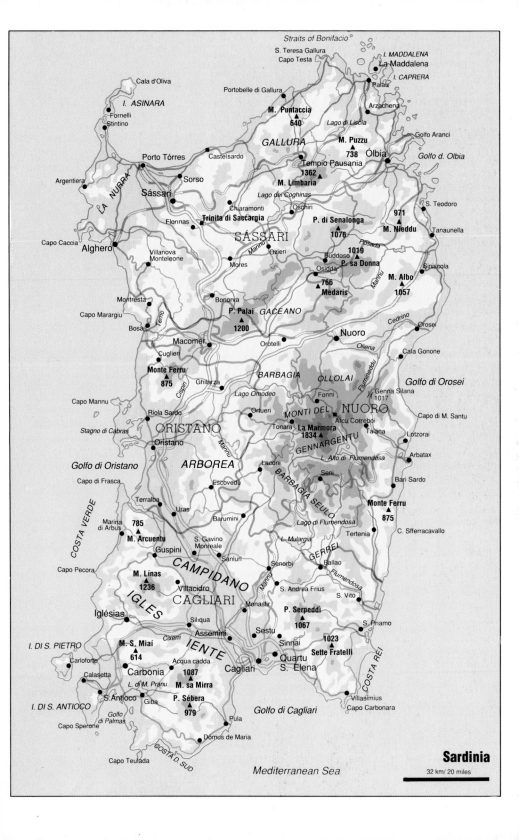

Sardinia

32 km/ 20 miles

Straits of Bonifacio

S. Teresa Gallura
Capo Testa
I. MADDALENA
La-Maddalena
I. CAPRERA
Palau
Portobelle di Gallura
Arzachena
Cala d'Oliva
I. ASINARA
M. Puntaccia
640
Lago di Liscia
Golfo Aranci
Fornelli
Stintino
M. Puzzu
738
Ólbia
Golfo d. Olbia
Porto Tórres
Castelsardo
GALLURA
Tempio Pausania
1362
Argentiera
Sorso
M. Limbaria
Lago del Coghinas
S. Teodoro
LA NURRA
Sássari
Chiaramonti
Oschiri
Tanaunella
Florinas
Trinita di Saccargia
971
M. Nieddu
Capo Caccia
SÁSSARI
Ozieri
Posada
Siniscola
Alghero
Villanova
Monteleone
Mores
P. di Senalonga
1076
Buddoso
1019
P. sa Donna
M. Albo
1057
Mannu
Osidda
766
Mannu
Montresta
Bonorva
Medaris
P. Palai
GACEANO
Cedrino
Orosei
Capo Marargiu
1200
Bosa
Teno
Macomer
Orotelli
Nuoro
Oliena
Cala Gonone
Cuglieri
Ghilarza
BARBAGIA
OLLOLAI
Golfo di Orosei
Monte Ferru
875
Cispiri
Lago Omodeo
Fonni
Genna Silana
1017
Capo Mannu
Ortueri
MONTI DEL
NUORO
Capo di M. Santu
Riola Sardo
Flumineddu
Arcu Correboi
Stagno di Cabras
ORISTANO
Tonara
La Marmora
1834
Talana
Lotzorai
Oristano
ARBOREA
GENNARGENTU
Arbatax
Golfo di Oristano
Laconi
Seni
L. Alto di Flumendosa
Bari Sardo
Capo di Frasca
Escovedu
BARBAGIA SEULO
Terralba
Uras
Monte Ferru
875
Marina
di Arbus
785
Barumini
Lago di Flumendosa
C. Sfferracavallo
M. Arcuentu
S. Gavino
Monreale
L. Mulargia
Tertenia
Capo Pecora
Guspini
Sanluri
GERREI
CAMPIDANO
Senorbi
Ballao
M. Linas
1236
Villacidro
Mannu
S. Andrea Frius
Flumendosa
S. Vito
IGLES
CAGLIARI
Monastir
I. DI S. PIETRO
Iglésias
Siliqua
P. Serpeddi
1067
S. Priamo
M. S. Miai
614
Assemini
Sestu
1023
Carloforte
Cixerri
Sinnai
Sette Fratelli
Calasetta
Acqua cadda
IENTE
1087
Quartu
S. Elena
COSTA REI
Carbonia
M. sa Mirra
Cagliari
L. di M. Pranu
S. Antioco
Giba
P. Sébera
979
Villasimius
I. DI S. ANTIOCO
Pula
Golfo di Cagliari
Capo Carbonara
Golfo
di Palmas
Dómus de Maria
Capo Sperone
COSTA D. SUD
Capo Teulada
Mediterranean Sea
COSTA VERDE

History

Features

Maps

TRAVEL TIPS

WHY SARDINIA IS DIFFERENT

Should you chance to encounter a Sardinian shepherd as he drives his flock across the parched and shimmering slopes of the Gennargentu in summer, you can expect to find yourself gazing into a pair of bleak, grim eyes. His face, bearing traces of a life of hardship, is marked by exposure to the sun and the elements. He tends to be suspicious of strangers – not because he does not appreciate the value of an hospitable gesture, but because he is careful by nature. For centuries strangers have come here, exploiting and taking advantage of the local population. For him, the tourists of today are no different – they, too, come from across the sea. And, according to a Sardinian proverb – those who "come from across the sea bring evil with them."

The island's history is characterised by a succession of foreign rulers and powers. Phoenicians and Romans, Arabs and Spaniards, Savoyards and Italians, and, last but not least, an army of international holidaymakers. Each has left his mark, seldom to the advantage of countryside and people. And so the Sardinians have learned to maintain a distance between themselves and external influences.

True Sardinians are more often brusque than warm, and of a melancholy disposition. You will rarely hear a Sardinian laugh out loud. With his *berretta* – the traditional headgear of the Sardinians and not the Basques – pulled well down over his face and his brow furrowed, he will stand with his friends, smoking and telling stories which they may well have heard hundreds of times before.

D.H. Lawrence visited Sardinia in 1921. After staying only a few days he was able to describe the island in his book *Sea and Sardinia* better than many other visitors: "Sardinia is not up-and-down at all, but running away into the distance… This gives a sense of space, which is so lacking in Italy… It is like liberty itself, after the peaky confinement of Sicily."

Little has changed since his visit – at least, as regards its fundamental character. It is not really an island at all, but rather a miniature continent. The individual regions are completely different from one another, and villages which may lie only a few miles from each other will often seem worlds apart. Today, modern development is slowly obscuring the traces of the past. *Insight Guide: Sardinia* is not intended as a catalogue of beaches but rather as a description of the culture and traditions of the island. It aims not to focus on tourism as such, but rather on Sardinia itself.

Preceding pages: weather-worn cliffs; even the walls are used for politics; strong winds make Sardinia's coast popular with surfers; rural workers during the *s'ardia* in Sedilo. Left, regional costume from Barbagia.

Sardinia is an island – a bald statement which nonetheless summarises the factor which has had the greatest influence on this "forgotten island" across the millennia; on its history, its civilisation and its economy. The natural boundary which the sea provides has often offered complete or partial protection from peace-shattering events taking place on the mainland, affording the island a considerable degree of cultural autonomy at all times. Fundamental changes came about largely as a result of outside influences; indeed, everything which was new and strange invariably came from "across the sea". As in virtually all other Romance languages, there is a Sardinian word for "stranger" (*istranzu*) based on the Latin (*estraneus*). It is, however, typical that even today one should encounter a preference for the euphemism *kie venit dae su mare*; for the Sardinian, everything which is "strange" inevitably "comes from across the sea".

The first Sardinians: There seems little doubt that the first inhabitants were themselves people who came from across the sea, but who they were and when the island was first settled is less certain. Until recently the accepted authoritative opinion was that the first colonists arrived here at the beginning of the Neolithic Era, i.e. approximately 8,000 years ago. But stone tools have now been found near Perfugas in northern Sardinia, and geological evidence so far suggests that they date from the warm inter-glacial period between the Riss and the Würm Ice Ages some 200,000 to 120,000 years ago. Latest finds could reach back still further into the Palaeolithic Era if their allocation to the so-called Early Clactonian Period (approximately 700,000 years ago) is confirmed. Fairly precise dating was possible, on the other hand, in the case of animal and human bones from the Late Palaeolithic Era (12,000 to 35,000 years ago), found in the Grotta Corbeddu, a cave near Oliena. These leave no doubt that Sardinia was already inhabited during the Old Stone Age.

Preceding pages: staircase to the well-temple of Santa Christina. Left, *domus de janas* in Ossi. Right, well-temple of Predio Canopoli.

It seems likely that the first "Sardinians" came from the European mainland. During glacial periods large quantities of water were frozen as ice sheets, causing the level of the sea to be lowered by more than 300 ft (100 metres). Thus Sardinia and Corsica formed one large island, only separated from the coast of Tuscany – which then jutted much further into the sea than it does now – by a relatively narrow strip of water. This proved to be no great obstacle for men, or for animals which were good swimmers, such as

deer. Evidence seems to indicate that, after this, Sardinia remained cut off from the continent for many thousands of years. It was not until the beginning of the Neolithic Era that a completely different race of men appeared on the island. They had already learned to make clay pots and clearly had reached a more advanced stage of civilisation. It may be that the first Sardinians suffered the same fate as the Indians of North America or the Amazon basin.

For the new arrivals, Sardinia must have seemed like a land of milk and honey. Here they found everything they needed for a peaceful existence: dense forests filled with game, broad lagoons with an inexhaustible supply of fish and shellfish, fertile plains and rolling hills for arable farming, cattle raising, and – above all – obsidian, their "black gold". Lumps of this black volcanic glass as big as a fist or even a head can be found in large quantities on Monte Arci, an extinct volcano east of Oristano. Razor-sharp splinters of obsidian were ideal for the manufacture of tools and weapons of all kinds, so that the substance became the most prized raw material of the New Stone Age, and was often traded across distances of more than 620 miles (1,000 km). Even 6,000 years BC the obsidian export routes radiating out from Monte Arci reached via Corsica as far as the

the first sites where each was discovered: the Bonu Ighinu Culture (*circa* 4000–3500 BC) and the Ozieri Culture (3500–2700 BC).

Some of the artefacts are true works of art: sophisticated pottery of remarkable quality, artistically decorated with pictorial and geometric forms, engraved or scratched before firing and sometimes filled out in colour; perfectly formed stone vessels or female cult statues, mostly of limestone – the older ones round and naturalistic, the younger ones slim and heavily stylised and bearing a strong resemblance to the more familiar religious effigies from the Eastern Mediterranean (the Cyclades and Anatolia). Their true significance is not clear; they are usually inter-

South of France – trade contacts which were doubtless an important reason for the high level of civilisation attained in Sardinia during the Neolithic Era.

Early Golden Age: During the fourth millennium BC, the farmers, shepherds and fishermen of Sardinia had already achieved a considerable degree of cultural independence and originality. Tools, pottery, burial gifts, funeral rites and way of life corresponded to a fairly uniform conception of lifestyle and customs which have been further developed and refined over the centuries. Archaeologists have named the two principal periods of this development after

preted as symbols of a mother goddess, but in any case they are obviously of religious importance.

Like the ceramic *objets d'art* – which are elaborately adorned with magic symbols – the idols were mostly found in graves, but also at places of worship: Monte d'Accodi, near Sassari, is a sort of tiered mound whose similarity to the ziggurats of Mesapotamia is as striking as it is inexplicable. The most remarkable relics of these deeply religious cultures are the burial chambers – well over 1,000 of them, hewn from the solid rock with primitive stone chisels.

The simplest of the tombs were constructed during the period of the Bonu Ighinu civilisation, i.e. the fourth millennium BC They consist merely of a hidden vertical entrance shaft and a small chamber, which was usually only large enough for one body. Because of their spherical shape these tombs were known in Sardinian as *forredus* (ovens). Later on several such chambers were linked together to form underground "burial apartments", with a common antechamber – often high enough to permit a man to stand – and an entrance corridor.

At the time it was believed that life continued after death on a different plane; the dead were therefore brought to their last resting place – often in skeletal form – with house-

lent. The walls of the tombs are often adorned with bas-reliefs of magic symbols: more or less stylised bulls' heads, motifs of horns, spirals and other geometric patterns; even remains of murals (mostly red ochre in colour) can often still be seen. A powerful torch is an essential item during any exploration. Particularly impressive are the necropolises of Sant'Andrea Priu near Bornova, and Montessu near Santadi, where several dozen tombs are linked, forming a town of the dead.

A violent transition: With the end of the Neolithic Era and the start of the Bronze Age there began a transitional period of approximately 1,000 years, often known as the Cop-

hold items and supplies of food. Some of the burial vaults consist of more than 20 chambers; many imitated so precisely on a smaller scale the wooden houses of the period, with ridge pole, roof spars, supporting columns, fireplace, sleeping area, doors and windows that the Sardinians called them *domus de janas*. According to local superstition the *janas* (fairies) are tiny female creatures who live in these houses (*domus*). They are powerful but unfortunately not always benevo-

per Stone Age. It was a time of violent change, about which very little is known, archaeologically speaking. The ramparts which were built around previously peaceful villages were typical of this restless epoch, as was the relatively rapid pace at which the various cultural periods succeeded each other: the Abealzu-Filigosa (*circa* 2700–2500 BC), the Monte Claro (*circa* 2500–2000 BC), and the Glockenbecher (*circa* 2000–1800 BC). New influences and new arrivals brought the entire "inventory" of western megalithic culture to the island: dolmens, standing graves, obelisks, stone circles, rows of menhirs and even well-de-

Left, the most famous Nuraghi village in Sardinia, **Su Nuraxi**. **Above**, Santa Sabina near Macomer, linking the Nuraghi with Christendom.

veloped menhir statues hitherto only found in some regions of Northern Italy and Southern France. This cultural heritage was to give birth to Sardinia's great Bronze Age civilisation, the earliest phase of which was known as the Bonnanaro Culture (*circa* 1800–1600 BC).

The Nuraghi Civilisation: This lasted from around 1800 to 500 BC. Sometime during the first half of the second millennium BC the first *nuraghi* appeared, dotted across the Sardinian countryside like upturned giant buckets. These squat circular towers were constructed without the use of mortar from massive blocks of stone. Even today, some of these structures up to 50ft (15 metres) high

are still standing, the largest and technically most perfect megalithic buildings in Europe. They are found only in Sardinia, in awe-inspiring profusion. Today some 7,000 are registered as historic monuments; 3,000 years ago, there must have been 10,000 of them. There is nowhere else in the world where travellers will find themselves so frequently confronted with prehistory. On average you can expect to come across a *nuraghe* every 6,600 ft (2,000 metres) of the island's 9,250 sq. miles (24,000 sq. km). In some places the towers are only a few hundred yards apart: on the high basalt plateau surrounding Macomer and Abbasanta, in the

fertile hills of the Trexenta and Marmilla, or on the Sinis peninsula near the modern town of Oristano.

What purpose was served by these thousands of towers – and who were the builders? The very fact that the men who constructed them are known as the Nuraghi, and their civilisation as the Nuraghi Culture, is indicative of the dilemma. The concept of the *nuraghe* dominates our entire picture of this people, whose lack of a written language meant they had no means of leaving records for us to decipher.

Throughout prehistoric times there is no comparable example of such frenzied building activity exercised by a people across several centuries. It is tempting to draw comparisons with the gigantic statues of Easter Island. It is certainly true that, stemming from their isolation and the resulting "cultural inbreeding", island societies do have a tendency to over-emphasise or even to produce monstrous exaggerations of elements also found in other societies. The *nuraghi*, however, are not the grotesque invention of some island race completely cut off from the rest of the world. The people traded vigorously with the other countries of the Mediterranean, and their civilisation produced a number of remarkable achievements, such as the exquisite spa temples, and the enchanting bronze statuettes which were placed in the temples as votive gifts. As far as we can judge today, the Nuraghi appear to have reached the highest standards of all Bronze Age cultures in the western Mediterranean, at least as regards architecture, metallurgy and sculpture.

The basic form of a *nuraghe* is a blunt-topped cone – a round tower which becomes narrower towards the top, and which ends in a platform. An entrance corridor at ground level leads to the interior, a more or less concentric circular room with a domed vaulted roof. This classic design is thus known as a Domed *nuraghe* or Tholos *nuraghe*. The *tholoi*, such as the famous "Treasury of Atreus", were beehive-shaped Mycenean tombs built of rings of stones; the diameter of each layer was smaller than the previous one, resulting in a dome in the shape of a pointed arch or an oval. The largest, and perhaps the finest dome, is that surmounting the Nuraghe Is Paras near Isili. Both the Myceneans and the Nuraghi built these domed structures from about the 16th century BC. Is there any connection? Recent investigations have shown that the basic principles on which the Myceneans built their underground vaulted tombs were quite different from those upon which the Nuraghi constructed their domes. The larger *nuraghi* towers consist of up to three storeys of rooms, each smaller than the one beneath. A staircase was then hollowed out of the walls – which were in any case constructed without the use of mortar. It led around the vaulted ceilings to the upper rooms and finally to the roof platform.

What purpose did these towers serve? Their ancient name, *nuraghi*, gives us no

frequently encountered suffix *kastru* (from the Latin *castrum*) indicates, the Romans regarded the *nuraghi* as "Kastelle" (forts).

In fact, apart from the solitary *nuraghe* towers there are also hundreds of *nuraghi* settlements of all sizes, ranging from a pair of neighbouring towers linked by two walls enclosing a courtyard to full-size fortresses consisting of a dozen *nuraghi* forming a turretted citadel and surrounded by a protective wall enclosing several courtyards, wells and storage rooms in case of siege. The largest and most interesting *nuraghe* complexes are the Nuraghe Santu Antine near Torralba, the Nuraghe Losa near Paulilatino, the Nuraghe Su Nuraxi near Barumini and

clue, for its original meaning has been lost across the millennia. Over the course of the centuries, travellers and scholars have produced a whole range of fanciful explanations or elaborated complex theories (and defended them with passion): tombs, mausoleums, "towers of silence" (where the dead were placed until they had been reduced to skeletons), "sleeping towers" (where one could escape the attacks of mosquitoes by sleeping at higher altitudes), sun temples, kilns or astronomic observatories. As the

Left, Nuraghi bronze figure in the museum in Cagliari. **Above**, Nuraghi stele in the museum.

the Nuraghe Arrubiu near Orroli. The function of these strongholds was probably similar to that of a medieval castle: in peacetime they may have been the official residence of a tribal chief, but were likely to serve as the centre of a wide range of communal activities (lookout, store, for the performance of religious rites etc.). In time of war they also provided a refuge for the inhabitants of the surrounding villages.

The military nature of these *nuraghi* fortresses is evident from the numerous defensive strategic features, such as the embrasures or the overhanging balustrades which once surmounted the towers and walls. Unfortunately no example of the latter has survived, but the island's museums contain a number of stone or bronze models of *nuraghi*, originally used for ritual purposes and showing their powerful overall impression and the method of construction used. The superstructures rested on huge stone bases and overhung the main tower by about one yard. On some *nuraghi* – for example, on the parapet of the well in the courtyard of the Nuraghe Su Nuraxi near Barumini – one can still see the stones employed, each weighing over a ton. Strategic refinements of this nature seem to be unique in the entire western Mediterranean, and apparently also in the Aegean. Thus for many years it was assumed

tion and agriculture flourished, and they mention the "numerous and magnificent buildings", referring to them as *daidaleia* – thus attributing them to Daedalus, their national hero. According to legend, the latter built the famous labyrinth for King Minos of Crete before fleeing to Sicily, whence he travelled on to Sardinia with a group of Greek settlers.

Whatever the truth of the matter, the Greek writers were apparently so impressed that they considered it imperative to deceive posterity into thinking that the achievements of the Nuraghi were the product of Greek intellectual and practical ingenuity. Even though, in recent years, archaeologists have

that these perfectly designed and highly complex *nuraghi* citadels must be of much more recent date. Today it has been proved beyond doubt that all *nuraghi* – even the largest complexes – were built during the second millennium BC. Recent excavations in Barumini even unearthed the remains of a balustrade that dated from the 13th/14th century BC.

Origins: The geographers and historians of Ancient Greece were among the first to try to solve the riddle as to who built the *nuraghi*. They believed Sardinia to be the largest island in the Mediterranean, describing it as a place of freedom and happiness. Civilisa-

found increasing evidence of close trading links between the Myceneans and the Nuraghi from at least the 14th century BC, it has nevertheless become clear that the Golden Age of the Nuraghian civilisation was the cause, and not merely the effect, of this contact. Comparatively insignificant cultures, such as that on the neighbouring island of Corsica, offered no attractions as trading partners.

Nuraghi can be found only on Sardinia. This means that their culture, too, must be indigenous. It obviously did not grow out of nothing, but was based on the existing cultural traditions of the western Mediterranean. Irrefutable evidence for this fact can be found in the so-called graves of the giants, a type of burial place whose origins go back to the beginning of the second millennium BC and which the Nuraghi developed and maintained for over 1,000 years.

Graves of the giants: The tombs of the men who built the *nuraghi* are as monumental as the towers themselves. The Sardinians call these burial places, which are 32–100 ft (10–30 metres) long, *tumbas de sos zigantes* (in Italian: *tombe di giganti*). The graves of the giants – like the *nuraghi* – have no obvious parallel on the mainland. The base of one such grave is formed by a burial chamber, between 16 and 50 ft (5 and 15 metres) long

tombs on Sardinia took on their characteristic form. On each side of the entrance, at right angles to the main chamber of the grave, a pair of walls was added. They demarcate a semicircular forecourt 32–65 ft (10–20 metres) wide, forming an imposing facade and lending the grave a monumental air.

In the case of the older graves (*circa* 1800–1400 BC) this impression is underlined by a finely chiselled stone stele some 10–13 ft (3–4 metres) tall, resembling an imposing doorway, with a tiny opening at ground level which could be closed by a stone and which served as an entrance to the grave. In the vicinity of the grave there are often vertical stone obelisks which may symbolise gods or

and 3–6 ft (1–2 metres) high. It is constructed from well-matched stones and is usually covered by a more carelessly constructed burial mound which looks from the outside like the hull of an upturned boat.

Thus far, the method of construction resembles the megalithic standing graves commonly found between France and southern Italy. At the beginning of the second millennium BC, however, during the early years of the Nuraghian civilisation, the

Left, Grave of the Giants Lu Coddu Cecchio near Arzachena. **Above**, archaeological site at the Grave of the Giants of San Cosimo near Arbus.

ancestors watching over the dead. These menhirs are known as *baityloi* (Italian: *betili*). The word is derived from the Hebrew *beth-el*, "Home of the Deity". The forecourt contains sacrificial graves, a fireplace and often an encircling stone platform used as a seat or table for the sacrificial offerings. This was where the funeral rites and commemorative ceremonies in honour of the dead were held. The members of a tribal group, clan or village met to pay their respects to the dead, who were buried here by the community without rank or privilege, and without funeral gifts of any value.

The graves of the giants constructed by the

Nuraghi should be seen rather as charnel houses, in which the bones of the dead were piled up after skeletonisation was complete. Some graves contain as many as 100 to 200 skeletons. Particularly worth visiting for their portal stelae are, amongst others, the giants' graves of Li Lolghi and Coddu Vecchiu (also known as "Capichera") near Arzachena; imposing menhirs can be seen next to the graves at Tamuli, near Macomer. Unique, too, is the cemetery of giants' graves at Madau not far from Fonni, where five graves dating from different periods are clustered together.

Water temples: A few hundred giants' graves are not the only remains which bear

water was collected. A staircase linked this pump room with the temple antechamber at ground level; the latter was ringed by small stone benches upon which votive gifts or cult objects were placed. There was also often a sacrificial stone with a small gully; this seems to point to blood sacrifices or possibly specific rites with "holy water".

Some water temples, presumably those of an earlier date, are built like the *nuraghi* from roughly hewn blocks of stone. There are, however, some particularly fine complexes such as the Temple of Predio Canopoli in Perfugas, Su Tempiesu near Orune, Santa Cristina near Paulilatino and Santa Vittoria near Serri. Such is the remarkable perfection

witness to the deeply religious nature of the Nuraghi. The most elaborate and remarkable structures from this era to be encountered in the Sardinian countryside reflect not only Nuraghian architecture but also the chronic water shortage on the island. The water temples built on the site of natural springs acted as a focal point for ritual gatherings or as places of pilgrimage. So far, approximately 50 of these unusual complexes have been identified; their design almost always followed the same basic plan. The heart of a spa temple (Italian: *tempio a pozzo*) is the Nuraghian domed vault, sometimes situated underground, in which the sacred spring

and precision of the limestone and lava blocks from which they are constructed that for many years these temples were regarded as stemming from the 8th–6th centuries BC, inviting comparison with Etruscan burial architecture. More recent finds, however, have led archaeologists to believe increasingly that the temples are several centuries older than this, and that they thus reach back into the time during which there was close contact with the late Mycenean kingdom in Greece and Cyprus.

The perfection of some water temples was clearly a reflection of their significance as a ceremonial meeting point or place of pilgrimage; it is surely no accident that the religious attraction of the most beautiful temples continued unbroken into the Christian era. In Perfugas, the Nuraghian pagan temple was discovered directly beneath the church square; Santa Cristina (Paulilatino) and Santa Vittoria (Serri) are places of pilgrimage even today – at festival time people travel long distances from the surrounding countryside in order to attend the church rituals (in the Christian church, of course). Even the celebrations take place more or less as they did 3,000 years ago – with wine and food, and song and dance.

Archaeological excavations have brought to light numerous secular facilities in the

pious visitors to the water temples left behind, a number of little bronze statues have survived. They represent not only the most beautiful and artistic examples of the Nuraghian culture, but are also one of the principal reasons for the traveller to allow plenty of time to visit at least one of the two most important archaeological museums in Sassari or Cagliari.

Bronze statues: Since most of the bronzes are only an inch or two tall, careful examination is essential. Like the votive plaques in the pilgrimage churches, these votive statues provide the observer with an insight into everyday life. One can admire not only miniature copies of household items, farming

vicinity of the water temples, which are not very different from those near any church in rural Sardinia. The best examples can be seen near Serri: simple accommodation for the faithful, who would stay near the temple during the festivals, some of which lasted for several days; more luxurious quarters for the dignitaries; meeting rooms; dance floors; arenas for competitions and market stalls, in which souvenirs and votive gifts were manufactured and offered for sale.

Of the countless votive gifts which the

implements, tools, weapons and magnificently decorated boats, but also exquisitely naturalistic representations of wild and domestic animals and, above all, people. With a little imagination we can glimpse their different activities and recognise the social strata: simple people, shepherds, farmers, workmen, musicians, mothers, people praying, sick people, mourners, priests and aristocratic-looking men and women – and particularly soldiers armed with a variety of weaponry, some of whom look like terrifying demons.

Each bronze statuette is a unique specimen of incalculable worth. And yet it is not diffi-

Left, interior of a fairy house on Montessu. **Above**, horn reliefs in a burial niche on Montesse.

cult to subdivide the Bronze-Age art of the Nuraghi into three distinct styles: the "Baroque", the "Geometric" and the "Popular". It is still uncertain as to whether these styles existed more or less simultaneously, or whether they represent a long period of technical and artistic development. Nor has it proved possible to date the figures with any precision. Many Nuraghian bronzes were found on the Italian mainland in Etruscan graves of the 8th to 6th centuries BC. Recently, more support has been won for the opinion that some Nuraghian bronze art is much older than that – considerably older, in fact, than anything comparable in the western Mediterranean. These assumptions,

however, do not fit into the generally accepted picture of the Nuraghi civilisation as one of the relatively unimportant fringe cultures of the Mediterranean region.

Metals, trade and culture: Latest research shows quite a different picture, and one in which the rich ore deposits of Sardinia, especially its lead and copper mines, play a key role. It is no coincidence that the Golden Age of Nuraghian culture in the middle of the second millennium BC should have occurred just as there was an upsurge in the importance of metalworking. It seems more likely that the "Bronze boom" and the resulting lively trading with the eastern Mediterra-

nean gave the island a valuable cultural impetus – to a greater extent than anywhere else in the west.

Even in the 19th century, speculation entertained the notion that the Nuraghi of Sardinia may have been the mysterious people known as the "Sardana". Recent opinions seem to lend credence to the idea. As long ago as the 14th century BC the Sardana are mentioned in some Egyptian texts as being enemies, and in others as mercenaries in the service of the Pharaoh. Archaeological evidence has proved that the Nuraghi had contact with the lands in the East at this time. It is not clear to what extent they relied on the Myceneans for these contacts, and to what extent they navigated the trading routes themselves. What is remarkable is the increased frequency of contacts with the eastern Mediterranean, especially with the island of Cyprus – even after the 12th century BC when, following the Trojan Wars and the eclipse of the royal house of Mycenae, Greece entered a "Dark Age" which was to last many centuries.

Thanks to its trading links, however, Sardinia continued to flourish culturally – a fact evident not only in the high standard of its bronze artefacts. Remarkable examples of the skill of the craftsmen are the statues of warriors found in 1974 on Monte Prama. They are exact copies of the little bronze statuettes, but are almost 10 ft (3 metres) tall and carved in stone. Those who are interested should see the fragments of these strange statues in the Archaeological Museum in Cagliari.

Art historians will have to await the results of further excavations in order to solve the mystery of whether the first large Nuraghian sculptures may have been created in the 8th century BC, which would make them predate even the oldest Greek sculptures. Examples of this kind of sculpture are the result of radical changes in the tribal-based society of the Nuraghi people, which in some places was already showing certain characteristics which were more typical of a city-based social structure. Archaeologists have no doubt that the reason for this development was the arrival of the first Phoenician settlements on the Sardinian coast.

Left, grave of the giants, Li Lolghi. **Right**, the main tower of the Nuraghe Losa.

The first Phoenician traders must have reached the coast of Sardinia in about 1100 BC. Excavations of Nuraghian sites have unearthed a number of bronze statuettes of Phoenician deities which were obviously imported from Syria or Palestine at around this time, and which doubtless influenced the Nuraghi in the development of their metalworking skills. The reason why the Phoenicians ventured so far westwards can be explained by the Orient's insatiable demand for raw materials, above all metals.

During the 9th and 8th centuries BC, at about the time when the city of Carthage was founded on the coast of what is now Tunisia, the Phoenicians built their first urban colonies around the principal harbours on the Sardinian coast: *Karali* (Cagliari), *Nora* and *Bithia* (near Pula), *Sulki* (Sant'Antioco), *Tharros* (near Oristano), possibly *Bosa* and others. It may be that in some places these settlements were built with the approval of the resident Nuraghi tribes. For the first time, however, excavations on Sardinia – as at the town of Sulki (the present-day Sant'Antioco) – have demonstrated just how incomplete is the traditional picture of the Phoenicians as industrious artisans, skilful traders and bold seafarers.

Scarcely 100 years after they founded the city, the colonists had conquered the entire fertile hinterland and the access routes to the lucrative mining areas, securing the region with a chain of smaller outposts and proper fortified towns. The dominant position of the garrison town on the high plateau of Monte Sirai near Carbonia makes clear to us the determination of the Phoenicians to create for themselves a new homeland here – almost 1,900 miles (3,000 km) west of their native ports on the Lebanese coast, where they had the Assyrians and Babylonians breathing down their necks.

The end of the Nuraghi: During the 6th century BC the Greeks, too, began to take an interest in Sicily. The writers of antiquity cite, for example, Olbia as a town founded by the Greeks – although to date no archaeological evidence has come to light in support of this claim.

The Phoenicians, for their part, tried to strengthen their hold on the island. It seems as if the Nuraghi finally realised the historic nature of the occurrences, banding together to counter-attack in an attempt to fight for their survival. These events did, in fact, mark the island's entry into the annals of history: classical literature provides us for the first time with a precise record of what happened on Sardinia.

In 540 BC Carthage sent an army of reinforcements to its Phoenician sister cities; the same troops had successfully fought under General Malchos against the Greeks on Sicily. Contrary to expectations, the expedition ended in disaster, with most of the army destroyed in a violent battle. The fortresses of the Nuraghi, incidentally, played no part in these struggles; they had lost their importance as defensive structures much earlier, in the 9th and 8th centuries BC, and had been largely left to decay. The success of the Nuraghi in open warfare is confirmed by finds excavated on Monte Sirai. They show that the Phoenician garrison was reduced to ashes at about the time of General Malchos's campaign.

In Carthage, the shock of this defeat gave rise to a reform of political and military institutions. The latter formed the basis for the increasing power aspirations of the Carthaginians, who subsequently sent well-organised armies of mercenaries to Sardinia. The island was soon so firmly under Carthaginian rule that in 509 BC the Romans were obliged to sign a contract that henceforth all trading with Sardinia was subject to Carthaginian control.

The Nuraghi were from now on virtually prisoners on their own island, with a choice between a life of bondage as serfs and mercenaries, or an impoverished but free existence as shepherds in the mountainous regions of the island, which were not agriculturally viable and therefore of no interest to the Carthaginians. The eclipse of the Nuraghi marked for the island the beginning of a period of almost uninterrupted occupa-

Preceding pages: the ruins of Tharros on the Sinis peninsula. Left, part of a lucky charm from a Punic necropolis.

tion, a period which was to extend almost into modern times and which would equate the history of Sardinia with that of its colonial powers.

Punic Sardinia: The Carthaginians quickly took advantage of their dominant position and secured their territorial gains with a sort of *limes* or frontier against the mountain-dwellers. By the 5th century BC a status quo had been established, in which the Carthaginians occupied two-thirds of the best parts of the island – not only the coastal regions, but also the entire south-west (Iglesiente) with its mining areas, and the fertile lowlands and hill slopes. Also under their control was classic sheep-farming country such

also pursued a policy of vigorous deforestation. Sardinia eventually became an overseas extension of Carthaginian territory, enjoying closer military, administrative, ethnic and cultural links with North Africa than did any other part of the Punic empire.

The joint role played by Sardinia and Carthage, the oldest and most important Phoenician centres in the West, explains the importance allotted to this cultural epoch in Sardinian museums. One of the most interesting aspects of Phoenician art is the often daring manner in which the artists adopted styles and forms from trading partners before blending them to create a highly individual work – although the dominant influ-

as the volcanic plateaux in the interior – a fact demonstrated by the foundation of towns such as *Macopsisa* (Macomer) as well as by the existence of numerous forts, including those on the northern boundary of the Campeda high plains near Bornova, on the Catena del Margine above Macomer, or in the northern Giara region of Gesturi, near Genoni. The agriculturally viable areas were criss-crossed by a remarkably dense network of paths and farmsteads, thus transforming the island into the granary of Carthage. According to classical sources, the Carthaginians not only used the services of immigrant Libyan farm labourers, but

ence of Egypt in sculpture is also evident to every museum visitor. If, however, he studies the miniature works of art in detail, he will discover that the proverbial wealth of the Phoenician empire was due not only to its seafaring traders, but also to the skills of its craftsmen. Most of the items are burial gifts: jewellery, amulets, talismans, incense burners, perfume flacons and unguent jars, but also frightening masks designed to keep evil spirits away from the dead. The most remarkable element of Phoenician architecture is its use of very large building blocks.

Outside the museums, traces of this period are not so accessible. The Romans destroyed virtually everything, and what little has remained is often only of interest to specialists. Worth a visit above all for their location and plan are Monte Sirai and Tharros. Monte Sirai is a perfect example of a self-sufficient garrison town complete with necropolis and its own sacrificial altar for burnt offerings. It lies on a high plateau and is interesting for its dominant strategic position and the clear-cut military plan of its acropolis. Tharros lies on a narrow promontory some 1 mile (2 km) long, with two hills: one for the town itself, and one for the necropolis. It is a classic example of a Phoenician coastal town, for it possesses a safe harbour, an easily defended single narrow land approach, shallow lakes

first tophet was not discovered until 1889 – and then not in Canaan, but near Nora in Sardinia. Here, and on half a dozen other *tephatim* which have since been discovered on the island, archaeologists found thousands of simple clay urns filled with charcoal and human remains, as well as hundreds of stone votive stelae recalling the sacrifice (with the object of prolonging its efficacy). Of these sites, only the *tophet* at Sulki on the island of Sant'Antioco has been left virtually untouched following excavations, so that the visitor can gain an impression of the original layout of the complex and the positioning of the urns and stelae.

Archaeologists have begun to question

with copious stocks of fish nearby and an extensive, fertile hinterland.

The child sacrifices: Little understood but nevertheless characteristic of the Phoenician religion was their custom of sacrificing young children by fire to the deity *Baal*, or later to the Carthaginian goddess *Tanit*. The Phoenicians called this ritual *molk* (known as *Moloch* in the Bible). The sacrificial altars were specially erected outside the towns; they are mentioned in the Bible as *tephatim* (the singular noun is *tophet*). However, the

whether the reactions of repulsion chronicled since ancient times are really appropriate in the face of these hundreds of child-sized urns. Not only do some urns contain remains of substitute animal sacrifices, mostly lambs or kids – after all, Abraham too sacrificed a lamb instead of his son, Isaac – but it is also evident that young children who died of natural causes were subsequently cremated in the *tophet*. This can be deduced from the fact that no babies were buried in Phoenician or Carthaginian necropolises.

In the light of this evidence, the 5,000 urns found in the *tophet* at Tharros lose something of their nightmare quality. It is even possible

Left, little bronze ship dating from 8th–7th century BC. **Above**, Phoenician bracelet from Tharros.

that the Phoenicians, faced by high infant mortality, regarded children up to a certain age as belonging to the deity.

Rome and Carthage first crossed swords with each other during the First Punic War (264–241 BC). The Romans had been forced to recognise the importance of Sardinia for the Carthaginians, both as a naval base and as a troop and grain store. They therefore did not hesitate when a mutiny by Sardinian mercenaries put pressure on the Carthaginians. Breaking the peace treaty, Roman troops annexed Sardinia in 238 BC without encountering much resistance. The island, however, was destined to suffer unrest for many years to come. On various occasions

between 236 and 231 BC, both consuls and their legions were forced to fight on the island; the situation was more or less repeated when there was another uprising in 226 BC.

During the Second Punic War (218–201 BC), several attempts by the Carthaginians on Sardinia to overthrow the Romans failed, although – as the Roman chronicler Livy reported – they were supported by the local mountain dwellers. This alliance between erstwhile enemies enmeshed the Romans ever deeper in endless guerrilla warfare. Caecilius Metellus, who had fought on occasion with two legions in Sardinia, was the

eighth and last general to be awarded the honour of a triumph by the Senate in recognition of his victories over the Sardinians. The fighting continued, but the Roman citizens started to view the island as a running sore, which was not worth trying to cure. They began to hate the island.

Sardinia as a Roman province: In 54 BC, when Cicero took on the defence of a certain Scaurus, a man who had acquired more than the usual degree of wealth during his time as governor of Sardinia, the lawyer's polemical plea for the defence echoed precisely the popular mood: Sardinia was the Roman province in which not a single town was friendly towards Rome – and in any case, the Sardinians as a race were the descendants of the sly Carthaginians.

In fact, towards the end of the Republic, Sardinia was the only one of the more than 30 provinces without a single city whose inhabitants were entitled to Roman citizenship. This shortcoming was not remedied until 27 BC, with the foundation of the Roman colony of *Turris Libisonis*. And Cicero was basically right, too, with his second statement. The year of the annexation of Sardinia was a date of purely political significance; culturally speaking, the Carthaginian influence on Sardinia remained evident for many centuries after Carthage had been destroyed by Rome. An inscription dating from the year AD 200 mentions a Sardinian *Sufete* (as the Carthaginian mayors were called) with the very un-Roman name of "Bodbaal".

The general situation on the island improved under the emperor Augustus. Many towns were awarded the right of Roman citizenship and a dramatic upsurge in the amount of building testifies to increasing prosperity. By now even the mountain folk had accepted Roman rule and the Romans could restrict their supervisory activities to mediating in the feuds between the sheep-farming tribes of the *barbaria* (known as the Barbagia today) and the Sardinian peasants on the Roman estates.

But Sardinia was doomed to remain a much-hated doormat on the doorstep of Rome, not least because of the prevalence of the dreaded malaria on the island.

<u>Left</u>, children's urns in the tophet of Sulcis. <u>Right</u>, mosaic floor in Nora.

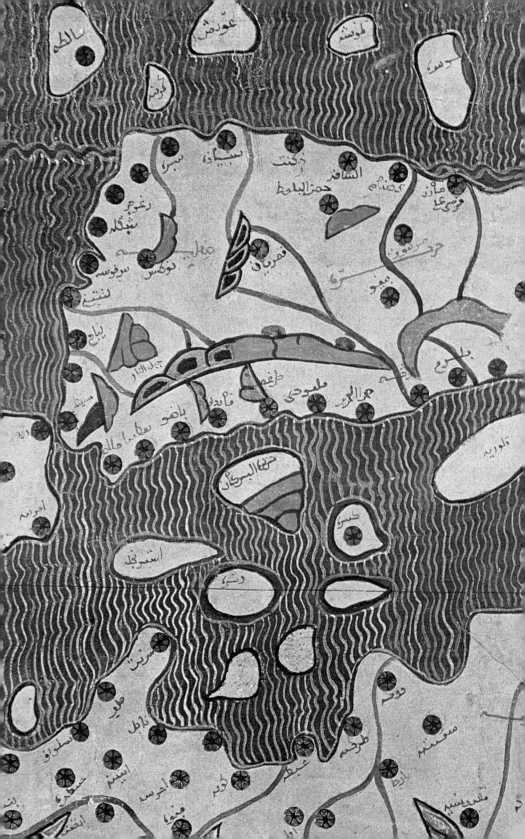

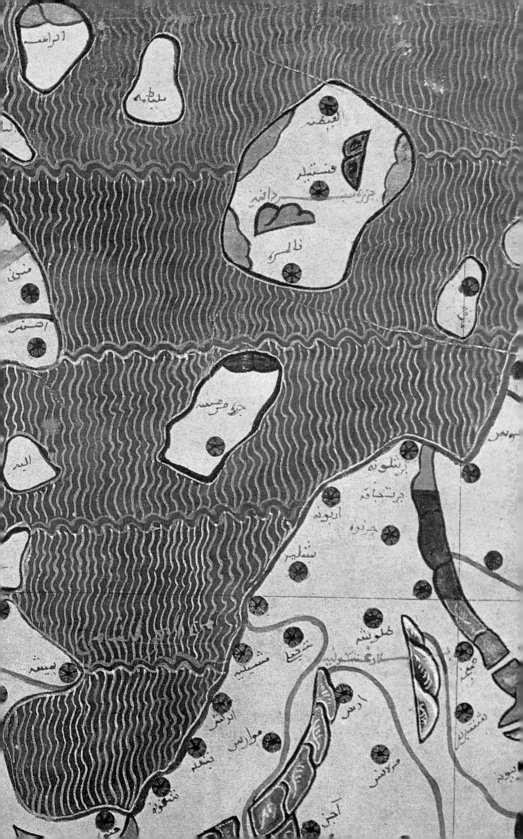

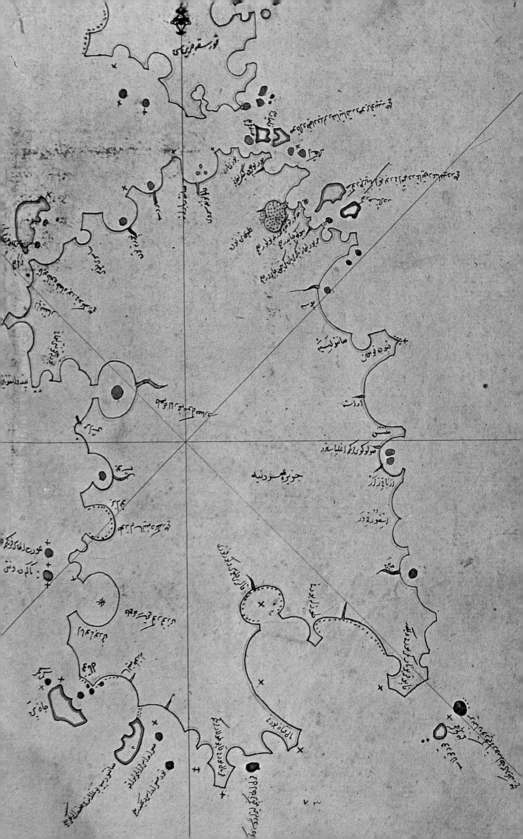

THE ARABS

Arabs first ventured ashore on Sardinia in AD 711; in that year the soldiers of Mussa-Ibn-Nucair captured the town of Cagliari and occupied various regions along the coast. Their visit was short-lived, however, and they set out to sea again shortly afterwards with considerable captured riches. It seems that the Saracens ran into a storm during the journey home, and that they and their booty ended up in a watery grave. Nonetheless, this mishap did not make the intrepid and warlike Arabs abandon their dreams of a vast empire. From their outposts in Spain, North Africa and Sicily they soon set out on their raids again, terrorising the coast, stealing food and kidnapping the natives, who were faced with the alternatives: "Your money or your life!" Those for whom no ransom was paid ended up in the slave markets of North Africa.

For 300 years, from 711 to 1015, not even the frequent storms deterred the Saracens from their plundering. The first raid on Sardinia in 711 was followed by others in 722 and 735–736. After yet another campaign in 752–753, Abd-ar-Rahaman decreed that a number of Sardinian towns which had already been sacked and laid waste should buy back their freedom.

In approximately 807 a Saracen fleet was ambushed and completely destroyed off the west coast of Sardinia near Sulcis. Only six years later the same fate befell the Arab general Abbu-el-Abbas and the armada of 100 ships under his command.

In spite of these naval victories, by 815 the Sardinians were so desperate that they sent a plea to the Emperor Louis the Pious, begging him for assistance in their struggle against the increasingly bold attacks of the Arabs. To no avail; after only a short interval, in 816 and 817 Cagliari was destroyed again. A Saracen chronicler commented tersely on the raid of 821–822: "They gave some beatings and received some in their turn; and then they departed from that place."

It was not until 1015–16 that the Sardinians were finally able to put an end to

this reign of terror. In alliance with the maritime republics of Genoa and Pisa they succeeded in routing the forces of the Prince of Mogeid-al-Amiri.

The latter, referred to as "Museto" in contemporary Italian records, had already conquered the Balearic Islands and Denia in Spain when he set sail from Mallorca with a fleet of 120 ships. Museto had recognised the strategic importance of Sardinia and was now toying with the idea of subjugating the island once and for all. The states bordering the Tyrrhenian Sea were roused from their lethargy by the fact that en route the Saracens had raided some of the Tuscan coastal towns, including Suni. What was more, the Italians feared that the invaders – forced to abandon temporarily their dreams of empire following defeat at Poitiers in 732 at the hand of Charles Martel – might revive their former ambitions and use Sardinia as a base from which they could set out to conquer Italy and the rest of Europe.

Pope Benedict VIII felt particularly threatened and used his influence over Pisa and Genoa to persuade them to unite in the common cause against the Arabs on Sardinia. The two republics would have had reason enough to go to war even without the Pope's intercession, for their aspirations to dominate the trading routes across the Tyrrhenian Sea were at stake. A Sardinia in Arab hands would represent an unacceptable threat. And so the fleets of Genoa and Pisa put to sea and routed the Saracens, together with the armies of the Sardinian *giudici* – the rulers of the four medieval *giudicati*, the defensive alliances of Cagliari, Arborea, Gallura and Torres – with whom they then proceeded to establish lively trading links.

In Arab hands: The occupation of Sicily by the Arabs in 827 marked a much darker chapter in the island's history, for it cut off the links with Byzantium and forced the island to rely on its own resources. The historian Alberto Boscolo has pointed out that the Arab supremacy at sea and the associated mass exodus from the coast to the island's interior radically changed the social structure. The abandoned towns were no longer focal points of trade and commerce as they had been during the time of the Vandals and the Byzantine era. In rural regions a land-based curtilage economy sprang up which was only able to supply the needs of a few villages. A fluctuating population led to the establishment of new farming communities in all areas. Even Cagliari was moved to Santa Igia, not far away but better protected, with marshes on one side and the ocean on the other.

The results of countless raids by a succession of new invaders were dramatic: many of the seaside towns and villages were destroyed or left to decay. Since the Sardinians believed even then that danger invariably came from across the sea, many of them left

raids were the regions surrounding Cagliari, Porto Torres and Olbia. The Sardinians fled and built new settlements not far from their devastated or burned-out cities. Sulcis and Bithia were founded in the hinterland of Cagliari on the site of what is now San Giovanni Suergiu; Tharros and Neapolis (the present-day Oristano and Terralba) lie in the hinterland of the Gulf of Oristano; Cornus (Cuglieri) and Bosa lie between Oristano and Alghero; Turris lies in the north-west; Coclearia (S. Teodoro) and Feronia (Posada) lie in the north-east. By contrast, it is maintained that Dorgali, in the hinterland of the Bay of Orosei, was founded in about 900 by the Saracen pirate Drugal.

the fertile coastal regions in order to make new homes in the rougher and less economically viable interior. They paid dearly for the security thus acquired: whilst life in the new settlements was marked by hardship and became progressively more depressing and monotonous, large stretches of the previously fertile coastal margin regressed into malarial swampland.

It was not only the pride and fear of the Sardinians which prevented the establishment of contact with the Arab invaders; the latter were also cruel and greedy, so that no true cultural exchange was possible.

Worst hit by the Saracens' plundering

The population in this area certainly displays a number of ethnic and linguistic characteristics which distinguish them from the other inhabitants of the island. Significantly, Islamic motifs can be found in the decoration of the Church of San Paolo di Dolianova in Cagliari, which dates from 1160–1289. They are ascribed to the Saracen stonemasons who helped build it.

The Genoese and the Pisans: The victory won in 1015–16 over the 120 ships of Sultan Museto's fleet established the naval supremacy of Genoa and Pisa over the Tyrrhenian Sea, vital for developing their extensive trading interests. The mainland republics quickly recognised the strategic value of Sardinia. The island could play a crucial role in their future military, economic and political plans.

At this time, Sardinia was divided into four *giudicati*: Torres, Gallura, Oristano and Cagliari. Each of these provinces, originally formed as a defensive alliance, had its own jurisdiction and its own social order. The ruler of the *giudicato* was known as the *giudice*; he lived with his family and an armed bodyguard in a castle. He was responsible for the administration of justice and the government of affairs of state. He was aided by the clergy and a secular civil service, as well as by the *curatores,* each of which governed in his name a *curatoria*, a region consisting of a number of villages and estates. The individual communities were run by the *majori*, men who enjoyed the trust of the *curatores.*

The *giudicati* were made up of state property (*rennu*) and the private property of the *giudice* (*depegugiare*). The status quo comprised a number of social classes. The hierarchy was divided into estates into which one was born: freemen – ranging from wealthy and powerful owners of large estates to the poor – and peasants and serfs. The latter estate was further subdivided into three groups, depending on how many days per week they were required to work for one or more masters. The *integri* had to work the whole day for their master, the *laterati* owed him half a day's work and the *pedati* worked for him for a quarter of the day. On their time off the *laterati* and *pedati* could work on their own plot of land – if they possessed one – or could undertake other work. The serfs' position was considerably better than it had been during the latter years of the Roman Empire. The villages, with their clearly defined administrative order, formed the kernel of the *giudicati*, together with the surrounding region consisting of private land, *latifundia* and village estates.

The arrival of the Genoese and Pisan forces on Sardinia marked their first encounter with this politico-administrative and economic system. And before long they, too, were delighted to discover that the island was rich in natural resources, with extensive

salt works as well as a flourishing agricultural economy, and above all plenty of scope for cattle farming.

The fierce rivalry between the two maritime republics also affected Sardinia. At the beginning, especially after the victory over the Saracens off the Balearic Islands (1113–15) Pisa had the upper hand. The city's superiority lay not only in military success but also in its archbishop: as the metropolitan of two Sardinian dioceses he was in a position to step in as arbiter in the frequent disputes between the powerful families within a *giudicato* and mediate between two warring *giudicati*.

After AD 1130 Genoa decided to bestow

its especial favour on one single *giudice*: it supported Comita d'Arborea in his attempt to unite the entire island under the aegis of the d'Arborea family. There was vigorous opposition to this plan from the other three *giudici* of Torres, Gallura and Cagliari; not until 1146 did the Archbishop of Pisa, Villario, manage to persuade the three of them to meet in Oristano to conclude a provisional peace treaty.

Only a few years after this, Barisone d'Arborea took up the family struggle for power on the island once more. The troops of the *giudicato* of Torres supported the Pisans; together, they besieged Barisone in his castle in Cabras. With Genoese help the latter finally succeeded in breaking the siege; he then appealed to the Emperor Frederick Barbarossa to proclaim him King of Sardinia. This was duely done and the coronation took place on 10 August 1164 in the Church of San Siro in Pavia.

Even this success was not enough to satisfy Genoa, which continued undaunted to cling to its dreams of hegemony. As a first step it took the precaution of ensuring the benevolence of the Papal States and then persuaded all four *giudici* to sign a number of treaties which declared them to be virtually the vassals of Genoa. This strengthening of the position of the Ligurian republic was a

Vallombrosians, Cistercians, followers of St Victor of Marseilles and Benedictines from Monte Cassino. They built abbeys and churches the length and breadth of the island. The presence of so many priests led to a rapid spread of the Catholic faith and to a blossoming of culture. Craftsmen and painters from the mainland were summoned to adorn the places of worship.

The monasteries soon began to attract unemployed labourers and local farmers anxious to learn the new agricultural methods which the monks had brought with them from Italy or other more advanced regions of Europe. They began to till fields which until now had never been cultivated, and land

severe blow for Pisa, which thereupon resumed the fight against its archrival. Once more, Emperor Frederick I intervened and divided the island into two separate dependent territories; Lugudoro and Campidano were subject to Genoa, and Gallura to Pisa. This event was a turning point in the history of the island. From this time onwards, wealthy Ligurian and Tuscan families with a long tradition of seafaring and trading brought increased prosperity to the island's economy.

Both Genoa and Pisa sent monks from a number of orders to convert the islanders to Catholicism: Benedictines Camaldulians,

which had long ago been fertile but now lay desolate. Yields were improved by the introduction of new strains.

The effort and the changes wrought proved worthwhile, for before long the sight of fields full of flowers attracted people's attention, reawakening and interest in the arts throughout the land. The churches built were hardly sophisticated Byzantine edifices, but they satisfied the needs of an agriculturally based society.

Foreign feuds: The feud between Genoa and Pisa, waged on Sardinian soil through the Sardinian *giudici*, was by no means forgotten. Towards the end of 1190, following a complicated dispute over the succession between Ugone Ponzio di Bas and Pietro d'Arborea, Barisone's son, the governor's throne in Cuglieri (Cagliari) was occupied for the first time by a man from the mainland, Oberto di Massa, who adopted a policy favouring Pisa. His successor, Guglielmo di Massa, declared war on Constantino di Torres. He forced him to surrender after laying prolonged siege to his stronghold, the Castello del Goceano.

The *giudicato* now fell victim to a campaign by the Genoese, who besieged and plundered Sant'Igia in 1194 before pressing on to Oristano. Ugone Ponzo di Bas was forced to flee, and the cathedral chapter had

new alliances with one of the warring parties or with other Sardinian families. In 1219 the Visconti routed the army of the *giudice* of Torres, subsequently hastening to secure their new position by means of a succession of marriages. The perpetual strife between the feuding families and rival power groups reached a climax in 1235, when a popular uprising led to the establishment of Sassari as a city state.

In 1238 Pope Gregory IX extracted from Ubaldo Visconti a formal declaration of loyalty and allegiance. Upon the latter's death he secured his position by proposing that Visconti's young widow, Adelasia, should marry Guelfo Porcari, a man who enjoyed

no option but to appoint Guglielmo as *giudice*. The two rivals were later to be brought closer to one another, not least through new family ties. At the end of the 12th century Sardinia was firmly under the control of Pisa.

In 1215 the death of Guglielmo di Massa revived the power struggle between the two seafaring republics, but this time the first families of Sardinia were also involved. They tried to gain an advantage by forming

Left, perfect defence technology: the Torre del Elefantei in Cagliari. **Above**, Santa Trinita di Saccargia: zebra patterns reminiscent of Tuscany.

his trust. Adelasia's choice, however, fell on Enzo, the illegitimate son of Frederick II of Swabia. Enzo's father had his son proclaimed King of Sardinia, whereupon the Pope avenged himself by excommunicating the couple.

By the middle of the 13th century, a complicated policy of arranged marriages, planned over a long period, brought virtually the entire island under Pisa's sway. Giovanni Visconti took up residence in Gallura, Guglielmo di Capraia in Arborea and the Dukes of Pisa themselves in the Castle of Cagliari. Supported by various Ligurian families – the Malaspinas, the

Dorias and the Spinolas – the *giudicato* Logudoro attempted to organise resistance to the Pisans.

And so a political wrangle slowly drew to a close, a scenario in which the principal actors – apart from the maritime republics striving for supremacy – were the most powerful families in the land. The majority of Sardinians, most of them involved with the everyday problems of town life, took no part in the affair. Thus came the end of a highly promising Golden Age in which culture, religion, the arts and the economy had flourished, without giving rise to a local political or economic power which would have been in a position to take control of the country's future.

Pisa struggles for control: The Pisans were forced to face a humiliating defeat between 1250 and 1260. The *giudice* Ghiano di Massa drove the Tuscans from Cagliari, settling into the town's castle himself and concluding a treaty with the Genoese, who soon sent an expeditionary force to reinforce his position.

Pisa transferred the representation of its interests to two *giudici*, Giovanni Visconti and Guglielmo di Capraia. Accompanied by a wild horde of soldiers, Gherardo di Donoreti was sent to Sardinia to support them. The decisive battle took place near Santa Igia. The Pisans won and moved back into the castle, taking Ghiano prisoner and eventually putting him to death. He was succeeded by his cousin, Guglielmo III Cepolla, who in 1257 was forced to sign a treaty of capitulation which guaranteed him a safe passage to Genoa or Sassari.

Towards the end of the 13th century the position of the factions in Pisa itself deteriorated; it was not long before the effects spread to Sardinia too. As a result of the bitter feud between the Guelphs and the Ghibellines, Anselmo di Capraia, Ugolino Donoratico and Giovanni Visconti found themselves faced with the humiliation of banishment and the expropriation of their estates on the island.

After the Battle of Meloria in 1284, the enmity between the Podestà of Pisa, Ugolino Donoratico, and his nephew Ugolino Visconti, who commanded the army, spread as far as Sardinia. The Pisans, however, were able to turn the feud to their own advantage by bringing under their direct control some regions and sections of the economy, especially mining.

Further to the north, the Genoese had not been idle during this time. They occupied the town of Sassari and the area of the Logudoro which was previously in the possession of Mariano d'Arborea.

In 1297 the Papal States intervened again in the dispute. On 4 April, during a formal ceremony in St. Peter's, Pope Boniface IV named James II of Aragon as seigneur in perpetuity over the islands of Sardinia and Corsica. At first this change of regency had little effect on the island, but during the early years of the 14th century James II saw his opportunity to take an active part in the affairs of the land. The population was still waiting and hoping for someone to put an end to the machinations of the representatives of the rulers of Pisa, which by this time had become intolerable.

Thus it was that, on 28 February 1323, the armed forces of Aragon and Pisa, both sailing across the sea towards Sardinia, actually met at the Santa Gilla Lagoon, just outside Cagliari. Pisa suffered defeat; later that year, on 19 June, a peace treaty was signed in which the vanquished state abandoned its claim to virtually all its rights associated with towns and estates on the island. Only a section of the fortress at Cagliari and the harbour remained in their possession, and that only for one more year.

This marked the beginning of the suzerainty of the Kingdom of Aragon, which was followed over four centuries by the kings of Spain in an institution which – as if by some irony of fate – came to be known as the *Regnum Sardiniae*.

In spite of the disadvantages resulting from the occupation of the island by Genoa and Pisa, there were many aspects of life which were enriched by their presence. The experience of the two maritime republics in seafaring and trade gave the Sardinians access to the mainland. A wide range of fine manufactured goods could thus be imported, of a better quality than those previously seen on the island: wooden and ceramic items, chopping boards, mortars and receptacles of every kind – and even fabrics from Tuscany, Flanders and Narbonne.

Right, the rural church of Santa Trinìta di Saccargia near Sassari.

SARDINIA UNDER THE SPANISH

In 1297, Pope Boniface VIII gave the *Regnum Sardiniae et Corsicae* in fief to the King of Aragon, James II. The two men knew each other personally, having previously both been in Sicily – James as King, and Boniface (still known at that stage as Cardinal Benedetto Caetani) as Papal Legate. They shared an antipathy to France and Anjou. Boniface claimed the right to dispose of Sardinia as he thought fit on the basis of a deed of gift of Louis the Pious, although the document was almost 500 years old and the subject of controversy. Dante Alighieri was not altogether wrong in his *Divine Comedy* when he accused Pope Boniface of selling high offices and depicted him in hell.

It could hardly be claimed that Sardinia was a no man's land at the time. It was subdivided into four independent administrative regions: the *giudicati* Logudoro and Gallura in the north, Arborea in the west, and Cagliari in the south. At the head of each region was a *giudice*, a judge, whose position – depending on the writer's historical perspective – has been variously described as almost that of an independent monarch or as a mere puppet of the mighty Pisan and Genoese republics. Sardinia was at this period under the control of the rival maritime city states. Both exploited the island and its people alike, valuing it for its rich salt, silver mines and its fields of corn.

King James II's first task was to take the reins of government from these mainland traders, who had a considerable vested interest in their Sardinian estates. Unfortunately, the Kingdom of Aragon, in spite of having just been awarded the island in fief, had no large fortune at its disposal. It was 26 years later that sufficient funds were raised for a campaign; half of the cost of the army was actually paid for by the Pope. Were it not for the fact that the ruler of Arborea appealed to Aragon for assistance against Pisa and Genoa, it might have been longer still before the King embarked on the military conquest

Preceding pages: putting on masks during the Sartiglia in Oristano. **Left**, map of Sardinia in the 16th-century *Cosmographia Universalis*. **Right**, detail from a *retablo*, a Spanish altar painting.

of Sardinia. As it was, in 1323 the Spaniards set foot on what was for them an unknown island. The Infante Don Alfonso set sail with 10,000 men and landed at the Bay of Palmas in the south-west of Sardinia. He captured Iglesias immediately and Cagliari during the following year, gradually advancing across the entire island. Here and there he encountered resistance from the Pisans and the Genoese, who were not prepared to relinquish without a struggle the influence and economic advantages they enjoyed here.

Division of the spoils: Once Sardinia had been appeased it was placed under the regency of a Viceroy from the Kingdom of Aragon. The land was subdivided into 376 fiefs. Half of them were awarded to Spanish noblemen whose one aim was to increase their fortunes at the expense of their Sardinian estates. The underpopulated, impoverished, malarial island was entirely at the mercy of foreign interests; its fate was decided in faraway Saragossa, over the heads of the local citizens.

Of Sardinia's former masters, only the rulers of Arborea had been able to maintain their previous position: Hugo II had acted as advisor to the Aragonese during their occupation of the island. However, this compact dynasty whose roots went back to Sardinia's earliest history was a thorn in the flesh of the Spanish, who wanted to fill positions with their own incumbents who were loyal to the throne. In order to destroy the Arboreas' power they sowed the seeds of discord between the two sons of the *giudice* Hugo II by favouring the younger son, Giovanni, rather than his elder brother Mariano.

The situation, however, did not develop as the Spanish had expected: Mariano was the one who came to power, despite the Aragonese preference for his brother. He summarily laid siege to Giovanni's castle

ing he was an ambitious man, Mariano agreed in 1367 that he should marry his daughter Eleonora. Subsequently christened the *"Giudica"*, Eleonora is still present in the minds of the populace today as a symbol of Sardinian independence.

After Mariano died of the plague he was initially succeeded not by Eleonora but by her sickly but strong-minded brother, Hugo III. He ruled harshly and strictly, imposing a high tax burden and rigid military conscription, for he was obsessed with the aim of freeing his country from the hated Aragonese. He, the little ruler of Arborea, swore to wage "perpetual war" against the Spanish, challenging alone the expanding

and held him prisoner for the rest of his life. Disillusioned at the greed of the new colonial rulers, the *giudice* Mariano IV declared: "The Sardinians were expecting a new king, but now found themselves faced with a new tyrant in each village." In an attempt to preserve the independence of his *giudicato*, he had no option but to change sides: instead of fighting with the Spanish against the Genoese Doria clan, he now decided to fight with the Doria against the Spanish. He received valuable assistance from one of the Dorias with the descriptive name Brancaleone, "The Lion-Catcher". In order to confirm the latter's allegiance, and know-

Aragonese-Catalan empire. He described himself as the *"signore de' Sardigna"*, the "Lord of Sardinia", declaring that he intended to transform his state into one where rich and poor would enjoy the same rights. His approach, however, was too dictatorial; his exaggerated sense of justice made him unpopular with many people. On 6 March 1383 he and his daughter were assassinated during an uprising in Oristano. Only three days later his son-in-law, Brancaleone Doria, appeared at the court of the King of Aragon in Saragossa and proposed that his son Frederick should succeed the murdered Hugo, with his wife Eleonora as Regent.

Judicious ruler: By means of a judicious mixture of concessions and tax relief, Eleonora brought the country under control within a few months. Her popularity increased when, in 1392, she published the *Carta de Logu*, a written constitution of common law on which her predecessors and their legal advisors had worked for half a century, and which was to remain in operation until the beginning of the 19th century. The glorification of this legal code, which basically contained no innovations, was due to the fact that it was written in the Sardinian language. It thus became one of the cornerstones of Sardinian national consciousness, both under the Spanish, who spread both

ing to face Aragon in battle shortly after arriving on the island. He and an army of 20,000 men confronted a much smaller force under the leadership of the King of Sicily, Martin of Aragon.

Despite their patriotic goodwill, the Sardinian soldiers under William III were no match for the better strategy and more modern weapons of the enemy. William conceded defeat and fled from Sardinia. King Martin died shortly afterwards, a victim of the malaria which was to plague the island into the 20th century. Legend, however, had it that he succumbed to the "Beauty of Sanluri", who had demanded of the Spanish ruler excessive feats of love.

Catalan and Castilian, and during the rule of the Kings of Savoy, who introduced Italian as the official language.

The *giudica* Eleonora died in 1404, followed by her son in 1407. It was rumoured that the latter was murdered on the orders of his megalomaniac father; Brancaleone Doria himself was to die in prison soon afterwards. Margrave William III of Narbonne took over the post of ruler in the *giudicato* of Arborea. He was a distant cousin of Eleonora who found himself hav-

William III thereupon returned to Sardinia, leaving the island for the last time in 1417 and abdicating his rights in return for adequate compensation some three years later. One hundred years after their first military invasion, the Kingdom of Aragon finally had the entire island under its control. For the Sardinians, however, this offered no prospect of a rosy, peaceful future.

Sardinia was ravaged by devastating epidemics of plague in 1404, 1477, 1529, 1582, 1652 and 1655. Failed harvests and famine claimed thousands of victims, so that in the middle of the 16th century Parliament lamented that the country was suffering from

Left, this metal star has to be picked up at full gallop. **Above**, rider at the Sartiglia of Oristano.

estrema pobreza, "utter poverty". The misery was compounded by the frequent uprisings which flared up across the land. The most violent was led by Leonardo Alagon, the Margrave of Arborea, who in 1478 suffered a crushing defeat on the plains near Macomer at the hands of an overwhelming joint army of Spanish and Sicilian troops.

Immigration: This meant that the population declined drastically; at the beginning of the 14th century, at the time of the Aragon conquest, there were 340,000 inhabitants; by 1483 this figure was reduced to 150,000 – representing only six inhabitants per square kilometre. In order to provide partial compensation for this decline and at the same

with Marseilles and Sicily. They also had a reputation as doctors; in the middle of the 15th century, a certain Ibrahim produced a scientific treatise on herbal remedies and the island's climate.

However, in spite of their contribution to the otherwise stagnant local cultural life the Jews were driven out towards the end of the 15th century. The few who preferred conversion to Christianity in order to remain were forced to face the Spanish Inquisition, which arrived at this time. Suspicious people were expropriated and sentenced to large fines – if they escaped being burned at the stake like Sigismondo Arquer.

He was born on Sardinia in 1525, and

time to increase the Spanish element on the island, settlers from the Iberian peninsula were transported to Sardinia. During the 14th century the town of Alghero was resettled with Catalan immigrants loyal to the throne, after the native population had been driven away in retaliation for an attempted coup against the Aragon rulers. (Even today, Catalan is spoken, written and sung by folk groups in this lively port.) Jewish immigrants had also reached Sardinia at about the same time as the Catalan settlers. They established themselves in Alghero and Cagliari as money-changers and traders and controlled the island's important trade links

studied law in Pisa and theology in Siena. During his travels across Europe he met Sebastian Münster in Basle. The latter, a Franciscan monk and geographer converted to Protestantism, was in the process of compiling his six-volume *Cosmographia Universalis*. Arquer himself wrote a *Compendio de las Historias de la Tenebrosa Serdenya*, a "Brief History of the Bleak Island of Sardinia", which was included in the second volume of Münster's world history. In correspondence with Protestants from the circle surrounding Erasmus of Rotterdam, Arquer not only supported Luther's theories, but also voiced energetic criticism of the deplorable behaviour of the Sardinian clergy – reason enough for the Church to have him tortured and condemned to death. In June 1571 he was burned at the stake in Toledo.

The case of the Sardinian Sigismondo Arquer is just one example of the lamentable activities of the Spanish Inquisition. Events of the time help to explain how a clerical institution came to enjoy such enormous political influence. In 1479, with the marriage of King Ferdinand of Aragon and Isabella of Castile, the linking of the two crowns created a unified Spanish kingdom. In order to be able to deal "appropriately" with the large numbers of Arabs and Jews in their land, the two monarchs – who were could, without undertaking any measures which might have led to an improvement in the standard of living on the island. Ferdinand and Isabella now ruled over an expanded united kingdom. In 1492, following the discovery of America, their interest was diverted from the Mediterranean towards the new, more promising territories in the West, and the mountainous, uneconomic island of Sardinia slipped still further into oblivion. Nor could the Sardinians expect a greater share of the attention of Charles V, the grandson of Ferdinand and Isabella of Spain on his mother's side and heir of the Hapsburg emperor Maximilian and Duchess Mary of Burgundy on his father's; he had

highly praised for their Christian virtues – asked the Pope to reintroduce the Inquisition, requesting the right to appoint the Inquisitors themselves. The long arm of the Inquisition reached even as far as Sardinia. Here, however, influential people were able to avoid its grasp thanks to their powerful protectors; those who landed in its net were mostly small fry: blasphemers, bigamists and women accused of witchcraft.

Forgotten island: The Spanish crown exploited the Sardinian population wherever it

inherited a difficult legacy with far-reaching consequences. Furthermore he was fully occupied by his wars against King François I of France, his struggles against Luther and problems caused by the spreading of the Reformation; he had no time to devote himself to his Mediterranean island. Sardinia was hardly more than a pebble on the beach of his world empire; since 1535 it had even lost its significance as a supplier of silver, for Hernando Cortez had discovered far more profitable deposits in Mexico.

Nonetheless, Charles V relieved the Sardinian populace of the humiliation of not even being master in their own country.

<u>Left</u>, Spanish fort (no longer standing) in Sassari. <u>Above</u>, the Piazza Eleonora d'Arborea in Oristano.

They had been allowed to enter Alghero, a Catalan settlement, only by daylight on their way to work. This restriction also applied to Castello, the fortified quarter of Cagliari, which all Sardinians had to leave by sunset. And anyone disobeying the cry *foras los Sards* – "Sardinians out!" – would be thrown unceremoniously over the castle wall. This prohibition – an example of the presumptuous arrogance of the foreign rulers – was lifted in 1535, when Charles V paid Sardinia one of his very occasional visits.

The monarch was, in fact, only passing through, for he was accompanying Andrea Doria, the Genoese mercenary leader. The latter set sail for Tunis with a 30,000-man

when attacks by pirates goaded on by the Turks were an everyday occurrence, Sardinia's totally inadequate system of defences lay in the hands of 86 men, who stood watch over the island from hilltops near the coast. Since the maintenance of a Spanish defence regiment would have been too expensive, the colonial rulers devised another method: instead of sending troops, they supplied the Sardinians with weapons. Since the latter were required to pay for the arquebuses and lances they received, the cost to the Spanish crown of the defence of their dominions on Sardinia was actually nil. Philip II, who had succeeded Charles V, imposed a high export duty on Sardinian cattle farmers in order to

army, eliminating Khair-El-Din, the notorious pirate Redbeard, plundering his fleet and freeing 20,000 Christian slaves. Six years later, Charles V and Andrea Doria set sail from the Sardinian port of Alghero once more on a joint expedition against the buccaneers of Algiers – this time without success. During his brief stay in Alghero, the Spanish-Hapsburg emperor described the local inhabitants as *todos caballeros* – flattering words – in a speech thanking the citizens for, as was the common practice of the day, supplying food for the mercenary forces while their ships lay in the bay.

In the turbulent years of the 16th century,

raise funds to cover the costs of repairs and munition supplies for Cagliari and Alghero, the two key towns in the Sardinian defence – thereby ensuring once again that no expenditure was involved.

The royal financial advisors found an equally neat solution in the case of the coastal watchtowers, which Philip had constructed towards the end of the 16th century. A survey indicated that to provide real protection against enemy attack, Sardinia would have needed 132 "Saracen towers", standing at roughly 9-mile (15-km) intervals along the coast. In fact, only 66 were built – in other words, only half the number required. The towers were financed by the barons or the town councils on whose property they stood.

A very detailed map of Sardinia entitled *Description de la Isla y Reyno de Sardena*, printed during the 17th century under Philip II and currently in the Bibliothèque Nationale in Paris, shows illustrations of these coastal towers. The map also depicts the coat of arms of the Kingdom of Sardinia: a shield with a red cross and four Moors' heads bearing a headband as a sign of their royal status (they represent the four dark-skinned regents conquered by the army of Aragon in the 11th century). Across the centuries, the band slipped down, so that the kings were transformed into slaves. Since

mine which aspects of art and culture could be imported, and which not. They permitted the Catalan Gothic style, which extended the art of the Middle Ages into the 16th century. They permitted the Spanish Baroque, which celebrated the triumph of the Counter-Reformation. But they banned the Italian Renaissance, through which man had discovered a new self-awareness.

Social changes: In order to keep close tabs on the better-educated classes, in the middle of the 16th century the Jesuits – known for their devotion to the King of Spain's cause – were sent to the island. They founded two colleges – one in Cagliari and the other in Sassari; both attracted large numbers of stu-

the 19th century the Moors' heads with the blindfolded eyes have remained as potent symbols of the Sardinian claim to the self-determination denied them for so long.

During the 400 years of Spanish colonial rule, the Sardinians were systematically deprived of their rights. Even in the cultural sphere strict censorship was imposed. Only the Spanish crown, the Spanish viceroys and the Parliament of the island, to which no Sardinian belonged, were allowed to deter-

dents and were promoted to the status of universities early in the 17th century. To prevent their being corrupted by alien philosophies, Sardinians were banned from studying at foreign universities which lay outside the Spanish empire. The Jesuits were responsible for two other measures. They imposed the use of Castilian (i.e. Spanish) as the official language, thus bringing some order to the Babel of languages under which the island laboured: until then the medieval *Carta de Logu* was written in Sardinian, announcements in the main towns were made in Spanish, the clergy conversed in Latin; in Cagliari and Alghero the upper classes spoke

Left, women wear Spanish mantillas for the Easter procession in Alghero. **Above**, the climax of the procession is the taking down of the cross.

Catalan whilst the common people spoke Sardinian, and in Sassari Catalan, Castilian, Italian, Corsican and Sardinian co-existed.

The country people spoke exclusively Sardinian, for the descendants of the early settlers had been unwilling to abandon their traditional tongue. In these times, in which they had been robbed of almost all they possessed, it represented their only wealth. The nomadic shepherds were impoverished and neglected; the peasants were equally poor, for they were exploited by everyone. The towns demanded their grain at cut-throat prices, the Church demanded its tithes, the nobles and merchants would only lend them money at exorbitant rates of interest, and the

Spanish monarchy commandeered soldiers, horses, grain and vegetables.

In the presumptuous arrogance and blatant injustice which characterised the attitude of the upper classes to the common people were sowed the seeds of Sardinian banditry. Totally lacking protection, but exposed to interference and corruption in every sphere of life, the poor had no option but to fall back on their own resources. They resorted to self-defence without recourse to – or sometimes directly against – the forces of law and order, since the latter were either unable or unwilling to fulfil their duties.

The alarming increase in robberies and cattle thefts first became a cause for serious concern to the authorities at the beginning of the 17th century. A particular problem was posed between 1610 and 1612 by the 20-strong band of robbers under Manuzio Flore from Bono. He incited the populace to refuse to pay its taxes, and, like a Sardinian counterpart to Robin Hood, directed his attacks especially against all officials who were "poor when they assumed office and rich when they retired."

During the 17th century, Spain went through a period of crisis: many of its colonies rebelled against the crown or declared independence, whilst the Thirty Years' War brought additional turmoil and losses. Once again, the rulers had more pressing problems than to tackle the plight of the exploited people of Sardinia.

Towards the end of the century, the attention of the major powers in Europe was directed towards the Iberian monarchy. Charles II, the last Spanish Hapsburg king, had no male heir. And then, in a final desperate attempt to ignore the inevitablility of death, the Spanish viceroy suddenly decided to try to revive his country's ailing Sardinian policy. Whilst, on the mainland, the prelude to the power struggles which would accompany the War of Spanish Succession began to make itself felt, on Sardinia a move was afoot to "repeal the old laws", to "encourage trade as the only true source of prosperity" and to "create a positive climate for agriculture in this patently fertile land", in order to "export its produce throughout Europe". Unfortunately time had run out for the Spanish rulers of Sardinia to translate their new theories into reality.

New owners: In 1708 the Spanish were forced to surrender to the English and the Austrians on Sardinia. Finally, in 1714, the Treaty of Radstadt ceded the island to Austria. In 1717 Giulio Alberoni, an Italian gardener's son and militant cleric who had risen to the rank of Minister of State under the Spanish, succeeded in winning back Sardinia for Spain, now ruled by the Bourbon dynasty. But then, in 1718, as part of the Treaty of London, Sardinia was passed from the Austrians to the Dukes of Savoy in exchange for the more useful island of Sicily.

Left, famous woman judge Eleonora d'Arborea.
Right, detail from the *retablo* of Castelsardo.

STAGNO DI CAGLIARI.

Saline

L'Annunziata

Fortini

di Ciarella

Ponte della Scaffa

Saline

Cialuppa parlamen

Vascello incagliato, e brucciato dà Franceli

GOLFO DI CA

STAGNO

S. Lorenzo

L. Polveriera

dei P. di Buc

S. Lucifero

Monticello

Monte Orpino

dei P. del Carmine

Stagno

S. Bardilio

E. redi di Filippo Pinna

Stagno

V. di Buonaria

Stagno

Cavalleria

G.ppe Umana

LIARI

Saline

G.ppe Passio

Co

Quartiere fanteria

V. di Luc

Fortini

Fanteria

Fortini

Avanguard Guastat

Paolico Pinna

Lazzaretto e Porto

di S.t Ignazio

di S.t Steffano

Fanteria

Pietra Aliada

di Calamoscas, o dei Segnali

Terre di C.

CA

ANCE S

During their almost 1,000-year history, the rulers of Savoy had managed no more than to extend their domains in the Isère Valley of France across the Alps into the Piedmont, and to acquire the title of Duke. The signing of the Treaty of London in 1718 ceded Sardinia to them, immediately doubling the area of land under their control and granting them the title of King.

Sardinia, however, was not a country to which they had aspired (they tried repeatedly to exchange it for territory on the mainland). They could arouse neither interest nor understanding for the island; nor could they make themselves understood there. The natives spoke Sardinian and the educated classes Castilian; the rulers of Savoy-Piedmont, however, spoke French. The regular reports sent from Sardinia to the capital, Turin, by the Baron de Saint-Rémy – the first Viceroy of the Piedmont – did not sound encouraging: "The nobles are poor, the country itself miserable and depopulated, its citizens idle and without any sort of trade – and the air is most unhealthy." Further on, he claimed: "The vices to which these people are most inclined are theft, murder and cheating." Nor do the 400 years of Spanish indifference seem to have been good for the clergy: the priests showed so little respect in their personal appearance "that they wear a peasant's cap and greatcoat in public, even at church during celebration of the Mass."

Mis-match: These reports echo the consternation and helplessness of the Piedmontese in the face of the unfavourable situation. At the same time, they indicate their determination to search for a solution. However, in one of the clauses of the Treaty of London the rulers of Savoy had had to agree to leave everything on Sardinia as it was: all laws, all decrees, all rights and privileges pertaining to the feudal lords were to remain untouched. Furthermore, quite apart from this promise, during the first years of their rule the Piedmontese were at great pains to avoid

Preceding pages: the French fleet depicted in the Gulf of Cagliari. **Left**, Alberto La Marmora, who gave his name to the highest mountain on the island.

interfering in local matters on Sardinia, lest they should provoke the already suspicious populace. Instead they observed, registered and sent precise and detailed weekly reports to Turin. Their aim was an honourable one: to get to know this new, unknown European country and to assist it towards more order and discipline by means of administrative reform. And so they measured reality, and the Sardinian mentality, against Piedmontese standards, and tried to make the Sardinians fit into a Piedmontese mould.

This lack of comprehension of the Sardinian psyche was a fundamental mistake, and one of which the order-loving Piedmontese were frequently guilty during their 130-year regency. They simply could not understand that it was impossible to reconcile these two such totally different worlds; that a Sardinian shepherd and a Piedmontese city-dweller could never be reduced to a common denominator.

Bandit problems: Apart from their concern at the poverty and the desolate economic and cultural state of the island, the Piedmontese were troubled at the internal unrest and the increasing incidence of lawlessness, which was rapidly getting out of hand. In some regions the bandits had formed regular armies. Particular notoriety was achieved by one feud involving families and gangs, which raged in the village of Nulvi in northern Sardinia during the 1730s. One side was led by a woman of about 40 called Lucia Delitala, who "had a moustache like a grenadier's and who had not married because she claimed that she did not want to be dependent on a man."

Problems of this nature were described by the Piedmontese viceroys in their reports. The quotation is taken from one produced by Signore de Rivarolo, who served as Viceroy of Sardinia between 1735 and 1738. The fact that his previous post was as governor of the Savoy prisons may help to explain his uncompromising severity in the bandit question, which he systematically tried to eradicate with military expeditions, accelerated trials and harsh punishments. In Oristano he left the corpses hanging on the gallows until they were consumed by flies. During the three years he was in office he had 432 people executed and more than 3,000 condemned to severe punishments. But his deterrents brought few results; the bandits fled to the neighbouring island of Corsica or into the impenetrable mountains of the island, returning to their native villages when things were quieter. The Piedmontese justified their lack of success with their attempt to bring Sardinia under control: the nomadic shepherds and the inaccessible mountainous terrain were the obstacles which doomed their project to failure.

The shepherds – who comprised more than half the entire population at the time – were portrayed as potential criminals. Decrees were issued restricting their freedom of movement: "All shepherds must erect their huts in easily accessible places, where they may easily be found." Some of the other official regulations were absurd: subjects were forbidden to wear a beard which was more than one month old, for a long beard of the type favoured by bandits and other outlaws altered the facial characteristics and made them unrecognisable.

That a decree should limit the period of mourning, traditionally lengthy on the island, was seen as an insulting infringement of an ancient and revered custom. And there was another problem: as judges employed on Sardinia confirmed, the bandits were able to pay for the clemency of the local dignitaries, who tolerated or even encouraged this state of affairs.

In order to master the situation, the Piedmontese had an idea which rapidly became an obsession: they wanted to transform the nomadic shepherds – whom they saw as the root of all evil – into settled (and therefore more easily controllable) peasants, and replace them by Piedmontese peasants. A first step in this direction was the colonisation of extensive, sparsely populated regions of northern Sardinia by Piedmontese peasants. What awaited the farming families from the mainland was not the fertile paradise they had been promised by the officials in Turin, but a sun-baked, malaria-infested land in which they, as immigrants, were completely ostracised by the native populace. They eventually gave up and returned disillusioned to their homes in Piedmont.

The Piedmontese regents had more success in 1736 with the settlement of fishing families of Ligurian origin on the island of San Pietro, and 30 years later on the island of Sant'Antioco. The settlers were the descendants of Ligurians from the Riviera village of Pegli, who had been kidnapped by pirates in the 16th century and taken to the coral-fishing town of Tabarka on the northern coast of Tunisia. They continued to ply their trade here in their new homeland and transformed the towns of Carloforte and Calasetta into flourishing fishing ports. Thus, for the first time, a scheme introduced by the Piedmontese government actually produced concrete results which were financially viable.

The reformist attitude which the rulers of

Savoy had long cultivated in their mainland territories spread to Sardinia as well at the middle of the 18th century. Count Giovanni Battista Bogino, who was appointed Minister of State of the Piedmont in 1759, was known for his open-mindedness; as his advisor in Sardinian affairs he chose Giuseppe Cossu, a lawyer and a native of Cagliari. Count Bogino, receiving an objective account of the true situation on the island, was the first member of the Piedmontese government to recognise that Sardinia's problems

Above, Piedmontese king Carlo Emanuele III founded the town of Carloforte on San Pietro.

were not so much due to the character of its inhabitants, but rather to the neglectful treatment the island had received at the hands of its former rulers, whose only interest had been in securing their own advantage. And so he began to introduce a programme of reforms: he improved the administration of justice, but attempted primarily to encourage agriculture by the distribution of seed and cheap loans for farmers.

Some progress was made thanks to Giuseppe Cossu, who travelled tirelessly the length and breadth of the island, pleading eloquently for modernisation of the hopelessly antiquated agricultural practices still employed. Not all reforms met with success: attempts to grow rice and tea failed because of the unsuitable climate, and the introduction of cotton and mulberry bushes for silkworm breeding were both abandoned due to violent opposition from the shepherds, who feared for the survival of their pastureland.

But generally the attitude of the Piedmontese continued unchanged, characterised by an inability or refusal to grasp the situation. In April 1780, only a few years later – after one of the failed harvests which were a regular occurrence on Sardinia – the starving peasants in Sassari rioted, plundering the granaries and storming the town hall. The revolt was quelled the very next day, however, not by force of arms, but by holding up a portrait of the King: a picture of the monarch and his ancestors was carried through the protesting mob, whereupon the latter reverently doffed their hats and fell down on their knees, calling out *Viva il re!* (Long live the King!).

During the last years of the 18th century the riots increased in frequency, and the prestige of the monarchy was no longer sufficient to calm the masses. This period of unrest coincided with the French Revolution, but the two phenomena are not strictly comparable. In Paris the revolt was against the monarchy, whilst on Sardinia the cause of the uprising was the presumptuousness of the feudal lords. Although they had never seen him in the flesh, the Sardinians remained loyal to a man to their sovereign in faraway Turin.

Sanctuary: The island populace finally had the chance to see their king and his retinue in 1799, when Charles Emmanuel III, driven from Turin by the French, realised his de-spised dominion was his only place of sanctuary. In order to gain the favour of the nobility and clergy, he and his successor, Victor Emmanuel I, bestowed honorary titles and decorations on all comers. Despite the stringency of the times, however, their extravagant household led a senior Sardinian official to note that "everyone was better off when the Viceroy ruled the island."

The ideas and aims of the French Revolution had only found resonance among the educated élite. Clubs with Jacobinic tendencies sprang up, and the first French constitution was even printed and distributed in Sardinian. And so the French troops who invaded the island from the south-west in 1793 believed that they had discovered a "revolutionary" land. They met with no resistance at all in Carloforte, on the island of San Pietro. They were able to erect their Tree of Freedom, re-christening the island "Freedom Isle" and establishing a republic which, however, was to prove short-lived. In some other districts of the island the French military campaign was to end in failure, however: for example, on the island of La Maddalena, where a promising young artillery captain by the name of Napoleon Bonaparte took part in the fighting.

The victory over the French army was solely due to the prompt intervention of a 4,000-man Sardinian regiment, called together overnight by the nobility and clergy. They feared that they would lose their privileges under French rule. The Sardinians were of the opinion that their courageous defence of their native land was worthy of a reward. They accordingly requested the King in Turin to appoint Sardinian natives to all public positions, and to grant them the right of direct involvement in all governmental affairs on the island. Their wishes and demands, however, were categorically denied. The Sardinians gave vent to their rage and disappointment at this ungrateful response: on 7 May 1794, 541 Piedmontese officials were arrested and shipped back to the mainland.

Now, for the first time in 500 years, Sardinia was under Sardinian rule again – but without breaking trust with the King. The royal standard still fluttered from all public buildings, and protestations of loyalty to the monarchy could be heard from all quarters. The revolution was directed against the hated feudal regime, which continued unchanged. The most energetic representative of the new Sardinian national consciousness, and the one who enjoyed the highest esteem, was the *giudice* Giovanni Maria Angioy. At the head of an army of peasants he marched in triumph across the island, finding widespread support for his appeasement policy.

In May 1796, however, the Piedmontese signed a peace treaty with France. Since their possessions on the island were no longer under threat, they did not need the support of the Sardinians. Angioy and his followers were proclaimed rebels. Accompanied by a small entourage, he set sail from Porto Torres and managed to flee via Corsica to

CAVOUR.
(From a contemporary print in Bianchi's *Cavour*.)

France. He died in exile in Paris in 1808, impoverished and forgotten.

In spite of considerable efforts, the Piedmontese had still not succeeded in giving the necessary impetus to Sardinian agriculture. All their attempts in this direction failed due to a peculiarity of the land use system in operation: there was no private ownership. For centuries the village communities had decided the distribution and right of use of land under their jurisdiction in accordance with the *Carta de Logu*, which was as sacred to them as the Bible. One year a field would be available to the peasants for agricultural purposes, and the next to the

shepherds as pasture. But the latent hostility between the peasants and the nomadic shepherds could not be checked by this means. And so, with their "Olive Tree Enactment" of 1806, the rulers of the Piedmont took a first cautious step along the road towards the privatisation of common land. A peasant who planted olive trees was granted the right to enclose his land; planting more than 4,000 trees gained him a title.

Property problems: The measure of success enjoyed by this edict – which was no doubt more directly attributable to the incentive of the title than to any sudden change in the traditionally conservative attitude of the Sardinian mentality – encouraged the Piedmontese to introduce in 1829 an "Enclosures Act", which turned out to have a sting in its tail. The *Editto delle Chiudende* was intended to put an end to the perpetual conflict between peasants and shepherds by providing a clear distinction between agricultural land and pasture, eliminating the traditional system of crop rotation and increasing yields by a more intensive use of the land. In addition, it was thought, the Sardinians would become accustomed to the concept of private property.

Within a very short period of the passing of the new act, however, the land was crisscrossed by the maze of dry-stone walls which are still a characteristic of the Sardinian countryside today. And once again it was the wealthy who gained the upper hand: with more labour at their disposal and more skill at cutting a path through the bureaucratic jungle, they were able to lay claim to larger areas of land. A peasant who had erected a fence round his fields with unseemly haste subsequently had to lease it from the new proprietors at inflated prices.

With this well-intentioned decree, which once again failed to take into account Sardinian traditions and customs, the Turin government succeeded in making the rich even richer and the poor even poorer. Once again riots broke out: whilst the women demonstrated in front of the municipal offices, the men were out in the countryside destroying the enclosures. In the first instance the Piedmontese were ruthless in quashing the unrest; in 1833, however, they were forced to repeal the edict, forbidding the rebuilding of the walls which had been destroyed for the time being. Six years were to pass before the enclosure of land was permitted again, as part of the large-scale reorganisation of property laws and the preparation of a land register following the abolition of the feudal system. Sardinia thus took an important and irreversible step forward into the modern world. But the traditional equilibrium within island society had been destroyed forever.

The gangs of bandits who came to the fore again represented true egalitarian ideals: during a visit by the archbishop of Sassari, the inhabitants of Orgosolo called upon divine justice and justified their cattle thefts by claiming that they led to a more equitable distribution of property: "How can it be that

charter so that they could use it as a base from which to lead the fight against the bandits, who were becoming increasingly concentrated in the Barbagia.

"Fusion with the motherland": The economic situation on the island was so catastrophic that the islanders could see only one way out of the dilemma: the incorporation of Sardinia into Piedmont, in order to guarantee the same treatment as the much wealthier mainland state. And so, in November 1847, a delegation of Sardinia's leading citizens made the journey to Turin, where they requested the island's "perfect fusion with the Motherland". Unification with Piedmont was proclaimed on 30 November.

God in his mercy, who is master over all living creatures, is prepared to observe how the shepherds in Gallura own 500, 800 or even 1,000 sheep, whereas we have only a tiny flock of 100 sheep?" Whereupon the archbishop commented: "The people here could lecture at the universities of Europe on the subject of communism!" The attitude of the Piedmontese regents to the increase in lawless banditry can be seen from the fact that in 1838 they granted Nuoro a municipal

Left, the first great statesman of the new Italian state, Camillo Cavour. **Above**, ceremony in Turin celebrating national liberation.

Instead of the hoped-for improvements, the Sardinians found themselves faced with still more disadavantages: nomadic sheep farming was banned, entire forests were felled, and the mines were exploited by foreign companies. It became increasingly difficult for the Sardinians to identify with the newly created nation state. In 1848 the Sardinian theologian, Frederico Fenu, explained the problem in graphic terms: "The attempt to transfer mainland laws and regulations to Sardinia, which is fundamentally totally different, can be compared to an attempt to make adult clothes fit a child or to dress a man in a woman's skirt."

Sardinia was now attached to the Piedmont, thus becoming part of the embryonic state of Italy. At this time the latter was being formed by a Piedmontese politician, Count Camillo Cavour, fought for by the leader of a volunteer army, Giuseppe Garibaldi, and ruled over by the House of Savoy. In 1848, however, when the deputies assembled in the Baroque Palazzo Carignano in Turin, there was no sign of the Sardinian coat of arms among the emblems of the Kingdom's other provinces.

Furthermore, Giovanni Siotto Pintor – the Sardinian senator who had been one of the most eloquent supporters of the "perfect fusion" between Sardinia and the Piedmont – was prevented from entering the Parliament building by a guard in gala uniform. He had arrived dressed – as was his wont on his native island – in a coarse woollen cloak and the *berretta*, the characteristic Sardinian headgear; such was the contrast with the elegant tailored suits of his fellow deputies from the Piedmont, Liguria and Savoy, that he was assumed to be a peasant, a stranger with no right of access to the hallowed parliamentary sanctum.

These episodes are not as trivial as they might seem, for they were typical of the permanent condescension characterising the attitude of the Piedmontese to the island which, 130 years previously, had entitled the Dukes of Savoy to the kingly crown. And hardly anyone bore in mind the trusting enthusiasm with which Sardinia had surrendered its ancient right of autonomy upon unification with the Piedmont in 1848. The islanders had high hopes that the Italian Risorgimento ("resurgence") would pave the way for a second "risorgimento" in their neglected homeland.

A sorry state: Conditions on Sardinia were deplorable – a fact also recognised by the entrepreneurs from the mainland who began to invest capital in the island. Count Carlo Baudi di Vesme, a Piedmontese nobleman, displayed a profound sympathy for Sardinia;

he revived the mining industry in Iglesias and attempted to establish model farms. "Sardinia is in a pitiful state," he wrote in 1848. "The fields lie fallow, the countryside abandoned, the cattle stocks largely destroyed. Poverty and famine are rife in most villages." Despite the exorbitant taxes levied, the communities received nothing in return. For this reason, explained Baudi di Vesme in his study, "the inhabitants are often forced to live on an unhealthy diet of herbs which they have gathered in the

countryside... Theft is a frequent occurrence, not because the people are wicked by nature, but because they are hungry."

In addition, there was enmity between the north and south of the island, especially between Sassari and Cagliari. The Piedmontese, expelled from Cagliari by the local citizens in 1794, would have been pleased to transfer the capital to Sassari, where most inhabitants were foreign immigrants from the mainland and therefore more favourably disposed towards them.

"The residents of the northern half of the island regard the south as less civilised," observed Alfonso La Marmora in 1838, in his *Voyage en Sardaigne*, for which he had also prepared a map of the island, "and sometimes they refer to them as 'Sards', which the southerners take as an insult, although it is actually the name of the islanders as a whole. The residents of the southern part of the island, on the other hand, although prepared to recognise the superiority of their northern compatriots in certain spheres of agriculture and trade, nevertheless consider them to be cruel and bloodthirsty."

Carlo Baudi di Vesme therefore proposed a solution: in administrative and religious affairs (except, incidentally, in sermons), the use of the Sardinian dialect should be banned and the use of Italian obligatory. "Unity of which must have reigned in the middle of the 19th century during the creation of the Italian national state.

Garibaldi speaks up: But Sardinia was not to become Piedmont and Italy as quickly as that – a fact which the Sardinians themselves were not slow to recognise. Their innate mistrust of the Piedmontese was transformed in 1860 into outright suspicion and ill-feeling. A rumour began to circulate upon the island that the Piedmont was hatching plans to cede Sardinia to France. Count Camillo Cavour, accused of secret negotiations in this respect, was energetic in his denials. He failed, however, to convince his gathering band of critics, so that eventually,

language would lead to a closer unity of spirit... thus overcoming the deep-rooted differences between the inhabitants of the various regions." In other words: since no one really knew what to do with the island as it was at the time, the plan was to destroy its national identity – an identity to which the Sardinians had clung despite enduring centuries of foreign rule, and which was also expressed in their native language. "Sardinia will become Piedmont, will become Italy", continued Baudi di Vesme. The powerful rhetoric of this assertion becomes comprehensible and forgivable in the light of the climate of over-enthusiastic exuberance after months of speculation, Giuseppe Garibaldi intervened.

Following guerrilla wars in South America, the successful defence of Rome against the French in 1848 and the death of his lifelong companion Anita, this "hero of two worlds" had settled on the little island of Caprera, off the north-eastern coast of Sardinia. The war hero had become an enthusiastic farmer. "Sardinia is the most important and strategically most significant place in the Mediterranean," he wrote in response to the rumours, and he expressed the conviction that as a "gentleman", Victor Emmanuel would neither agree to the cession of any more territories, nor to the division "of this Italy, which we all wish to see united".

Garibaldi remained loyal to Sardinia. To avoid diplomatic confusion, in the autumn of 1849 he was detained on La Maddelena. From here he embarked upon his revolutionary odyssey across almost every continent. Six years later he returned to Caprera, his banishment partially lifted. He was permitted to return to Italy as a private citizen – in fact, as the captain of a small cutter – providing he refrained from political involvement. Garibaldi's ship enabled him to establish a transport route between his native town, Nice, and Sardinia. By means of an inheritance he was able to purchase parts of the

"very uncertain appendix of Italy". On 17 March 1861 it became part of the new unified Italian state. Victor Emmanuel II proclaimed himself King of Italy, and Sardinia ceased to be the kingdom in its own right which it had been for the previous 650 years. The newly-formed nation inherited a starving, exhausted, exploited island.

Exploitation: Camillo Cavour, who is regarded as the founding father of modern Italy, had imposed on Sardinia an unprecedented tax burden, demanding high property taxes based on a confused, incorrect and therefore unjust Land Register. He had also allowed foreign speculators to gain possession of the pastureland so essential for the

island of Caprera in 1855; one year later, he and his companions settled there. Less than four years after this he was back in politics. Although this exercised an irresistible spell on him, he always missed his island of Caprera and visited it frequently. And here it was that Giuseppe Garibaldi, the tireless fighter for Italian freedom, finally fell asleep for the last time.

In spite of its worst suspicions, Sardinia remained a part of Piedmont, albeit as a

Left, an historic shoulder-to-shoulder: Vittorio Emanuele and Giuseppe Garibaldi. **Above**, this is how people imagined Sardinian bandits.

Sardinian economy, and had awarded Genoese, Piedmontese and overseas investors' licences for the clearing of the island's forests – an overfelling which has continued today with the development of tourism. The cereals harvested were sold to mainland traders at high prices on the open market, although food supplies on the island grew increasingly scarce. The cost of living rose rapidly. The starving inhabitants of the towns revolted openly, whilst the impoverished country dwellers demanded a return to the old common law. The shepherds, deprived of their livelihood by the ban on nomadic sheep rearing, ended up as bandits.

The Sardinian senator Giovanni Siotto Pintor, who proudly insisted on wearing the local costume despite frequent exclusion from the Parliamentary building in Turin, summarised the situation on his native island after its unification with the Piedmont: "They wanted to suck milk from a withered breast at any price, but what they sucked was blood!"

Even so, Italy started to improve conditions on Sardinia. The road network was completed in 1862. Shortly afterwards, work on the first railway was begun; the line was finished in 1880. But the antiquated methods of production in agriculture and the management of pastureland defied all attempts at

was the establishment of dairies on the island by Neapolitan and Roman businessmen. The *pecorino sardo*, the traditional Sardinian sheep's milk cheese, proved universally popular. Since this led to an increased demand for sheep's milk, there was a revival of the nomadic sheep farming, which the Italian government had originally intended to abolish altogether.

Popular bandits: Once again the island was without just and impartial rulers, so some of the local inhabitants took it upon themselves to assume the reins of power: this was the real reason why banditry escalated. There was scarcely a village on the island which escaped terrorisation by one of them.

progress. Estates were often split up into tiny parcels of land, frequently some distance from each other; additional problems were presented by plagues of locusts, a series of failed harvests, famine and the age-old menace of malaria – which spread with renewed virulence across the land deforested by foreign speculators.

Once again the Sardinians felt they were being exploited by foreigners – this time by the investors from the mainland or overseas, whose aim was to export from the island a maximum quantity of charcoal, cheese and ore for a minimum financial investment. One of the few bright spots on the horizon

Berrina ruled in Dorgali; Oliena was under the sway of Corbeddu, the King of the Macchia, and Ottana under the viceroy of the Macchia, Salvatore Dettore. In Sarule, Giovanni Moni Goddi and Dionigi Mariani fought for supremacy; in Nuoro, it was necessary to obey the Carta brothers to survive. The Sardinian poet Sebastiano Satta (1867–1914) immortalised the bandits during the last century as *"belli, feroci, prodi"* – "handsome, wild and bold". His thinly disguised sympathy echoed the sentiments of many Sardinians.

The poems of Sebastiano Satta, like the novels of Grazia Deledda (1871–1936), who was to receive the Nobel Prize for Literature in 1926, attracted the attention of Italian intellectuals to the island's culture. Researchers began to study Sardinia's archaic language as well as its folklore, which retained numerous traces of pagan influence. And the new political parties, especially the Socialists, also began to take an interest in the island – not in the shepherds and peasants, who were still wholly wrapped up in the past, but in the miners.

Sardinia's mines could have brought the island prosperity. Too small a percentage of the profits, however, was reinvested here. The novelist Grazia Deledda saw them as a factor which had a destructive influence on

better, more decent working and living conditions. In 1900 miners went on strike in their hundreds following in the footsteps of the ferry crews of Carloforte – who had lost their jobs upon the introduction of a steamship – and the printers of Sassari. The wave of strikes reached a tragic climax in 1904 in Buggerru, when three men were killed and several more injured during violent clashes between the strikers and the army. But repression didn't contain the problems. The protest rallies spread from the mines to the towns, and from the towns to the surrounding countryside. The entire working population of Sardinia was in a state of unrest; as a result of all the strikes and demonstrations, a

the primitive but harmonious island world. "The horizon spread out, broad and pure," she wrote in *Elias Portulu*, "the fragrant breeze wafted gently across the deep green pastures: an indescribable dream of peace and untamed solitude… And then, suddenly, this noble landscape, desecrated and laid waste by the black entrances and slag heaps of the mines."

The miners, well known for their rebellious nature, began to voice demands for

Left, women loading coal from the Iglesiente on to sailing boats. **Above**, typical kitchen in a 19th-century farmhouse.

new political awareness was dawning.

During World War I, thousands of Sardinia's inhabitants laid down their lives for their country. The dauntless men of the Brigata "Sassari" were even mentioned in a dispatch; 13,000 of them died on the battlefield. Disenchantment with the government, which once again failed to keep its promises, embittered the ranks of returning troops. They united to form the "Partito Sardo d'Azione", the "Action Party of Sardinia". At long last, after centuries of inaction, Sardinians were once more sufficiently conscious of their national identity to take their fate into their own hands.

MARZO
APRILE
1914

The events of World War I were to provide the main impetus for Sardinia to abandon its insular existence and enter the modern world. This transition was marked by success and failure in equal measure.

The number of Sardinians who took part in the war was unusually high. So, too, was the number of casualties. Almost one-eighth of the entire population, approximately 100,000 soldiers, saw active service; 13,602 of these never returned. This represents a casualty rate of roughly 14 percent, compared with a national average of 10.5 percent. At the same time, these bare statistics indicate that fundamental changes in the Sardinian attitude to life had already taken place. Suddenly the island's residents saw that they could not ignore what was happening on mainland Italy if they were to rise out of the poverty they had so long endured. They realised that Italy and Sardinia shared a common heritage; and that, they must also accept joint responsibility for the fate of Italy as a whole.

Brave men: The four years of warfare in the trenches brought together for the first time officers and soldiers from the various regions of Italy. They were suddenly confronted with the necessity of learning strange new customs as they faced people whose culture and history were quite different from their own. These encounters with non-Sardinians were to leave a more lasting impression on the islanders than any others in their history to date. They fought from first to last for a country which they hoped would not forget their valour after the war was over, and which would help them end the reign of misery on their native shores.

And indeed, their country had no choice but to tackle the problem of Sardinia and acknowledge its brave soldiers. The legendary Sardinian *Brigata Sassari*, which included in its ranks nine holders of the *medaglia d'oro* (corresponding to the medal "Pour le Mérite"), 450 holders of the silver medal, the *medaglia d'argento*, and 551

holders of the bronze medal for bravery, the *medaglia di bronzo*, was also awarded four gold medals for regimental courage, and was mentioned four times in dispatches.

Historians are agreed that the regiment's almost uncanny success was attributable to two factors: not only to the exemplary bravery of the individual soldiers, but also – and more importantly – to the unique spirit of warm-hearted mutual cooperation between officers and men in the illustrious *Brigata*. This latter quality is seen primarily as a

symbol of the moral virtues of the Sardinians rather than of their military superiority.

This feeling of ethnic unity, underlined by their common cultural heritage, intensified during the postwar years. It was fanned by a renewed interest in culture and the arts as well as by various political groups and movements, especially the *Partito Sardo d'Azione*, the Sardinian Action Party.

The men returning from the war during which they had fought so unquestioningly and uncomplainingly for so long, expected to reap in peacetime their reward for the service they had rendered their country. The encounter with other people who had already

Preceding pages: railways played a key role in the transport of coal. **Left,** cover of the magazine *Sardegna*. **Right,** Grazia Deledda.

profited from economic progress and whose standard of living was much better than their own was bound to make the demobilised Sardinian soldiers ponder their lot and draw comparisons. Very soon they found that even their medals and the memories of their bold deeds could no longer console them for the fact that their country did not intend to carry out its promises. Above all, the government was not prepared to grant farmers permission to till fallow land.

Many ex-soldiers joined together to form a *Movimento Combattentistico*, a movement of front-line fighters. They held their first congress in May 1919 in Nuoro. A few months later, three members of the party

his back on the Socialists in order to found the Italian Communist Party, in 1921 the Sardinian front-line fighters decided at their congress in Oristano to form the Sardinian Action Party, the *Partito Sardo d'Azione*. The central elements of the party programme were a varied array of demands directed towards Rome, plus the concept of self-determination for Sardinia.

One of the prime achievements of the *Movimento* and later of the *Partito Sardo d'Azione* was their encouragement of an active political awareness in large numbers of young people and peasants who had lost patience with the old liberal democratic order. As the population at large became more

were elected to the Italian Parliament. Many cherished the secret hope that they would finally be allowed to carry the island's economy and society forward into the 20th century. Of course it was not only the members of the *Movimento Combattentistico* who believed that the party represented the only chance for a sufficiently powerful front to bring about a radical change in the national policy towards the island.

The Sardinian Action Party: For Antonio Gramsci from Cagliari (1891–1937), the movement was "the first people's country party, above all in central and southern Italy". Although Gramsci was about to turn

politically active, so their representatives put into practice with greater fervour the view acquired in the trenches, that a unified Sardinia was a powerful regional entity. And so, for the first time, Sardinia possessed a strong people's party. Tightly organised, it opened meeting rooms and local groups throughout the island and carried the political arguments from the towns to the remotest corners of the countryside.

Even the rural population gathered together to form its own movement, which seemed to be in a position at last to lure the peasants and shepherds out of their traditional exile from political and social life.

Initially among the front-line fighters' movement and the rural people's movement, and subsequently in the *Partito Sardo d'Azione*, there was a maturing concept of a decentralised, democratic particularism. This soon led to demands for a special statute of autonomy for Sardinia, not only by virtue of its geographic location but also its specific history and culture.

The period between 1919 and 1921 was dominated by a continuous spirit of republicanism. During this time, however, the particularist doctrine flourished in many different forms: there remained a strong monarchist faction, supported above all by intellectuals and lawyers, as well as various anti-working class, anti-Bolshevist and middle-class factions.

In the wake of Fascism: In 1923 Paolo Pili, the leader of the wing with Fascist sympathies, brought about a split in the party when he and fellow-sympathisers left to join the PNF, the *Partito Nazionale Fascista*, the Fascist party. That this schism should occur at all was a major setback for General Asclepio Gandolfo, Mussolini's authorised representative. He had been responsible for the island's affairs since 1922 and had been instructed to use his good offices behind the scenes with the aim of promoting unification between autonomists, Fascists and militant front-line fighters in both camps.

Since the fusion of the various particularist factions with the Fascist party had now failed, the changed allegiance of Pili's group aroused widespread interest among the population at large. Pili himself had been appointed Party Secretary of the PNF for Cagliari. Under his leadership was formed *Fedlac*, the *Federazione delle Cooperative Lattiero-Casearie della Sardegna* (the Sardinian Dairy Cooperative). The aim of this new institution was to protect shepherds' yields from the near-monopoly of a few large concerns.

Fedlac was an unqualified success; between 1925 and 1927 it even achieved a breakthrough with the export of sheep's milk cheese, *pecorino,* to the American market, where it was a huge success. This embryonic contact was to gain in value particularly after World War II, when cooperatives, such as

the *Consorzio Caseario Regionale* (the Regional Dairy Consortium) sprang up across the entire island.

Pili was skilful in taking advantage of Fascist policies as well as part of the cooperative programme of the Sardinian Independence Movement in order to further his own cause, until he fell from favour and was expelled from the PNF. Only a short while later, *Fedlac*, which had been formed on his initiative, fell victim to the world recession, followed one by one by less ambitious initiatives which had sprung up to protect wine and corn production.

The declared political aim, that of "providing a new framework for some aspects of

the *Partito Sardo d'Azione* within the Fascist party", was never achieved. In the 1924 elections the Sardinian Action Party did less well than the Fascist unified list of candidates, but it was still represented – much to the chagrin of the Fascists. Thanks to the influence of Emilio Lussu and Camillo Bellieni, the Sardinian Independence Movement became more popular and more anti-Fascist in tone.

After the assassination of the Socialist Giacomo Matteotti, Lussu became aware of the dangers of continued isolationism in spite of his reservations towards Marxism. He thus sought increased contact with the

Left, rural workers at the end of the 19th century. **Right**, basket-weaver in the Barbagia, *c*. 1900.

Communists, whilst Gramsci's Socialists desperately attempted to acquire the support not only of factory hands but also of farm labourers, despite their traditional suspicion of industrial workers. Gramsci made no secret of his intention of luring voters away from the Sardinian Action Party; at the Rural Internationale of the Fifth Sardinian Action Party Congress, he gave an inflammatory speech aimed at producing this split.

Political extremes: During the 1924 elections, the list with the five-pointed star contained the names of candidates representing widely conflicting interests – progressive liberals and constitutional monarchists and men like Mario Berlinguer, who was able to

emphasis on including in their own programme some of the characteristic demands of the Sardinian Independence Movement, e.g. the abolition of unemployment and the increasing of productivity. On 6 November 1924, the Royal Edict no. 1931 was proclaimed. It was later to be known as the *Legge del Miliardo*, the "Law of the Milliard": promulgated at the instigation of the Fascists, it was designed to remove, or at least to minimise, the most glaring causes of Sardinian unrest.

Indeed, the state of the island at the time was in many respects truly wretched. In 260 of the 364 communities there was no running water; only seven communities had their

assert himself against older, more moderate leaders, and who had won a seat whilst he was still a young man. But the hope that all these widely differing approaches might be united in a common cause proved short-lived. It was not long before the Fascist dictatorship held sway on Sardinia too, despite its clearly ambivalent policy as regards the island. On the one hand, the Fascists were anxious to solve Sardinia's prevailing economic and social problems, but at the same time they were also determined to quell at source even the most modest attempts at autonomy.

From 1924 the Fascist Party laid great

own sewage system, and 156 communities had no primary school. Statistically speaking, there were not even enough teachers to allow for one per school. In 1925, an investigation of educational standards on the island revealed that more than half the 870,000 natives of Sardinia (58 percent) were illiterate. Of the 120,000 school-age children on the island, only 81,000 were registered at a school; of these, barely 60,000 attended with any degree of regularity.

In 1925, the Inspectorate of Public Works – the *Provveditorato alle Opere Pubbliche* – was established as part of the attempt to give priority to the Sardinian "Renaissance". A number of state undertakings which had been put into abeyance during the war were now revived. Progress was made especially in the region around Terralba, where 25,000 acres (10,000 hectares) of land had already been developed by the Società Bonifiche Sarde, and in the vicinity of Sanluri, where 5,000 acres (2,000 hectares) were available for development. In the Nurra, too, the town of Fertilia sprang up in the middle of 5,700 acres (2,300 hectares) of what was now agricultural land. Near Terralbas 4,000 settlers built the town of Mussolinia, known these days as Arborea.

Considerable efforts were made to overcome the island's chronic water shortage: in

proved impossible to equal the record set by the Fascists in this respect.

Mussolini's Sardinian policy: Following Mussolini's declaration of absolute rule exploitation of the metal and coal mines on the island was intensified, especially in the Sulcis Basin, where the town of Carbonia was founded in 1938. From here coal was exported via the port of Sant'Antioco. The settlement grew rapidly, acting as a magnet for Sardinia's unemployed as well as for workers, peasants and shepherds from all over the island, who left their homes in the hope of finding permanent employment. The development naturally led to the rapid formation of a working class – the first in the

1923 the King officially commissioned the Tirso Dam, in 1926 the Coghinas Dam was put into operation, and construction work began on the present hydraulic station on the Flumendosa. The rate at which these ambitious projects were completed was intended to put in the shade all irrigation projects on Sardinia, past and future. And indeed, despite the continuously increasing demand for water – a prerequisite for progress of every kind on the island – to date it has

Left, coal sailing boats on the beach of the Iglesiente, 19th century. **Above**, in those days the *matanza* harvested a great many fish.

country; it was well organised along trade union lines.

Nuoro became the provincial capital in 1926, but failed to develop to meet expectations and requirements. In the interior of the island things remained as they had always been: the inhabitants eked out a meagre existence as labourers and shepherds, while many of the more august leading citizens discovered an unexpected taste for Fascism, using their position as head of the district council or as mayor to promote their own interests. Corruption was rife.

The efforts of the Fascists to bring about a rapid integration of the island were most successful in places where economic measures were implemented and where their propaganda reached the people. They failed utterly in the most remote country areas, where the population continued to adhere to traditional work methods and social forms, and where the restless mood of the towns could not arouse support.

The Fascists attempted to quash all Sardinian attempts at independence by limiting the influence of its most dangerous representatives and by encouraging the islanders to adopt a more centralised culture and way of thought.

Mussolini's representatives fought with particular determination against the *bandit-*

June 1923, Mussolini harangued the crowd with the message that he had not come to Sardinia merely to get to know the island. Forty-eight hours would hardly be long enough for that, and especially not to get to the bottom of the intractable problems of the inhabitants.

He, Mussolini, was aware of them – as all those who had ruled the island during the past 50 years had also been aware of them. Indeed, the entire nation was aware of the problems, and if no solutions had been found so far, then it was only because until that day they had lacked the iron will of renewal which constituted the heart, the essence and the credo of the Fascist government.

ismo. The public safety regulations of 1931 transformed what was hitherto a compulsory domicile order under the local magistrate into house arrest supervised by the police. This meant that all suspects lost virtually all their rights, and that they were utterly at the mercy of the whims of the prefect, quaestor, commander of the *carabinieri* or chief of the militia. Even a hint of suspicion was sufficient to put someone behind bars; informers flourished and old feuds were revived – only to be unreported by the heavily censored press. Problems swept aside in one place had a habit of reappearing again somewhere else.

In a speech delivered in Cagliari on 11

What Mussolini failed to appreciate was that even men like Cavour had had a clear understanding of Sardinia's problems. In 1849 he had replied to the urgent requests of Sardinian members of Parliament for help for their country: "I do not question that Sardinia's situation could be improved by investing a great deal of money. If the Kingdom were a great power instead of a small state, perhaps I might not blanch at demanding of the cabinet a few millions for the island's development."

Even a master-demagogue like Mussolini took cover behind a torrent of words. And yet it would be wrong to maintain that the Fascists were unaware of the true situation on Sardinia, or that they had failed to undertake any measures which might have improved the islanders' lot.

In 1935, 40 million lire were made available for major development projects; the money disappeared in Sassari and Cagliari. In spite of an apparent lack of interest, Nuoro managed to achieve a modest degree of prosperity and some progress during this period, whilst Fascist policies were working towards independent free enterprise, especially in agriculture. A few contemporary statistics will serve to prove the point.

The economy of the Thirties: The farmers' greatest wealth lay in their livestock:

cially for women. In the province of Nuoro alone, 734 weaving frames produced a surplus of 110,000 yards (100,000 metres) of fabric, for the weaving factories in Prato and Biella produced cheaper fabric of poorer quality. The population increased only minimally – by 6,000 people – between 1911 and 1921. There were numerous reasons for this unusually low rate of increase: the large number of war victims, high infant mortality – which was also a result of the deplorable sanitary conditions and malnutrition – and, as always, a depressingly high total of malaria victims (98 deaths compared with a total of 12 for the rest of the country).

Of 328,000 Sardinians in full-time em-

608,000 sheep, 160,000 goats, 60,000 cattle, 35,000 pigs, 8,000 donkeys and 13,000 horses. They also harvested 240,000 hundredweight (12,200 tonnes) of barley, 270,000 hundredweight (14,000 tonnes) of wheat, 200,000 hundredweight (12,000 tonnes) of potatoes, 36,000 hundredweight (1,800 tonnes) of oil, 90,000 hundredweight (4,600 tonnes) of almonds and 34,000 hundredweight (1,700 tonnes) of grapes.

The production of coarse woollen fabrics created a large number of new jobs, espe-

Left, Mussolini inspects the model of the city of Carbonia. **Above**, canteen in an Iglesiente mine.

ployment, at least 200,000 worked in agriculture and sheep farming, 15,000 in trade, 13,000 in the transport industries, 62,000 in industry and 41,000 in miscellaneous professions. This figure decreased by a total of 9,000 between 1911 and 1920 due to reduced demand and the recession linked to the war.

The Serpieri Laws of 1924 and 1933 were aimed at the development of all cultivable land on the island, much of which lay fallow or, if it was tilled at all, was frequently divided into uneconomically small parcels. Although pastural agriculture and free-range cattle farming continued to predominate, in 1930 it was noted that of a total of

127,000 agricultural concerns, more than 70,000 farmed less than 7 acres (3 hectares) of land.

The Fascist land reform was intended to bring about an increase in the population. This did, in fact, occur; a further change was the introduction of new crops, such as the cultivation of rice near Arborea. Between 1921 and 1931 the population grew by 1.2 percent, and from 1931 until the census in 1936 by a further 1.26 percent, resulting in a total figure of 1,004,000.

In 1936, 376,000 Sardinians were in full-time employment in the following areas: 16,000 in the transport industry, 78,000 in industry, 211,000 in agriculture and 46,000

50,000 mark, and smaller towns – Olbia, Alghero, Oristano, Tempio, Iglesias and Carbonia, also gained in significance.

Rural concerns: The interior of the island and the smaller towns were of no particular interest to the Fascists; they left things here much as they had always been. After the *Podestà*, as the mayor was called under the Fascists, the most powerful man was the Party Secretary. It was his task to supervise official duties in conjunction with the mayor, and to preserve for the principal families a certain number of privileges and a modicum of respect.

The inhabitants of the interior devoted themselves exclusively to their own prob-

in miscellaneous professions. Italy exhibited a diminished concern for the island's problems for a number of years, but showed a revived interest during the years leading up to World War II. The island acquired strategic importance, in particular as a military base and as a supplier of raw materials which were to contribute towards the realisation of Mussolini's long-held dreams of an all-powerful Italy.

The Fascists were most active in the most densely populated towns. Between 1921 and 1931 the population of Cagliari almost doubled, reaching a total of almost 100,000. During the same period Sassari topped the

lems rather than to national politics. Orgosolo was the scene of a bloody feud; between 1925 and 1935 there was further unrest, the causes of which had never really been settled. This was the heyday of the legendary bandits, who were soon translated by folk tales and popular song into resolute, philanthropic heroes. The best-known of these Sardinian Robin Hoods were undoubtedly Samuelo Stocchino from Arzana and the Pintore brothers from Bitti.

During the years leading up to World War II, the Ethiopia Campaign and the Spanish Civil War led large numbers of Sardinians to join the armed forces for the second time.

There was a shortage of male labour in all areas of industry; many projects begun by the Fascists were never completed, and the lack of men to work on the land made farming even less productive than it had been. Furthermore, a fresh malaria epidemic on Sardinia took a heavy toll of victims.

In 1936 only 24,623 workers were still employed in cattle farming, compared with 42,103 in 1921. A number of the Sardinian working class was employed not in industry but in agricultural concerns which had sprung up as part of the land reform, or in small or medium-sized dairy farms. Few of them were permanently employed. The interior regions were firmly in the hands of semi-

holder) usually brought neither equipment nor capital into the arrangement.

The contracts for leasehold cooperatives mostly ran for only two years. It often happened that a farmer or reaper would work virtually all the farmland in his native community during the course of his working life. Strictly speaking they were no longer sons of the soil, but could farm any of the land belonging to a considerably larger community, i.e. that of their rural district. Not only did this leasehold system allow even the poorest Sardinian peasants to make a reasonable living for their families; it also gave the landowners a greater degree of freedom in permitting them to adapt the use of their

leaseholders, leaseholders and settlers who had been allocated their own plot of land by the Fascists.

Land reforms: The parcelling out of cultivable land typical for Sardinia prevented the establishment of the semi-leasehold system in extensive regions. More common was the so-called *Compartecipazione* (leasehold cooperative). By and large the system had much in common with the tilling of land by paid hands; the *Compartecipante* (co-lease-

Left, Emilio Lusso, a leading Sardinian political intellectual. **Above**, communist leader Enrico Berlinguer, who also came from Sardinia.

fields to the constantly changing conditions.

Serious attempts to improve Sardinian agriculture were put into operation following the "Mussolini Law" of 24 December 1928. More than one-third of the island was affected by the land reform. In all, 449,194 acres (181,339 hectares) of land were placed under irrigation, 1,791,000 acres (725,000 hectares) were subject to the local government reform and 19,440 acres (7,867 hectares) of mountainous territory were developed for the first time. The Land Reform Ordinance for the whole of Sardinia dated 13 December 1933 had the ambitious aim of developing 2,185,883 acres (884,615 hectares) of land – in other words, one-quarter of the entire island. But progress was slower than had been hoped, and by 1938 about 10 percent of the target had been developed.

In general, the Fascists used public works as a means of exerting direct control over the poorer classes and the unemployed. Some prefects even instituted forced labour groups for the maintenance of the roads within a community; this was the case, for example, in Cagliari in 1931 and 1932. During the final years before the outbreak of World War II, ever-increasing numbers of islanders were caught in the poverty trap or got into debt. More and more people were forced to take out large mortgages on their homes, to

culture, which allowed the population by and large to continue to exist in dignity. Unrest seldom penetrated into this world, except when some ancient feud flared up again, when the alarming deeds of Samuele Stocchino, the Pintore brothers or some other bandits attracted attention, or when thousands of young men were required to join the armed forces in Ethiopia, Spain or to take part in World War II. By an ironic stroke of fate, Sardinia had to pay a high price – two wars and thousands of dead – in order to buy its way into the 20th century.

Sardinian autonomy: Article 116 of the Italian Constitution states that "Sicily, Sardinia, Trentino-Alto Adige, Friuli-Venezia-Giulia

put their property up for auction, or even to flee the country.

To summarise, it would be correct to say that between the two world wars Sardinia was dominated by the Fascists, who succeeded in taking the wind out of the sails of the independence movements which had arisen after World War I, the so-called front-line fighters and the Sardinian Action Party.

Life in the towns followed the middle-class pattern found elsewhere in Italy, supporting Fascism and being rewarded with a wide range of advantages and privileges. By contrast, life in the country retained its reactionary outlook and its own, self-contained

and the Valle d'Aosta shall be awarded particular forms and conditions of autonomy according to separate constitutional laws and statutes." At the end of World War II, the worst effects of which the island was largely spared, Sardinia felt itself more isolated than ever from the political and economic situation of mainland Italy. And so the hopes of all became concentrated on autonomy, universally considered to be the only way of tackling the province's numerous unsolved problems.

In 1944 the Rome government appointed a High Commissioner to supervise the running of the island. It was his task to coordinate the activities of the prefects, to act as local representative for the central government and to assume the ultimate control of both civil and military administration. Later on, six members of an executive committee assisted the High Commissioner in the performance of his duties.

In December 1944 a regional assembly was created to advise the High Commissioner. It consisted originally of 18, and later of 24 members of the political parties and trades unions as well as representatives of industry and the arts. This body remained in operation until 8 May 1949 – the day on which the Sardinian people elected its first regional parliament. Shortly afterwards, following the formation of the first regional committee, the High Commissioner resigned from his post.

The regional advisory committee had two main functions: to produce a draft for a Statute of Autonomy which would then be presented to the central government for approval, and in close cooperation with the High Commissioner to submit a plan to improve the island's economy as well as helping the large numbers of unemployed and needy inhabitants and malaria victims, whose position was hopeless at the time.

The final draft of the Statute of Autonomy was passed by the regional committee in April 1947 and passed on by its president to the National Constitutional Committee. On 20 June, they approved Article 116, in which Sardinia – along with a number of other regions – was awarded special status. In a plenary session on 21 July, the Constitutional Committee discussed an application submitted by a number of Sardinian members of parliament. They came to the conclusion that the Sardinian statute should be investigated immediately.

The commission of the Constitutional Committee responsible for the statute produced a new draft, which was accepted by the full committee on 31 January 1948 – one day before the committee was disbanded. The Sardinian Statute became Constitutional Law No. 3 on 26 February 1948. The gist of the first of the 58 articles of the statute states that Sardinia and its islands is an autonomous region, which can lay claim to its own legal responsibility within the framework of the indivisible political unity of the Republic of Italy and the conditions laid down by constitutional law.

The Sardinian Statute: The statute itself is subdivided into eight sections: (1) the structure of the autonomous region, (2) its function, (3) its official bodies, (4) the smaller local authorities, (5) the relationship between religion and the State, (6) the ways of revising the statute and (7) and (8) interim measures.

Article 3 is of particular importance, for it lists a series of areas which the region is entitled to administer entirely independently

from central government. Among these are:
● the organisation of offices and administrative bodies within the region, including the legal position and pecuniary situation of its employees
● the local districts
● the local community or town police force and the regional police force
● agriculture and forestry, small development measures and projects aimed at increased yields or soil quality improvement
● public works affecting only the region
● building construction and town planning
● public transport by bus or tram
● thermal springs and medicinal spas

Left, even today transport is difficult. **Right**, the Ferrovia Sarde is these days only of limited local importance.

- hunting and fishing
- the right of administration of public waterways as if they were public property
- the right of administration of mines, quarries and salt works as if they were public property
- customs and morals
- crafts
- tourism and gastronomy
- local authority libraries and museums.

Emphasis should be placed on Article 13 of the statute, which declared that, with the approval of the region, the State had drawn up a plan designed to eradicate the economic and social problems of the province.

A cherished dream: The Sardinians' hope especially from the Republicans and other progressives.

However, what we should nowadays call an economic revival actually took place at a very slow pace indeed. It was not until 1951 that the central government, with the long-awaited approval of the regional committee, at last formed an "advisory commission", with the task of "studying the island's resources and planning economic development in the spheres of agriculture, mining, industry, trade, transport, banking and credit, and the social structure of education."

The work of the "Study Commission", as it was usually called by the islanders, made very slow progress. One problem was the

that at some time in the future their land will see better times again is as old as the history of the island. It was a great source of strength in dark times, and supplied during the past 200 years the motivation for the best-informed and most progressive section of Sardinian society, which was in no way inferior to the intellectual and political elite of the rest of the country. Giorgio Asproni, for example, was one of Giuseppe Mazzini's most intelligent and influential advisors. He boldly supported Sardinia's interests as senator under the monarchy in Turin, opposing the centralist policies of Cavour and gaining for his native island much sympathy,

alterations to instructions and strategy issued by Rome; another was the difficulty experienced by the region itself when it was required to produce a clear analysis of the most urgent tasks. Finally, in 1958, the Commission presented its "Final Report on Investigations Preliminary to an Economic Revival". In the report, the Commission demanded the investment of 862 billion lire (at contemporary values), of which 546 billion should be made available by the state during the course of the following decade.

Still no positive action was taken, however. In 1959 another commission was instituted, with instructions to formulate a more precise plan of action. During the same year, Statute No.7 created a regional civil service department. The latter soon produced results and presented a "Final Report" during the year in which it was formed. The report demonstrated the need for measures to support 18 separate areas, especially industry. These areas would then exert a positive effect on the remaining areas, finally putting an end to the traditional economic underdevelopment of Sardinia.

Surprisingly, although several years had passed, the total sum to be invested was considerably less than that quoted in the first report. Suddenly, only 670 billion lire would be required. This did not mean, however,

Statute no. 522. It bore the title "Extraordinary Project to Further the Economic and Social Development of Sardinia in Execution of Article 13 of Constitutional Statute no.3 of 26 February 1948".

By now, 16 years had passed since the beginning of the negotiations. The sum of money to be invested had shrunk once more, to 400 billion lire, to be spread over 12 instead of 10 years.

The period after 1945, in other words the time since the implementation of the Statute of Autonomy, divides into three distinct phases according to the historian Manlio Brigaglia. During the first of these, "between 1945 and 1955, the island gradually adapted

that action would be taken immediately to precipitate the longed-for upswing. On 17 January 1961, the Italian government agreed a draft law which was then presented to Parliament and the Sardinian local assembly. During a skilfully engineered discussion, the region insisted on the execution of the plan.

After protracted discussions between the Senate and the House of Representatives the bill finally became law on 2 June 1962, as

Left, the modern European port of Cagliari. **Above**, the price of ruthless industrialisation: petrochemical plants at Porto Torres.

to the conditions and lifestyle of the rest of the nation. During the second phase, between 1956 and 1966, conditions on the island changed more rapidly and social patterns altered considerably. The third phase, from 1966 until the present day, is characterised by a discrepancy between development as it has actually taken place and a desire to limit those aspects which have no direct relevance to the local culture of Sardinia, and which would lead to a long-term subordination to the mainland system."

Despite all the mistakes and delays, for which some blame can also be attributed to the local government, Sardinia has made remarkable progress in all spheres of its public life and economy since the war. The three public censuses in 1951, 1961 and 1971 listed a total population of 1,269,000, 1,419,000 and 1,474,000 respectively. Despite this increase, the number of illiterates decreased from 221,000 in 1951 to 177,000 in 1961. In 1961 the number of people in employment totalled 433,000; 51 percent of these worked in agriculture. Ten years later the distribution looked quite different: the percentage employed on the land had shrunk to 33.2 percent, with 31.7 percent of workers employed in industry and 35.1 percent in miscellaneous professions.

Considerable progress was achieved on

the educational front. In 1963, 163,000 pupils were being taught in primary schools; by 1970 the figure had grown to 166,000. Some 17,000 children attended middle schools in 1951; by 1970, 75,500 did so. Whilst there were only 9,000 pupils enrolled at secondary schools in 1951, by 1970 the number had risen to 49,000; and the number of students attending the two universities in Cagliari and Sassari multiplied tenfold between 1951 (just over 2,000) and 1970 (20,000). This figure does not include the large numbers of students following courses at a mainland university in Rome, Florence, Pisa, Milan, Turin, Genoa or Bologna.

In many areas the growth rate in Sardinia lies above the national average: in the number of telephone lines in use, for example, the numbers of radios and television sets, the amount of printed matter and the number of private cars.

There was also a remarkable increase in sea transport. In 1954, 429,000 passengers were carried across to the island; 10 years later, the figure had reached over one million. Contributing to this total were not only the increasing numbers of Sardinian emigrants returning home on holiday, but also the rising numbers of tourist visitors. Within a few years it seemed as if the entire world had suddenly heard of Sardinia; businessmen were also attracted to the island and a full-scale tourist industry blossomed, enthusiastically transforming previously uninhabited or uninhabitable regions such as the Costa Smeralda – the "Emerald Coast", developed by the Aga Khan.

Booming tourism, industrialisation and the rapid transition from agriculture to the service industries, the equally rapid spread of the high-spending consumer society, and the introduction of universal education and transport systems, coupled with the population shift from the poorer regions to the industrial conurbations have altered Sardinia's countenance more profoundly during the past 30 years than the previous two centuries had done.

There seems little doubt that the lifestyle and character of the Sardinian population have undergone profound changes – changes which are still under way (unfortunately not always for the better). Particularly in the remote regions of the interior, they have precipitated a crisis in the native culture and behaviour patterns based on traditions reaching back over thousands of years. Bearing in mind the rapid pace of change typical of our era, which seems set to drag Sardinia into the contemporary history of the western hemisphere complete with all its victims, homeless and new poor, it is by no means certain whether this progress will prove to be to the advantage of the Sardinians as a whole. For the time being, at least, the fulfilment of their long-cherished dream of independence and self-reliance seems uncertain.

Left and right, murals are expressions of cultural identity, rebellion or just plain fun.

Sardinia's history has always been closely bound to that of its shepherds, whose lifestyle is as fascinating as it is full of privations. Even today, this little island – the home of about one-third of Italy's entire sheep population – produces almost half the country's sheep's milk. Some 3.8 million sheep graze the hillsides of Sardinia, compared with 11 million in the whole of Italy. The native Sardinian sheep is small and hardy, able to withstand the harsh conditions, and produces a high milk yield in spite of often poor pastures.

Sheep rearing has a long and honourable tradition here. It was the subject of considerable attention under the Romans, in the Middle Ages and especially under Spanish rule. At other times it was further developed by various religious orders; the Benedictines, in particular, were very diligent in this respect. Absurdly enough, it also profited from the migration from the land; previously fertile fields were left fallow and reverted to pasture which could be taken over at leisure by the shepherds and their flocks. Although the Enclosure Laws of the 19th century portioned off much of the plateau land, most of the mountainous area remains wild and unfenced. As today, these parts were largely too inaccessible and barren for any form of arable farming.

Sheep farming enjoyed a further upsurge as a result of the involvement of a group of enterprising businessmen from Rome who established industrial cheese factories between 1885 and 1890. Here they produced on a large-scale basis the *pecorino romano* (sheep's milk cheese), popular in Italy since Roman times (Pliny refers to it in his *Historia Naturalis*). With the help of aggressive marketing, the cheese was an immediate hit in the United States where it was warmly welcomed by the large number of Italian immigrants. Today it is popular throughout the entire world. Pungent and tangy, it is eaten with bread, grated over pasta and fre-

quently used in cooking, especially in *pesto*.

At the turn of the century the success of the *pecorino romano* transformed many of the antiquated sheep farming methods employed on the island. New production techniques and modern ideas gave the entire profession a new lease of life, forcing it out of its traditional lethargy. But – as is often the case in times of rapid change – even as the first dairy production cooperatives were being formed, there were still extensive areas of land where farmers clung to the old order.

The shepherd was upheld as a symbol of an entire culture which was in danger of disappearing as a result of the links being forged with other spheres of industry. The sinister innovations were met with reactions ranging from suspicion to outright hostility. As a rule shepherds are deeply conservative people; even today a few still wear national dress as a matter of course (those who don't tend to wear a brown corduroy suit). They were extremely reluctant to have their affairs regulated by an outside force.

Popular cheese: Sheep and *pecorino* together form one of the oldest and steadiest pillars of the island economy. The following

Preceding pages: candle-light procession in Alghero; workers in the fields. Left, shepherd in his house with pecorino moulds. Right, flock on its way into a feudal pen.

figures will prove the point. During the first 28 years of this century, the quantities of *pecorino romano* exported by Sardinia rose from 1,000 to 4,000 tonnes. And in 1980 – despite increasing industrialisation and the development of tourism as a source of income – sheep and dairy farming was still a highly profitable business accounting for a substantial slice of the gross national product. It provided 30,000 people with work and produced a turnover of 580 billion lire.

The encouraging statistics disguise the fact that the entire industry has as much difficulty in ensuring that its organisation moves with the times, as in introducing modern production methods.

improved breeding methods, for instance, or working in closer cooperation with fellow-shepherds, or creating areas of pastureland which would not only serve as a source of food for the animals in winter, but which – more importantly – would be available during the six to eight-month periods of drought in summer.

A Sardinian flock averages only 100–400 animals – a total which is more frequently undercut than surpassed. And yet the trade as a whole, contrary to popular impressions, is profitable and continues to attract young Sardinians, who sometimes even abandon jobs in the factories and mines to wander across the countryside with their sheep. One

The biggest problem of all, and the most insoluble, is the individualistic nature of the Sardinian shepherds. In spite of everything, they continue to live in their pastures or their sheep sheds, completely cut off from the rest of the world. They may wander for months on end with their flocks, and some, usually those whose pastures are particularly remote, still make the cheese themselves, in their own *ovili* (sheepfolds) – stone huts attached to brushwood milking enclosures. Most are not even remotely interested in modern discoveries which could help them and therefore the industry as a whole – developing more resistant animals as a result of

reason why the industry is so attractive is that it has prestige. Independence is considered more valuable than monetary gain. Unlike the factory worker, a shepherd takes orders from no-one. In addition, these young urban workers tend to nurse romantic images of banditry and the Codice Barbaricino, the unwritten law of resolving conflict through brigandage, vendettas and kidnapping. Altogether some 28,000–30,000 people are employed in Sardinia's sheep and dairy farming industries.

The products: A Sardinian sheep gives large quantities of milk; if the profits from this are added to those from the wool and lambs produced, the value of a sheep can double in a single year.

Virtually all the sheep's milk produced is made into cheese, either by the shepherd himself or by cooperatives, or by the increasing numbers of small companies which are flexible enough to be able to adapt to the rapidly changing requirements of their Italian and overseas customers.

The first cooperative was formed in 1907 in Bortigali, near Macomer. Its aim was to protect local shepherds from the Roman businessmen who, adept at making capital of their own financial resources as well as the Sardinians' poverty and lack of unity, were poised to monopolise the sheep industry.

These days marketing of the sheep's milk cheese is largely supervised by the *Consorzio Caseario Sardegna*, the consortium of the Sardinian sheep and dairy farming industry. The advantages of an organisation of this kind are obvious. As a result of its being able to exclude the grasping middlemen whose services were previously indispensable, it can make much more money available to the shepherds and breeders.

Medium-sized and large private cheese-making factories can claim particular success. Forty-five factories produce 60 percent of the *pecorino romano* as well as most *tipo toscanello* and *canestrato*. Private concerns undertake the marketing of their own prod-

Today there are more than 50 cheese-making factories on the island, the majority of which are situated away from the coast. Apart from *pecorino romano* (40 percent), they also produce a sweet white variety known as *pecorino tipo toscanello* and *canestrato*, a cylindrical sheep's milk cheese. The district around Gavoi is famous for its *pecorino fiore-sardo*, nowadays mostly exported to Apulia, where it is sold in quantity as a great delicacy. In the Abruzzi it is served with pears.

Left, preparation of the famous *pecorino* cheese. **Above**, moulds in a *pecorino* dairy in Dorgali.

ucts at home and abroad and many have been very successful at extending their markets. The cheese exported in largest quantities is still the *pecorino romano*, which is famous not only in Latium, Liguria, Apulia, Tuscany, Umbria and Lombardy, but also in the United States, France, Greece, Canada and Germany.

But recently, increased production of *pecorino romano* has resulted in a surplus, for it is difficult to find a market for all of the 6,000 tonnes produced annually. Attention has therefore turned to increasing the quantities of sweet and soft cheeses, since they are finding favour with a wider circle of devotees. In spite of their relatively high price, these cheeses have gained popularity not only the length and breadth of Italy and abroad, but also on Sardinia itself. This is due in part to the increased prosperity of the islanders and the steadily rising numbers of tourist visitors, which in high season equal the residents themselves. In other regions of Italy – for example, in Latium – in order to meet this increased demand, a proportion of the milk yield is frozen during the months of highest production and turned into cheese during the summer and early autumn when production falls.

An excellent curd cheese (*ricotta*) is also made from the *pecorino*. Light and bland, it

date – the relatively high prices fetched by cheese, *ricotta*, wool and lamb, and the favourable market situation – should not be allowed to distract attention from some of the unsolved problems in the sheep and dairy farming industry. The work environment and working conditions of the shepherds are still not conducive to an appropriate standard of living for the 1990s, although big improvements have been a matter of course in other spheres of industry.

What's more, modernisation of the industry could help to solve the problem of banditry, which in some areas is tantamount to a profitable sideline for the shepherds. Seasonal trends in crime have traditionally cor-

makes a good accompaniment to *pane carausa*, the crisp thin bread – at one time shepherds virtually lived on this and *ricotta* on their long wanderings – and is used in cooking. One particular use of *ricotta* is in the preparation of ravioli and *sebadas*, the typical Sardinian hors d'oeuvres popular with Italians and foreigners alike. Initially only on the menu in a few specialist restaurants in Oliena and Nuoro, *sebadas* have since won over the palates of the entire island – even on Costa Smeralda, not known for its gastronomic excellence despite its many expensive hotels.

It is important, however, that success to

responded to transhumance movements. The increase in winter crime in lowland grazing areas has always coincided with the presence of transhumant shepherds. Some studies have noted an incease in crime when shepherds' rents fall due.

There is still plenty of room for action; an economic infrastructure must be created, and sheep rearing must be organised differently, for – despite the financial gains to be made – at some stage in the foreseeable future there may be no one left who is willing to wander across the countryside with his flock for months on end.

The regional government has been talking

for years about undertaking the necessary measures, but – as is so often the case – these good intentions are not enough. The 1950s saw substantial improvements in other areas of agriculture, with incentives for farmers, the completion of numerous irrigation projects and an increasing level of mechanisation, but the pastoral areas received little help from the authorities.

Fundamental changes must be brought about, and modern businesses created, with sufficient pasture at their disposal and efficiently-planned livestock sheds equipped with all the lastest facilities, from lighting to running water to milking machines, and regular veterinary care for the flocks.

It is time to admit that the national and regional reform statutes of 1974 and 1976 have largely failed. Only a sensible distribution of credit and the creation of a number of medium-sized companies are likely to permit the ancient vocation of sheep rearing to enter the 20th century.

Quick solutions are required – ones which will have sufficient impact to break through the rigidity of established traditions. They should also guarantee those employed in this sector an appropriate standard of living and a new niche in modern society.

Only by these means can a traditional livelihood and a culture which has existed for thousands of years be saved. If nothing is

Fifteen years ago, a parliamentary investigative committee demanded the immediate implementation of some of the measures listed above. At the time, however, it was stated that the establishment of estates or even designated areas of pasture would be a serious mistake, less from an economic than from a cultural point of view. It was considered sufficient if the government intervened financially in the case of exceptional cold or drought, or a livestock epidemic.

Left, a Sardinian shepherd's profession involves plenty of hard work. **Above**, shepherds know and love every animal of their flock.

undertaken, the inevitable invasion of Sardinian villages by modernity, the continuing migration from the land, the industrialisation of the island and the growing numbers of local inhabitants employed in the service industries will ensure that the shepherd is increasingly isolated from society, and possibly even excluded altogether.

Furthermore, a dangerous gap could arise between an increasingly impoverished interior, where sheep and dairy farming would still be the main source of income, and the comparatively wealthy regions of the island – not to mention a booming mainland Italy or the rest of Europe.

The *Dizionario Archivistico per la Sardegna* (Historical Dictionary of Sardinia) by Francesco Loddo Canepa, which was first published by the Historical Archive of Sardinia in 1926, explains the term *bandito* in the following way: "The word is derived from the Catalan word *bandejat*, Spanish *bandeado*. Bandits were men condemned to a prison sentence without the fact being made publicly known; or else they were men sought by the police in connection with a serious felony with an equally severe sentence, who had already been questioned concerning the crimes of which they were suspected. But bandits also included men for whom an arrest warrant had been issued by the local judge, but who had fled into the *Macchia* in order to avoid arrest."

Loddo Canepa's definition summarises the main categories as they were listed by Sardinian law between 1394 and 1927. It is more precise than Eleonora d'Arborea's *Carta di Logu* and the civil and criminal legal code drawn up by Charles Felix. Nowadays, the term "bandit" is still used to describe someone who flees justice following a crime, taking refuge in the *macchia* – usually

in the company of a band of like-minded individuals. In Sardinia the latter is mostly a short-lived unit with clearly defined aims, in contrast with the *Camorra* or the *Mafia* of mainland Italy, which are stable criminal groups that have a well-established organisational structure.

In Roman times: As long ago as Roman times, bandits plagued these regions. The Greek historian and geographer Strabo, writing in the 1st century BC, talks of the "thwarting of gangs of robbers". He was

referring primarily to preventing thefts committed by bands of belligerent shepherds living in the mountains and directed almost exclusively against the more peaceful peasants dwelling on the plains.

Strabo tells how the army was brought in to act as a police force, "waiting for the days on which the barbarians gathered together for their traditional festivals in order to attack them. Thus many were taken prisoner." For centuries the bandits' existence on Sardinia depended upon the state of tension which prevailed between shepherds and peasants. Their conflicting interests – cultivation of the land on the one side and sheep and cattle grazing on the other – lay at the root of the strife.

A further aspect of traditional *banditismo* is the *bardana*, which may be derived from the *gualdana* of Tuscany. It was a vendetta directed either against an entire village, or against a single wealthy landowner who possessed not only cattle stocks but also a fortune in gold – a rarity in those days. The *bardana* prevailed in Sardinia until the beginning of the 20th century, and still occurs from time to time today in the form of cattle end. Such attacks became commonplace in the middle of the 19th century, but they continued to occur sporadically until relatively recently.

After each of the two world wars there was an increase in robbery with violence. One of the most notorious cases, which provoked international outrage, took place in the village of Sa Ferula on the Nuoro-Bitti plain. The ambush was directed at the jeeps of ERLAS, a Sardinian organisation which, with the assistance of the American Rockefeller

stealing or kidnapping. It is a lucrative form of crime which for a variety of reason entails relatively low risks.

Robbery, categorised under this heading since the 16th century, usually occurred on the open road. Bands of thieves would lie in wait for travellers. Their aim was to extract money or goods from the victim by force; if he resisted, matters often came to a bloody

Preceding pages: mural depicting the police crackdown on bandits. **Left**, the land-eating landowner of Orgosolo. **Above**, Sardinian newspapers announcing that a girl has been rescued from her kidnappers.

Foundation, was leading a successful programme to eradicate malaria. Several workers and the armed escort were killed during the attack.

Cattle stealing: There were originally two reasons for cattle stealing: need on the part of the thief, or – more commonly – revenge. By taking justice into his own hands, the robber sought personal vengeance for a previous theft. By and large, Sardinian society does not regard the stealing of livestock "amongst us shepherds" as a grave offence. This attitude is due in part to the frequency with which such thefts occur, and in part to the generally accepted right of retaliation. The shepherds are far quicker to condemn the theft of family pets or basic items of work equipment, or of items essential for the everyday existence of a poor family: their goat, for example, since it provides milk for children as well as adults, or the pig, or the yoke for a peasant's ox.

Nonetheless, these basic rules of Sardinian banditry are not always strictly observed. On occasions, a moderate crime of this nature is followed by an act of far greater violence, with blood being spilt – especially if the thief refuses to offer adequate compensation for his deed. Many blood feuds originated in this kind of escalation of violence. They could last for generations.

Kidnapping is increasingly used by bandits as a means of blackmail. They have the reputation of being quite ruthless, even in cases when they merely carry out the plans of a third party, or when their only duty is to guard the hostages in an isolated shack or cottage. The theft of livestock is a relatively straightforward affair, but the abduction of a person requires much more planning and strategic ability on the part of the perpetrator. The victim must be carefully chosen, ransom negotiations must be cunning and tough, and – last but not least – the perpetrators must have the wit to forsee obstacles; for one thing, their success depends on the "laun-

dering" of large sums of marked banknotes.

And the groundwork is equally important. The bandits of Sardinia need the shepherds. They know every stone of the wild countryside, the gorges, caves, forests – the areas where a kidnap victim can be kept for days or months on end without being discovered, which he or she may have to cross during arduous forced marches through the night or where the endless waiting period will be spent, gagged and tied to a tree or a rock.

The meagre diet of a hostage will perforce be that of his shepherd captors: flat bread, sheep's milk cheese and – if he is lucky – roast lamb, mutton, goat or wild boar. But even if a kidnap victim is kept prisoner in an inhabited area – perhaps in a cottage in one of the remote villages – he will know that such a village is surrounded by vast tracts of lonely countryside, mute and sun-baked and sometimes deadly.

Kidnappers have few difficulties organising their crimes in the inaccessible regions of the *Gennargentu*, or in the other hill and mountain areas, since here they are more mobile than the police or the *carabinieri*. A comparison of kidnapping statistics over the past 50 years provides impressive evidence of their success. Even more remarkable – and depressing – are the figures for the years following World War II. During a 20-year period (1945–65), there were 58 kidnappings on Sardinia – and not a single one took place on mainland Italy. During 1966–68 alone there were 33 on the island, but none on the mainland.

But the year 1970 marked the beginning of a new, very different chapter in Italian banditry. The kidnapping of human victims for ransom ceased to be confined to the island, but spread across to the mainland, where the number of cases escalated with startling speed. Between 1969 and 1973 there were 18 kidnappings on Sardinia and 77 in the rest of Italy; between 1974 and 1978, the respective figures were 35 and 382. And between 1979 and 1982 there were 22 abductions on Sardinia and a staggering 919 on the mainland. Unless something fairly drastic is done quickly by the Italian government, it seems likely that the trend represented by these figures will continue.

Left, and right, the long white beard is the pride of every traditional Sardinian.

At the end of the 18th century, Sardinia was known as an *India de por acá*, an "India in the midst of the Western World". And thus, strictly speaking, it was to remain at least until the end of World War I: an exotic culture, about which virtually nothing was known, even by the few visitors whose spirit of adventure drove them to explore the island. Sardinia fitted into no specific category except perhaps that of "living antiquity", a place in which time had stopped dead, somewhere between the Old Testament period and Homer.

The island's character seemed contradictory; it possessed a hidden homogeneity that was only understood by those who knew it well. It remained inaccessible to the simple, direct approach adopted by scientists and other travellers. Even Goethe omitted the island from his "Italian Journey", the famous tour of Italy and its islands that he undertook between 1786 and 1788. He travelled the length and breadth of Sicily and described it in epic detail, but Sardinia failed to pull him. Perhaps it wasn't sufficiently Classical. Indeed, a visitor to Sardinia after Goethe's time described it as "foreign to Italy".

The English Romantics – Byron, Shelley, Keats and Wordsworth among them – also gave Sardinia a miss when they rushed off to Italy in the 19th century. It wasn't until D.H. Lawrence visited the island in 1921 – in a spur-of-the-moment bid to escape winter in Sicily – and wrote *Sea and Sardinia* that it was brought to the attention of the English-reading world. Many, including Anthony Burgess, have felt that Lawrence managed in six days what others failed to do in years: "A single week's visit was enough for him to extract the very essence of the island and its people." But Lawrence's conclusions were in part grounded in the inscrutability of the island and islanders that had confounded others. "Lost between Europe and Africa and belonging to nowhere… as if it never really had a fate. No fate. Left outside of time and history," he pronounced.

Preceding pages: Desulo is famous for its colourful traditional costumes. Left, Whitsun preparations.

Even today, it is true to say that it is a difficult task to form a really fair impression of Sardinia. One runs the risk of getting tangled up in a web of relationships and interrelationships; in the Sardinian maze, one may be caught up like Theseus in the Minotaur's labyrinth during the search for Ariadne's thread.

Folk roots: Inevitably, observers look for clues in Sardinia's ancient folklore. But it is difficult even to define what is meant by local "folklore". It does not mean that everything here is rooted in the soil or natural, as is so often maintained in the folklore described in panegyrics. The truth is the very opposite. Over the years the traditions of this Mediterranean island have been amassed layer upon layer, shifting perpetually so that their survival until modern times should be assured. It is a heterogeneity which is universally acknowledged, and which according to Lucien Febvre justifies Sardinia's inclusion in the category of *îles-conservatoires*.

Strictly speaking, a large proportion of Sardinian folklore is already condemned to disappear as a result of the furious pace at which industrialisation is taking place on the island. Particularly at risk are forms of native poetry, handicrafts, customs associated with everyday life, even the most jealously guarded traits of the national mentality. As they assume the form of relics deprived of their original context, they inevitably lose their ritual value. In particular, the traditional customs marking the fundamental events of human life – birth, marriage and death – are losing more and more of the internal motivation which lent them their intensity. In some cases, what is left are gestures, sometimes ugly travesties of what they have replaced.

Tourism has played an equivocal role. Undoubtedly some community celebrations have been revived and rejuvenated by the tourist industry, and a few would have died a natural death without it. In other cases, it has led to distortion and adulteration, ancient customs exploited in order to make money.

Genuine folklore and its essential links with the island's traditions are a colourful and complex aspect of the Sardinian national heritage. They are, however, all related to each other, as well as being inextricably interwoven with both the civilisation and the legal, economic and social structures of the country. It would thus be wrong simply to dismiss Sardinian folklore as a mere cultural phenomenon which developed among the lower social classes of the community and is of concern only to them.

To a greater extent than in many other societies, the roots of Sardinia's cultural heritage lie in both folk culture and the customs of the so-called upper-classes. Modern research has confirmed that the cultural heritage is proudly seen by all strata of society as their common inheritance.

sense, touching off on almost every page illuminating truths about the Nuorese peasantry, their customs, ideas, ways of feeling… [They] are the best substitute for Sardinia landscape painting."

All classes of society see the shepherd as a symbol of their cultural heritage. The historian Manlio Brigaglia makes an interesting observation in this respect. He reports that, shortly after World War I, the artist Mario Delitala had suggested that the Sardinian coat of arms should be changed. He proposed that the four blindfolded Moors, dating from the time when Sardinia was ruled by the house of Aragon, should be replaced by motifs representing the island's "four

No other folkloric tradition has been so lovingly immortalised by the literature and art of its own area, whilst at the same time exerting such a profound influence on its artists. Writers such as Sebastiano Satta, Grazia Deledda and Giuseppe Dessì spring to mind, as do artists like Antonio Ballero, Giuseppe Biasi, Francesco Ciusa and Filippo Figari. Writing and painting during the 19th and 20th centuries, they belonged to an era in the island's history characterised by an exceptional degree of creativity. Alan Ross, in *Bandit on the Billiard Table – a Journey through Sardinia,* said of Grazia Deledda's novels: "They are local in the best

traditional occupations" – a shepherd, a farmer, a mountain-dweller and a fisherman. The idea was a good one, but it found little support on the island: in the eyes of the islanders, from the highest to the lowest born, the shepherd performed a far more important role than the other three.

And so the scheme fell flat, and things remained as they were. Sardinia retained its "imported" coat of arms with the four Moors. Rather than allowing other members of the coummunity a share of the limelight, the islanders preferred these foreign symbols. It is a typical attitude which recurs regularly throughout Sardinia's history; the shepherd is the dominant figure of island society. Stubborn and jealous, he is the originator of one of the harshest and most disturbing local proverbs: *Furat chi benit dae su mare* – "He who comes from across the sea is a thief". The only riposte one can make to that must be the Spanish saying *pocos, locos y malunidos* – "small, mad and at odds with each other".

The land of poetry: One typical characteristic of Sardinian folklore is its penchant for pointed remarks. It would be no exaggeration to claim that language is the second, secret master of the island. From everyday encounters to special occasions, every event is accompanied, underlined and explained by a verbal commentary. Few peoples possess such a broad palette of set phrases and such an extensive and colourful vocabulary as the Sardinians. Significantly enough, another Sardinian expression describes the island as *Terra di Poesia* (The Land of Poetry).

Unsurprising, then, that folkloric poetry, existing in a wide variety of genres, are such a strong part of the island's culture. The rigid metricity of virtually all forms of expression is particularly noticeable, even in simple incantations, curses, excommunications and teasing rhymes (*Berbos*), in lullabies (*Ninnias*), lamentations for the dead (*Attitidus*) or eulogies of the saints (*Gosos*). It extends to various elaborate forms of love poetry such as the *Mutos*, the miniature variations of which are called *Muttettus* or *Battorinas*. The rhythmical pattern of the *Mutu* resembles that of the *Strambotti* and *Stornelli* of Tuscany (short traditional love songs written in the 17th century). It consists of two parts: the *Isterria* (exposition) and the *Torrada* (response).

The finest *Mutos* possess "a note of fantasy"; they resound with "poetic intelligence", an expression of "a higher plane and great sensitivity" which moved Pier Paolo Pasolini to describe them as essentially a "female" lyric form, a form of poetry "which knows neither brute force nor Orgosolo."

By contrast, the lament for the dead, the *Attitidu*, is often unmistakably aggressive in tone. Usually the chant of the *Attitadoras* (the wailing women who perform a similar function to the *Voceratrici* of Corsica, but

who in Sardinia are usually related to the deceased) is simply a tribute to the deceased's qualities, complimenting his virtues and those of his ancestors and imagining the great deeds he would have accomplished had death not snatched him away – but not when the deceased is the victim of a vendetta. Then the job of the *Attitadoras is to* stir up feelings of hatred and vengeance (*Attizzare*, to stir up/to fan, may well explain the origins of the word).

J.W.W. Tyndale, a 19th-century traveller in Sardinia, noted how "the feelings of the relatives are appealed to with the utmost earnestness by the Prefiche, who enumerate the murdered members of each family, reca-

pitulate the wrongs and injuries, appeal to God, honour, and duty, and use every argument for revenge."

Even as long ago as the mid-19th century the government was trying to prohibit these incitements to revenge but the ceremony of the *Attitidu*, which forms part of the wake (*Sarja*), continues to be practised, particularly in the more remote regions of the Barbagia. Nonetheless, persistent pressure by the church has resulted in the abandoning of the most violent curses in favour of a "quieter, more sorrowful almost liturgical" lamentation (Gino Bottiglioni).

Max Leopold Wagner saw the *Mutu* as an

Left, the Ballu Tundu, traditional round dance, in the 1950s. **Right**, a prelude to hunting.

expression of the Sardinian tendency to melancholy, which assumes concrete form in the "grim solemnity" of the *nuraghi,* the ancient towers dating from the 2nd millennium BC that are dotted all over the island. Not every visitor, however, is of the opinion that the Sardinians are a melancholy people – although it is a trait which somehow seems in keeping with the rugged desolation of much of the countryside. Some observers, including Gino Bottiglioni, maintain that the islanders are fundamentally a cheerful and out-going race. Many would say both attitudes are correct, for the soul of the typical Sardinian – who celebrates with such gusto, who is so full of vitality and who organises

Sardonico – a sardonic, spiteful laughter which is neither amusing nor an expression of light-hearted *joie de vivre.*

Their tragedy, some maintain, is expressed by the masks of the *Mamuthones* and those of their companions, the *Issocadores*, both of which are characteristic of the village of Mamoiada in the Barbagia, the heart of traditional Sardinia. (In Ottana and other villages in the same region the carnival processions are mostly dominated by the presence of another mask, the *Boes, Boetones* or *Merdules*, based on an ox's head.) If we are to accept the theories of researchers, these masks represent an allegorical reference to the tragically recurring events of Sardinian

horse shows and poetry competitions between the shrewdest *Improvvisatori* – is remarkably contradictory.

In a work which is in essence an essay on the nature of the Sardinian, published under the meaningful title *Miele Amaro* ("Bitter Honey"), the writer Salvatore Cambosu maintains that the Sardinians do indeed enjoy festivals, but only because such celebrations act as an anaesthetic, numbing the painful consciousness of their tragic existence – and not because they regard them as a means of amusement. If a Sardinian actually laughs, then more often than not the result is the almost proverbial *Ghigno*

history. The wild, cumbersome *Mamuthones*, they say, are caught by the *Laccio* (or *Soca*) of the nimble, mocking *Issocadores* who are nothing less than images of the island's countless foreign conquerors. Francesco Masala, one of the principal writers of Sardinia's so-called "Ideology of the Vanquished", has made this grim interpretation his very own.

The Ballu Tundu: Another remarkable manifestation of the contradictory combination of sadness and mirth is the *Ballu*, the dance – a traditional form of expression held in high esteem by the Sardinians and still popular on high days and holidays. Though similar to the national dances of Greece and Romania, the Sardinian version is usually executed more solemnly. Traditionally, only men and women who were betrothed or married were allowed to link fingers or touch palms – though J.W.W. Tyndale noticed that this rule was not respected in the village of Osidda in the province of Nuoro, where "whether by uniform usage, or by a peculiar dispensation from the patron saint of the day, the greater part danced with their hands round waists."

Here, too, the observations of travellers and researchers are in blatant contradiction to each other. It is perhaps interesting to note that the comments of the "Interpreters" of

ologist Leonardo Sole drew attention to what he called the significant "mythical silence" which still surrounds the *Ballu Tundu*, and which bears a certain resemblance to a "sacred chorus".

Ethnographer Francesco Alziator, who has made a study of the age of the *Ballu Tundu*, has this to say: "Two basic features of this round dance support the theory that it is very ancient: firstly the *launeddas* (flutes), which traditionally accompany the dance throughout almost a quarter of the island, and secondly the association of the dance with fire. For in the olden days there was almost always a fire in the centre of the circle of dancers." It is easy enough to imagine the

Sardinia, to adopt the phrase coined by the cultural anthropologist Alberto M. Cirese, formed for many years an utter dichotomy: their attitudes fell into the category of either calumny or eulogy. Some writers – like Baldessare Luciano – regarded the *Ballu Tundu*, the "national dance" of Sardinia, as lascivious; others, such as Pater Bresciani, insisted that it was on the contrary dignified, serious and solemn, despite the occasional interludes of frivolity. Recently the semi-

scene; all one needs to do is to study the paintings by Mario Delitala, Stanis Dessy, Carmelo Floris or one of the other 20th-century Sardinian artists. All the painters mentioned have frequently found inspiration in the symbolic representation of the *Ballu Tundu*.

The art historian Carlo Aru has discovered what may be the earliest portrayal of the Sardinian *Ballu Tundu* in an interesting painting that hangs in the medieval chapel of San Pietro di Zuri which was built in 1291 by Anselmo da Como (the ruins of the adjoining historic village are now, alas, completely submerged beneath a reservoir). Aru re-

Left, traditional costumes are essential for family celebrations in the country. **Above**, *launeddas* players at the St Efiso festival held in Cagliari.

marks that "On the outermost right-hand pillar, on the apse side, is a painting of people dancing: tiny figures holding hands; on their heads they are wearing the *berretta* (the traditional beret of Sardinia). "

Musical instruments: The *launeddas*, the musical instruments which provide the accompaniment for the *Ballu Tundu*, are thought to be very ancient indeed, possibly dating from as long ago as the time of the Nuraghi. They are also unique, occurring only on Sardinia. In a detailed study of the *launedda*, distinguished ethno-musicologists Giulio Fara and Gavino Gabriel speculate that this "triple-piped" *Tibia* (an ancient Roman musical instrument resembling a

shawm), which looks like a bagpipe without the sound bladder, might in fact be closely related to the *Fistula disparibus compacta arundibus* – the shepherd's flute with pipes of varying length – described by Virgil. Tyndale, although worried that the "great exertion required to blow the *launedda* has considerable effect upon the health of the musicians, who frequently play for hours together", pronounced the sound of the *launedda* "though strange and wild, not disagreeable to the ear."

In his remarkable summary of the island's cultural heritage, a work which has assumed the form of an ethnographic stream of con-sciousness, Salvatore Cambosu attributes more sinister qualities to the sound of the *launedda* than the amiable Tyndale does, defining it as an existential metaphor for an "historic illness". All of a sudden we see again before us the terrifying, grim expression of the Sardinian with the evil eye, whose character has supposedly left its mark so irrevocably on the island's history.

Today the cohesive strength of this culture – which is so introverted that it has earned the nicknames "Culture of Stone" in addition to the "Culture of Loneliness" – has suffered a damaging blow which threatens to destroy an entire folkloric tradition. Tourism has taken over some aspects of Sardinian folklore and, as in so many other places, has transformed them into mere entertainment.

This took place, as already indicated, within the framework of the continuing changes that have taken place in Sardinia this century. But it is also a process which – according to the ethnologist Giulio Angioni – is the result of two "conspicuous historic turning points" on Sardinia: the abolition of the feudal system at the beginning of the 19th century and the monopolisation of cheese production by the large cheese-making companies on the Italian mainland during the 20th century.

These two events challenged the entire basis of island society and its foundation in the pastoral culture. Journalists Gaspare Barbiellini Amidei and Bachisio Bandinu noted the alarming, tangible way in which the incompatible symbols of two extremely different cultures – cork and plastic – simultaneously determined everyday life and manufacturing techniques on the island in the 1960s.

Nowadays, Sardinia's great folkloric traditions are virtually restricted to the most important religious *Sagre* (folk festivals), such as the processions of the *Redentore* ("Saviour"), *Candelieri* (the "Candlelight Procession") and *Sant'Efisio* (the biggest festival on the entire island, held in Cagliari each May), or the principal feudal tournaments such as the *Sartiglia* which takes place every spring in Oristano. These are festivals in which sacred and profane elements co-exist. Their effect is powerful.

Left, mask from the famous carnival of Mamoiada. **Right**, folk dancers dressed for the part.

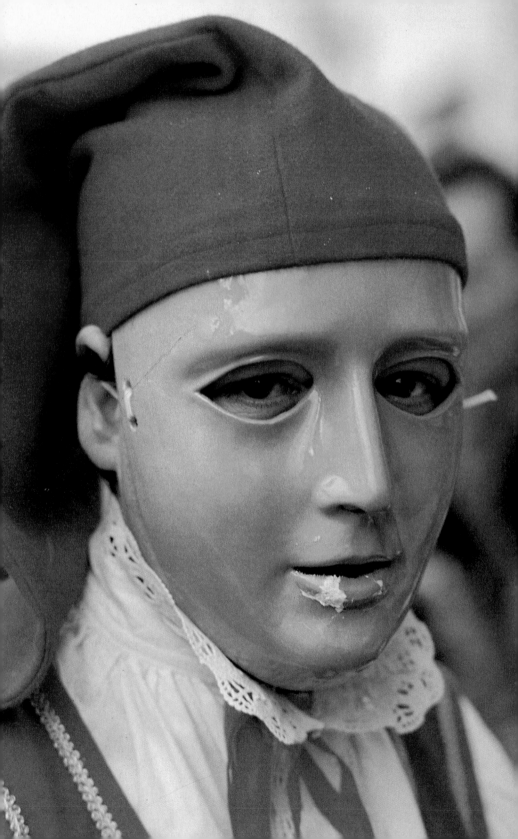

There is no better way of gaining an insight into the character and moods of a country than taking part in its festivals. Statistically Sardinia offers its visitors the opportunity of attending at least 2.73 celebrations per day; a brochure published by the Sardinian Tourist Authority (ESIT) is even called *1,000 Feste*. Festivals provide an ideal starting point for an exploration of the Sardinian soul; they are nostalgic, religious and full of contradictions.

It is remarkable how so varied a people celebrate so much within such a small area. The marked contrasts between the coastal region and the interior are matched by the diverse characters of the inhabitants. What do the descendants of settlers who arrived from North Africa many centuries ago (Sant'Antioco) have in common with those of long-established residents whose first language is Catalan (Alghero)? Both communities cling to their own traditions, and not only in the food they eat – from couscous to lobster Catalane.

The island's most famous festival, dating from 1656, is that of St Efisio, the martyr and patron saint of Cagliari. On 1 May, in a grandiose procession, his statue is borne from the capital to Pula, the place where he was executed. Local residents in traditional costume join his train. The festival is an annual highlight in the lives of many of Cagliari's citizens, but even this, the most spectacular festival, isn't treated as a bean-feast. Sardinia's festivals are like many of the islanders themselves – frequently sombre, rarely to be taken lightly. "None of the suave Greek-Italian charms, none of the airs and graces, none of the glamour," said D.H. Lawrence of a *festa* in Cagliari. "Rather bare, rather stark, rather cold and yellow," he continued. They are fiercely Christian but often their traditions make reference to pagan roots. The pre-Lenten carnivals – the best-known are those of Mamoiada and Ottana – don't just suggest Christian pen-

ance. The *boes* (sinister wooden masks with twisted mouths) and *merdules* (masks in the form of a bull's head) owe much to paganism

Equally sober are the ceremonies of the Easter cycle, where the *confraternitate*, the brotherhoods, dressed in hoods and penitential robes file solemnly through the narrow streets and alleys of the towns and villages. They leave an impression of deep piety and penitence – not only the elderly among the spectators genuflect before the crucifix – but again the accompanying torch processions and bonfires date from pre-Christian times.

The strong element of machismo (which Lawrence claimed, as early as 1921, was extinct outside Sardinia and Spain) can be observed in the *matanza*, the catching of the tuna in early summer when shoals of the fish migrate east. The fishermen begin their elaborate preparations for the bloody massacre weeks beforehand; their mood is one of anticipation, excitement. And in the equestrian festival of San Costantino, which takes place in Sedilo in July, religiosity and male pride combine. Many a rider has paid with his life for taking part in the wild horseback entry into the pilgrimage church.

The lives of many Sardinians are simple and marked by privation. Nevertheless, once the visitor has grown accustomed to their rough, somewhat obstinate manner, he will usually find them friendly and even warmhearted. The mountain villages of the interior, however, leave little opportunity for fleeting encounters between locals and foreigners – nor are such meetings considered desirable. Sardinians have often suffered from the effects of their stubbornness, manifest in their perpetual tendency to mutter and grumble; nonetheless, to this day they see no reason to change their attitude.

Why should things be different? Foreigners are still the source of no good, for their presence means increased income primarily for the islanders living along the coast – most of whom are not natives. Sardinians themselves are frequently charged with the term "bandits", which understandably annoys them. The entire island is riddled with clichés which are no more appropriate now than they ever were.

Preceding pages: horse riding festival in Sedilo; the carnival of Mamoiada; during the *redentore*-festival in Nuoro; old and young. Left, masks like these are worn at the *sartiglia* in Oristano.

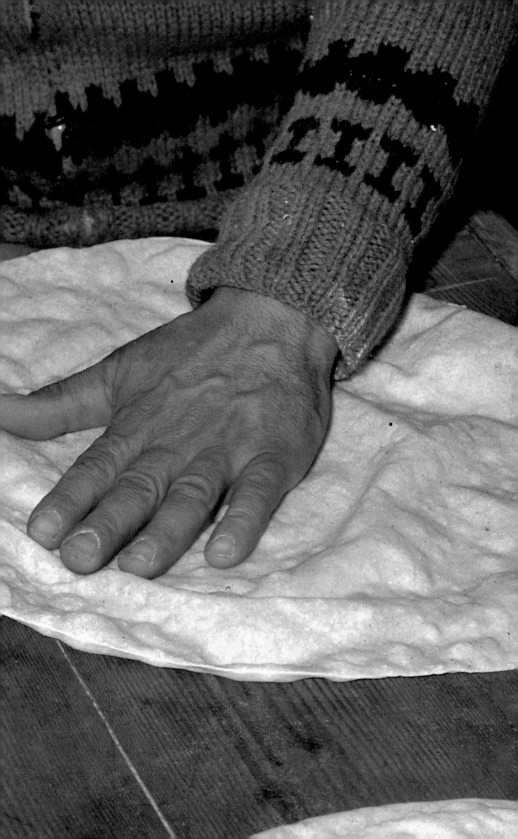

The Sardinians are a nation of shepherds; therefore any account of their food and drink is also an account of three staple foods: bread, meat and cheese. In times past, society was divided into two main classes on the island – the masters and the servants – and which one you belonged to determined the proportion of meat to cheese and bread and level of culinary refinement you enjoyed.

Alfonso La Marmora, one of Sardinia's most diligent researchers, travelled and explored the remotest corners of the island during the 19th century. He reported that the bourgeoisie, locally known as the *prinzipales*, was served white bread made from wheat flour, whilst the servants and labourers – in other words, the rest of the islanders – ate bread baked from barley or acorns, with the addition of plenty of bran. D.H. Lawrence, on his visit to Sardinia in 1921, observed that most of the bread was "course and brown, with a hard, hard crust". He noticed that a man who could afford to have a wheat loaf with his broth considered himself a swell.

The meat requirements of the time were met by hunting or by keeping animals such as pigs, sheep, cattle and goats or even occasionally horses. White meat, especially poultry, was consumed only in small quantities: roast or boiling fowl was regarded as suitable food only for invalids or women in childbed. Surprisingly for an island, fish fared no better (though the island did give the name to sardines, fished in copious number off its shores).

It is possible that the lack of appetite for seafood is explained by the fact that the Sardinians have never been a nation of seafarers. They have always regarded the sea as an enemy, ever bringing new waves of conquerors to their island. Even today the owners of the fishing fleets operating in Sardinian waters tend to come from Ponza, Naples, Genoa or Carloforte. The annual *matanza*, tuna harvest, an event dating from Roman times, is these days mainly to supply

the export market and is by and large backed by Japanese funds.

That said, recent trends have led to a greater emphasis on fish in restaurants on the coast; around Cagliari, in particular, you will find establishements serving excellent lobster, red and grey mullet, and in the Oristano-Cabras region, eel.

A variety of kneading techniques, handed down from generation to generation, and widely differing forms and contrasting types of leavening explain the remarkable range of

breads available on the island. The artistically shaped loaf of bread is a typical example of Sardinia's culinary heritage. On festivals, people try to outdo one another with the intricacy of their designs.

Each area in the patchwork of regions boasts its own characteristically shaped loaf, so it would be difficult to attempt to produce even a semi-complete list. The best-known – not least because it is successfully marketed on the mainland – is the *pane carasau*, the "sheet of music" – two crisp, round, flat loaves. As this type of bread keeps fresh for long periods, shepherds have traditionally taken a few *pane carasau* with them as pro-

Preceding pages: cutting the shepherd's bread. Left, Sardinian cheese is still made by hand and, right, the olives are still hand-picked.

visions on their long wanderings. In recent years families of all social classes have discovered the bread; most restaurants serving typical Sardinian cooking list it among their local specialities.

Roast specialities: Deserving of more detailed study are the *arrosti*, the roast and grilled meat specialities which are a highlight of Sardinian gastronomy, particularly in the island's interior. The principal characteristic is that only the meat of young animals – lamb, kid, suckling pig and veal – is used. There are two main methods of preparation. In the first, shared by other Mediterranean countries (in particular Turkey), a hole is dug in the ground (stakes are laid on its base and

ensure that the meat cooks evenly. In some districts the finishing touch is provided by a lump of bacon fat, which is wrapped in paper and then ignited. As it drips down on to the spit, the fat colours the meat golden brown and makes it crisp. One of the few good things D.H Lawrence had to say about Sardinia was about such a kid roast.

The most impressive *arrosti* are those served on special occasions: country festivals, saints' days or weddings. For the Sardinians, any cause for celebration presents a social duty to provide good and plentiful food.

You can sample an *arrosto*, usually described as a typical Sardinian speciality, in

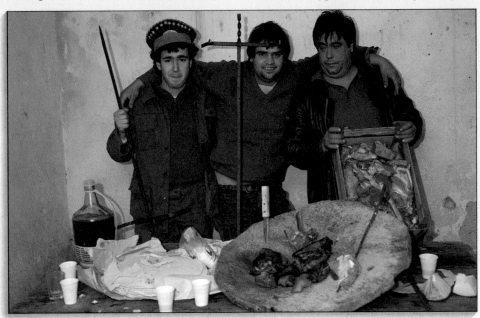

driven round the inside to shore back the earth) and a deep trench is then dug round the hole, leaving about six inches of soil as a "wall". The meat, usually the whole carcass, is placed inside the hole (which is liberally lined with herbs), and a fire is lit above. When this is sufficiently hot, the live ashes are raked into the trench. The heat bakes the meat evenly; the herbs lend it a delicious aromatic flavour.

In the second method, the suckling pig, lamb, kid or veal is placed on wooden or metal spits. These are then positioned vertically or horizontally around the central fire. The spits are turned from time to time to

virtually every restaurant on the island. Although not the only true Sardinian dish, the *arrosti* are the only ones which boast a centuries-old tradition.

These days traditional dishes are no longer standard fare in the homes of the island. The changes which have taken place in the social, economic and cultural history – the restructuring and reorganisation of the food sales and supply networks, and new agricultural and farming methods – are refected in the eating habits of the Sardinian populace. It has had to adapt to all these developments. Increased purchasing power and advertising of convenince foods in the mass media have also helped to bring about fundamental changes. That said, three meals a day – a light breakfast of coffee (espresso or *caffe latte*) and a breadroll or plain cake, followed by a substantial three-course lunch *and* dinner – are still the norm.

A guide to the menu: Sampling the food and drink on Sardinia remains an exciting experience. Visitors are spoilt for choice deciding which specialities from the four provinces – Cagliari, Sassari, Nuoro and Oristano – not to mention the wide range of dishes common to mainland Italy, they should sample next. The recommendations which follow should help to simplify selection from the dishes most commonly found on menus.

without pasta is unthinkable. Here it is almost always home-made; the three most popular types are *mallureddos* (small dumplings of wheat and potato flour), *maccarrones cravaos* (dumplings) and *maccarrones de busa* (a type of very fine cannelloni). All three are served in a sauce of fresh tomatoes with chunks of meat or pieces of smoked sausage and herbs. Equally common are thick broths of vegetables, meat and herbs; they are substantial, often meals in themselves.

The main dish is usually an *arrosto*. Apart from the more usual suckling pig, lamb, kid or veal, wild boar – with a spicy sauce – is increasingly popular. Vegetable accompani-

The most popular *antipasto* (hors d'oeuvre), the *antipasto di terra*, offers a selection of "earthy" *amuse-gueules*: ham, smoked sausages, olives, chicken liver, heart, *sa cordula* (lamb tripe, served rolled up and grilled or fried with peas), mushrooms and brawn. Visitors not prepared to do without seafood can usually opt for a sophisticated but unfortunately not typically Sardinian *antipasto di mare,* a recent innovation designed with tourists in mind.

As elsewhere in Italy, in Sardinia a meal

Left, shepherds' feast. **Above**, *malfatti* (cheese dumplings) are the speciality of Villasimius.

ments are likely to include lettuce, fennel, celery, radishes and, a speciality of Sardinia, globe artichokes.

A traditional lunch *alla sarda* – Sardinian style – will conclude with cheese and dessert. The islanders have been manufacturing dairy products for more than 5,000 years, so it is not surprising that the range of fine cheeses made from sheep's, goat's or cow's milk is extensive. Gourmets will delight in the discovery of *caprino, fiore sardo, calcagno, bonassai, semicotto, pepato, toscanello, foggiano, romano* and *crotonese.* All types are available, from soft curd to hard cheeses, with flavours ranging from slightly acid to mild and aromatic to piquant. Some are eaten simply with bread; others are grated generously over pasta.

Desserts are another Sardinian speciality; one particular favourite, *sebada*, consists of two circles of pastry the size of a fruit plate; dipped in honey (Sardinia is famous for its aromatically-flavoured bitter honey) and sometimes sprinkled with sugar, they are filled with a layer of curd cheese and fried in deep fat.

Invariably, a selection of fruit is offered at the end of a meal. This varies according to season; popular, too, are the dried fruits and nuts: almonds, hazelnuts and dried figs. A favourite confection at *festa* time consists of

almonds and orange peel dipped in honey.

The most commonly served digestif has always been *aquavite*, an aromatic grappa with a high alcohol content. Lawrence described it as tasting like "sweetened petroleum with a dash of aniseed: filthy". The Sardinians like it, though, and you will see them settling down for a glass or two at any time of day.

Another powerfully flavoured liqueur has also become popular among Sardinians in recent years: *liquore di mirto*, distilled from myrtle. It is red in colour when it is manufactured from the berries, and clear if only the leaves of the plant are used.

Which wine?: There is a wide variety of local wines; most have a high alcohol content and are full-bodied and smooth. There are, however, a number of young wines available which are worth trying; they are fairly sweet, slightly sparkling and completely pure.

The best-known bear the description *Cannonau*. Wines bottled in the cooperative cellars bear the *DOC* label guaranteeing quality; this certificate of authenticity is only awarded to wines from specific wine-growing areas. The varieties available range from heavy and lighter red wines, through rosés to whites. Most tend to be on the dry side rather than sweet or heavy; some are decidedly tangy. The areas in which the *Cannonau* wines are grown lie in the provinces of Cagliari, Sassari and Nuoro: *Dorgali, Jerzu, Oliena, Tortolì, Sorso, Sennori* and in the *Baronia* and the *Sarabus* regions.

Three wines from the district around Cagliari – *Girò, Monica* and *Nasco* – are all fairly sweet or sweet. Light and frothy by contrast are the *Vermentino* wines, the *Moscato*, Sardinia's exquisitely dry *Spumanti* and the *Semidano*. *Vernaccia*, rather like a dry sherry and relatively expensive, and *Malvasia*, sweet dessert wine, from the provinces of Oristano and Nuoro also enjoy a first-class reputation; new fermentation methods have permitted the production recently of a bubbling *Spumante* which, when drunk as an apéritif, can stand comparison with Italy's other dry sparkling wines.

This brief journey through the kitchens of Sardinia has perforce been limited to a small number of typical dishes. Those whose appetites have been whetted and who want not only to see at first hand Sardinia's Arcadian landscapes, countryside, its archaeological sights and the customs and traditions of its people, but also to sample the authentic cuisine and taste the island's wines, are urged to study the many works published on this subject, including the gastronomic travel guides. Their advice and tips will prove invaluable to all travellers visiting the island for the first time. Many include restaurant recommendations for each region, each province and often even for the remotest areas of the island's interior.

Left, the traditional shepherd's bread, *pane carasau*. **Right**, wine tasting.

THE LANGUAGE

The most comprehensive research into Sardinian, including a scientific analysis of its significance as a language, is essentially the work of a German linguist. Even in the remotest corners of the island, virtually everyone knows the name of Max Leopold Wagner (1880–1962).

From the age of 25, in a series of lengthy journeys, he combed every region of Sardinia, talking to the inhabitants, persuading them to recite for him traditional poems and stories. He recorded these, analysed them scientifically and compared them with the scattered records of other researchers, mostly Sardinians. Wagner's results were published in two major works: *La Lingua Sarda* (1950) and *Dizionario Etimologico Sardo* (1960–64).

Sardinian is an old Romance language with a highly original and in some cases extremely archaic vocabulary. Historical linguists consider it to be the most characteristic of all Romance languages, far more so than the Rhaeto-Romanic of South Tyrol, or Provençal. The only thing that links Sardinian with Italian and all other Romance languages is their common ancestor, the Latin of Roman times.

This heritage is far more obvious on Sardinia than in other regions of Europe. In fact, as recently as the 1960s visitors to the island often found schoolboy Latin more helpful than Italian evening classes when it came to understanding the local inhabitants.

Apart from its Latin skeleton, the vocabulary of Sardinian reflects the entire history of the island. Place names, in particular, have retained many Indo-Germanic roots from prehistoric times, as have names of objects, such as *nuraghe*. There are few remnants of Phoenician and Etruscan, and the number of words with a Greek derivation dating from the Byzantine era can be counted on the fingers of two hands.

By the 14th century, over the course of the island's long and sometimes obscure history, Sardinian had developed from vulgar Latin. Then for 400 years first Catalan and then Castilian were the official languages.

Left, the older generation enjoys a daily chat.

Amalgam of dialects: During the 13th and 14th centuries a sort of official Sardinian also established itself, for the laws promulgated in Sardinian by the ruler-kings of Arborea were valid almost everywhere on the island. Nowadays, more than in earlier times, the language is an amalgam of the island's many dialects. Broadly speaking, the latter can be divided into the dialects of Logudoro in the northern central region, that of Campidania in the south, and a number of very ancient dialects in the mountainous region around Nuoro.

The dialects spoken in Sassari and Galluro to the north reveal closer links with the languages of Tuscany and Corsica. Apart from that, there are also two language "oases" as a result of early settlers on Sardinia: since the 14th century, Catalan has been spoken in Alghero, and since 1736 an ancient Ligurian dialect on the little island of San Pietro.

This fragmentation of Sardinian is a major problem for the island's writers and poets. Montanaru (1878–1957), a popular poet with a following throughout the island, was forced to append a liberal quantity of footnotes to his verse in order to make it comprehensible to the majority of his readers, despite his efforts to write in "Standard Sardinian". All the great Sardinian writers, including Sebastiano Satta, Grazia Deledda, Giuseppe Dessì and Gavino Ledda, have felt obliged to write in Italian.

Today, the main threat to Sardinian's survival is undoubtedly posed by the media. Children learn Italian even before they go to school. Apparently in an attempt to counter this development, the Regional Assembly in Cagliari voted in 1981 to award Sardinian equal status to Italian. And yet, this in itself presents problems.

Since the time when modern Italy was formed from the Kingdom of Savoy, all regions of Sardinia have been bilingual – for example, the dialect of Nuoro coexisted with Italian, and that of Galluro with Italian. No law was necessary in this respect. But now the question confronting the linguist experts is this: which of the many Sardinian dialects shall become the official one?

Grazia Deledda, Sardinia's Nobel Prize-winning novelist, was born on 21 September 1871 in Nuoro, the daughter of Giovanni Antonio Deledda and Francesca Cambosu. For four years she attended the primary school in her native town. The teachers there recognised her lively intelligence, but complained of a certain insolence which their pupil was wont to display when she was required to learn subject matter by rote without asking questions. At the end of her public education, her father engaged a private tutor

published her first juvenile stories too early. In them she attempted to describe the life of the people who lived in her native town, recording certain habits and customs. Inevitably in a small community, such observations sometimes caused offence. Some of her fellow-citizens felt themselves slighted and indicated to young Grazia their opinion of her criticism of their lifestyle.

Grazia, however, was a determined young woman, who was not to be intimidated as easily as that. Whilst quietly continuing to

to teach her literature. Giovanni Antonio Deledda was not a particularly learned man, but in a little town with only 6,000 inhabitants, the majority of whom could neither read nor write, he was certainly to be numbered among the few with a good basic education.

Little Grazia, however, was soon bored by this supervised learning and persuaded her father that it would be better to dismiss the tutor. She continued to read widely if unsystematically, acquiring books primarily from the library of her maternal uncle, Canon Cambosu.

It could be claimed that she wrote and

study the great works of Italian and European literature, she developed her writing skills. She became aware of a desire to tell a wider audience about her native land, and in particular of the town in which she was born. She therefore decided that from then on she would write not in Sardinian as she had until then, but in Italian.

At the age of just 15 she produced her first major work. She painstakingly described and, when necessary, interpreted the characteristic customs of the inhabitants of Nuoro

Above, the novelist who did most to promote Sardinia in the outside world.

and its surroundings for the *Rivista delle Tradizioni Popolari Italiane*, Angelo de Gubernatis's periodical for Italian folkloric culture. It was an impressive work detailing curses and oaths, sayings and proverbs, incantations, prayers, lullabies and nursery rhymes, *attitos* (songs of mourning), beliefs and superstitions, traditional remedies, greetings and congratulations, death announcements, charity customs, festivals, poems and eulogies.

This treasure chest of knowledge, including some of the earliest records of Sardinian civilisation which had been passed down the generations for thousands of years, was to provide the basis for her books. Totalling almost 50 in number, their action virtually always takes place in Nuoro, at the very heart of the island.

Before 1900 Grazia Deledda wrote a great deal, publishing parts of her work in Sardinian or Italian periodicals. Some of her novels, such as *Fior di Sardegna* and *Anime Oneste*, reaped some harsh criticism from her fellow-citizens, but also encouraging praise from well-known Sardinian and Italian intellectuals.

She was determined not to accept the role traditionally demanded of a woman in Sardinian society. The customs of the time had the force of ancient, unwritten law. The man represented the family in public, tilled the fields and tried, within his means, to increase the family fortune. It was the woman's duty to bear children and to bring them up to conform to the rules of the clan or village. She should be a careful housekeeper and, ideally, augment the family income by means of traditional female occupations – sewing, weaving or the cultivation of a vegetable garden.

Grazia Deledda allowed the authors of the works she read to transport her into foreign worlds. She dreamed of the fame which she hoped would one day be hers. She wanted to describe her beloved Sardinia for posterity, as her role model, Leo Tolstoy, had done for his native Russia.

New life in Rome: During a visit to a friend in the historic capital of Cagliari, Grazia made the acquaintance of Palmiro Madesani, a ministry official. It was not long before he asked her to marry him. Grazia agreed, but laid down two conditions: that the wedding should take place a few months later, and that they should move to Rome. For Grazia the writer, the Holy City was a sort of mecca of the arts. Madesani willingly agreed to his future wife's requests, and so, following their marriage in Nuoro, the newly-weds moved to the capital in 1900. In her luggage Grazia had packed notes and sketches for several important, as yet unfinished works, including *Elias Portolu*, which was to be published a few years later in 1903. It was followed the next year by *Cinders* (*Cenere*, 1904).

Reeds in the Wind (*Canne al vento*, 1913) continues the realist style of her early works. In Rome she divided her attention between her writing and her family, which soon increased in size with the births of her sons Sardus and Francesco ("Fran"). She worked indefatigably on her novels until her death from breast cancer in 1936.

The move to Rome marked the start of a period of reflection on her faraway home, which she was to visit annually until 1911. The distance seemed to fuel the fires of her creativity, lending her works their characteristic depth and maturity. She wrote of stirring, sun-drenched landscapes, of the awe-inspiring solitude of some regions, of the silence pervading the island and the lives and deaths of its inhabitants, inextricably linked to the core of the earth's existence and the rhythm of the seasons.

Receiving the Nobel Prize for Literature in 1926, she achieved the fame she had longed for in her youth. She made Sardinia famous throughout the world. Through her novels, European literary circles as well as Italian became aware of the unique life of the island's shepherds, of the happiness and disappointments of its young men and girls, and of the lords and ladies of this ancient nation. Her characters were not presented as leading static lives, as though sitting motionless in a Homeric pastoral idyll in accordance with the popular myth, but as setting out on a journey towards the intellectual and cultural achievements of modern times.

CAGLIARI

The name Cagliari is derived from the 12th-century Spanish *callaris* or *callari*, which in turn comes from *karalis, karale* or *karali* – even older expressions meaning "a rocky place". Looking across to the limestone hill of the *Castello* from Sant'Elia, the observer can see how appropriate the name is.

Accurately dated archaeological finds from Sant'Elia, Santa Gilla, San Bartolomeo and Calamosca prove beyond doubt that the first inhabitants settled on this part of the island at the end of the 3rd millennium BC.

The Phoenicians, plying their trading routes between their native shores (the present-day Lebanon) and the Iberian peninsula, moored their ships in Cagliari in the **Golfo degli Angeli**. The coast here formed a perfect natural harbour which afforded their fleet not only a safe and sheltered anchorage, but also the opportunity to take aboard fresh provisions. The Phoenicians colonised the area and built a series of trading ports along its coast.

Cagliari soon developed into one of the most important trading centres on the East-West Mediterranean axis. Ships laden with goods from the East dropped anchor here in order to exchange some of their cargo for local products such as wool, cheese, minerals and cereals.

In order to accelerate the spread of their culture across the island, the next conquerors – the Carthaginians, descendants of the sea-faring Phoenicians – criss-crossed Sardinia with an important network of roads radiating from Cagliari. Evidence seems to indicate that the structure of the town administration here was modelled on that of Carthage itself: two *Sufeti* – native members of the urban aristocracy – were given the task of ruling the city. This was a clever move on the part of the invaders, for they chose two governors who belonged to families which had made their fortunes from trading (and

were thus likely to be amenable to the Carthaginians), and who were also held in high esteem by the rank and file of the populace.

Witnesses of the past: When the Romans arrived the castle area, which must have formed the heart of the city under the Carthaginians, as it was to do later under Pisan rule, became the site of a *castrum* (fort) built to protect the coast. Sardinia remained vulnerable to Carthaginian attack and sound defences were a priority for the Romans.

Not until the arrival of the Pisans would foreign invaders feel at home here. Following the decline of the Roman Empire, the town entered a prolonged period of stagnation. Since the Roman towns were more complex in design and of greater architectural merit than those of their successors, the colony they built on the coast was doomed to remain isolated and untouched by the newcomers whose more modest accommodation would have looked as out of place as the new residents in such splendid surroundings.

Excavations carried out between 1958 and 1978 enabled archaeologists to unearth numerous items supplying clues to the city's past: **wells** in the del Carmine Church, and later the walls of a **Late Carthaginian Temple** dating from the 3rd century BC, and **Thermal Baths** dating from the 2nd century AD in Largo San Felice as well as a group of houses from the period between the end of the Republic and the 4th century AD. Further finds included a **Punic Temple** and **Theatre** – where religious plays were performed – and two **Necropolises** (in the Sant'Avendrace district and on the Colle di Bonaria).

The discovery of the necropolis on the Colle di Bonaria was a particular source of jubilation in archaeological circles, for the site yielded numerous ancient inscriptions, especially from tombs. The **Thermal Baths** in the Viale Trieste are worth a detour. The spaciousness of the site is an indication of the prosperity and vitality of the town in Roman times. An aqueduct carried water for the citizens' daily needs through the sub-districts of Siliqua, Decimo, Assemini and Elmas as far as the Stampace district.

During the Byzantine era and the occupation by the Vandals the town continued to grow in importance, so that it was on the point of dominating the entire southern half of the island. The spread of Christianity rapidly elevated Cagliari to a sort of spiritual and moral capital. This occurred long before it was created the official capital of the *gudicato* of the same name – an event which was not to occur until the high Middle Ages – and enabled the town to demonstrate its superiority over its despised neighbour, Nora.

The most significant traces of the period when the Vandals ruled Sardinia (AD 455–553) bear witness to the triumphal march of Christianity. The Vandal king Thrasamund banished all strict Catholic bishops whose views he did not share to southern Sardinia. They were not permitted to leave.

The year AD 827 marked the first long-term Arab occupation of the island

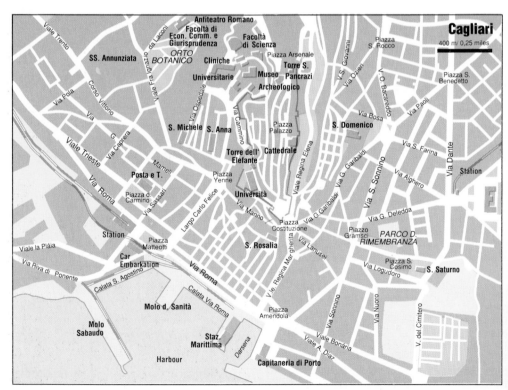

and the subsequent flight of the population from the towns – including Cagliari – to the interior, especially to the little island of San Simone and to the Lagune Santa Gilla.

Fear of the sea and the invaders it carried to the island wrought fundamental changes in the character of this typical coastal town; they were to prove so long-lasting that for almost three centuries Cagliari was to remain cut off from world history. This isolation may have been why Sardinia's first *giudicato,* a defensive alliance with its own jurisdiction, was formed around Cagliari.

It was not until the arrival of settlers belonging to various religious orders, such as the Benedictine monks from Montecassino, or the followers of St Victor of Marseilles, that the town seemed prepared to open itself to Western influence again. Mindful of its commercial history, it established contact with the French towns along the Mediterranean coast and began trading with the city states of Genoa and Pisa, which were subsequently to dominate

The neo-Catalan Town Hall of Cagliari.

the history of Cagliari and even Sardinia itself, first as partners and then as conquerors.

Under Pisan rule, the town enjoyed a considerable demographic, artistic and economic revival. For the Tuscan visitors the town's layout had a familiar air, and they expanded it enthusiastically. It became one of the most important ports on the Tyrrhenian Sea; secular and sacred buildings such as the new Cathedral were erected, and the fortifications with their three defensive towers were built around the castle.

The Spanish conquest: In 1326, following the decline of Pisa, Cagliari fell into the hands of the royal house of Aragon. Their first action was to expel all native Sardinians from the castle, and it was occupied by foreign noblemen whose job it was to decide the fate of the town. In 1418 it became the official residence of the Viceroy of Sardinia, who replaced the Governor General. In 1421, in the presence of the King of Aragon, Alfonso V "The Magnanimous", the Viceroy of Sardinia, Ber-

nardo de Centelles, inaugurated the island's first parliament.

Under Aragonese rule the city's administrative system built up by Pisa was dismantled and replaced by a new arrangement resembling that of Barcelona. The administration of justice was in the hands of a governor and a *Bàilo*, who later assumed overall control of the professional associations and the guilds, and eventually also of customs and excise. .

The *Amostassen* was responsible for the town's food supplies; he was assisted by two *Clavari*, who were in charge of the slaughterhouses and the granaries. Public works were carried out by *Obrieri*, and a consulate for marine affairs dealt with matters concerning overseas trade and regulated disputes between merchants.

Under Aragonese and Spanish rule, Cagliari's position as an important port and trading town was reinforced. Such was its expansion that the neighbouring *Villae* of Stampace and Villanova were completely swallowed up by its sub-urbs, thereby losing their original function as refuges or *Oppida*. Between 1620 and 1626, Philip III encouraged the foundation of a university.

At this time, too, Cagliari was the scene of feuds, sometimes bloody, between powerful local families and the Spanish newcomers. This violence culminated in 1668 in the assassination of the Viceroy, Manuel de los Cobos, and the Marchese Agostino di Locani. One of the Viceroy's murderers, Jacopo di Castelvi, Marchese di Cea, was sentenced to death and beheaded in 1671 on what is now the Piazza Carlo Alberto. In due course the other conspirators were also arrested and handed over to the executioner.

The plot against the Viceroy was the most obvious manifestation of the latent tension smouldering between the Sardinian populace and the Spanish colonial power. What's more, the ruling Spanish tried to introduce a number of unwelcome minor administrative reforms, which aggravated matters further. As a consequence, the population

Red blinds in the arcades of the Via Roma protect from the sun.

in the northern half of the island, in particular, openly supported Austria in its ambitions to make Spain part of the vast Hapsburg Empire.

On 12 August 1708, the British naval fleet under Admiral Lake approached the town of Cagliari and opened fire. Ten years later, following the Peace of Utrecht (1713), Duke Victor Amadeus II of Savoy became the sovereign of the *Regno di Sardegna*, the Kingdom of Savoy. On 4 August 1720 Sardinia, along with Naples, Milan and the Spanish Netherlands, was formally handed over to the Austrian Empire by the Spanish; on 8 August the island was passed on to Luigi Departes, the emissary from Savoy.

The House of Savoy: Under the Kingdom of Savoy, Cagliari suddenly became an international political arena. On 28 January 1793 it was forced to fend off an attack by the French fleet under Lorenzo Giovanni Truguet. Following heavy fire from the ships' cannons and an attempted landing, the invaders were repulsed by the hastily summoned militia under the command of Gerolamo Pitzolo.

In the wake of the turmoil which Napoleon spread across the whole of Europe, including Italy, Cagliari was to become the refuge of Charles Emmanuel IV of Savoy, the King of Sardinia. He lived for seven months in the Viceroy's palace on the Piazza Palazzo. On another occasion the town was again called upon to provide a King of Savoy with hospitality and protection (which unfortunately was not always reciprocated). On this second occasion, the recipient was Victor Emmanuel I, returning from exile in Gaeta and Rome following the abdication of his weak brother, Charles Emmanuel IV. He was a guest in the Viceroy's palace from 17 February until 7 May 1814.

The town chronicles relate a series of dramatic events in the middle of the 19th century: there was a succession of famines and epidemics which plagued the inhabitants, exacerbated by the indescribable sanitary conditions under which the population lived, a series of

The ideal place for a café, under the arcades of the Via Roma.

violent riots, and hangings ordered without ceremony by the increasingly nervous rulers and their bands of compliant henchmen.

In spite of these drawbacks, during this period the town gradually acquired its modern countenance. Each of the new buildings erected after 1840 and designed for purely peaceful purposes helped to shake off the image of "fortress Cagliari", an image that the city had endured since Roman times.

The heart of the city: Cagliari is a treasure trove for visitors interested in art or archaeology. The wealth of precious objects to be found here tells of the city's colourful history, which on more than one occasion has determined the fate of the entire island.

The town and its surroundings offer sights of every kind, plus the attractions of the Sardinian countryside: gently rolling hills, the **Golfo degli Angeli**, historic districts such as the **Castello** or *Castrum Caralis*, the **Bastion**, which seems to hover weightlessly above the town, surveying one of the loveliest natural landscapes in Europe. Its views over the city are as breathtaking as any to be had over Barcelona, Nice, Genoa or Taormina.

Worthy of special mention is the **Citadella dei Musei** – the Museum Citadel – in the heart of the old town. Until 1966–67, when it was allocated to its present role as a documentary and cultural witness of local history, the building itself experienced a very turbulent past. The present structure rises above the remains of the old bastion which the blessed Emmanuel had constructed. It is a perfect example of a successful synthesis between past and present. Since the museum also stands on the highest point of Cagliari, it affords a spectacular view of the town and the bay.

The two architects, Gazzola and Cecchini, were successful not only in creating an harmonious blend of elements from a number of different architectural periods, but also in adapting historic elements to new uses, as can be seen in the case of the fine Renaissance

To save space, the washing is sometimes dried across the street.

portal and splendid statue of St Barbara.

The Citadella houses the **Regional Ethnographic Collection** (*Raccolta Etnografica della Regione*), the **National Gallery of Art** (*Pinacoteca Nazionale*), the *Museo Siamese Cardu* and the **Institute of Ancient History** (*Istituto di Antichità*). The **Museo Siamese Cardu** was donated to the municipality in 1917. Stefano Cardu, a Sardinian at the court of the King of Siam, bequeathed the town – apart from a collection of 1,306 gold and silver coins – various Chinese and Siamese ivory *objets d'art*, some dating back to the 11th century and now on view in the museum which bears his name.

Not to be missed is the **National Archaeological Museum** (*Museo Archeologica Nazionale*) on the Piazza Indipendenza, built in 1800 on the orders of Charles Felix of Savoy. The exhibition rooms contain displays of prehistoric and early finds as well as a large number of objects illustrating the history of the island.

The first gallery contains Neolithic and early Bronze Age stone, copper and ceramic exhibits from the necropolis of **Angelo Ruiu**, near Alghero. In other cabinets are displayed female cult figures from the Cyclades, from the *domus de janas* which were also discovered near Alghero. The term *domus de janas* derives from an ancient folk superstition, according to which the modest graves or "houses" hewn from rock by the island's early inhabitants, were in fact the homes of *janas* – supernatural beings, usually referred to as fairies. Other interesting exhibits include scale models of stone *nuraghi* dating from the 8th and 7th century BC from the regions surrounding Barumini, Cabras and San Sperate.

Also worth seeing are statues of wrestlers and warriors from the period between 800 and 600 BC, the largest statue of a maternal deity yet to be found on Sardinia, and a variety of bronzes, especially the *Navicelle Nuragiche*, mostly votive gifts from *nuraghi* and Nuraghe villages, graves, temples and sites of sacred springs.

Gallery III contains the finest exhibits from Phoenician and Carthaginian Sardinia, found at sites scattered the length and breadth of the island. The Etruscan Bucchero vases of fragrant clay were found at Tharros, as were the Phoenician ceramic jugs with their mushroom-shaped rim.

The Phoenician epigraphs dedicated to the deity *Sid* and the bronze tablet on which the *Father of Sardinia* is invoked were found in the temple at Antas; the juniper-wood statuette of a *kore* (a girl wearing festive dress) was discovered in the former Punic settlement of Olbia, as was a particularly well-preserved example of the apotropaic terracotta masks which were manufactured extensively by the Phoenicians to ward off malevolent spirits.

Continuing through the museum, the visitor enters the rooms containing exhibits from Roman times. These include a mosaic dating from the period AD 100–200 discovered during excavations at the former Forum Traiani (Fordongianus), as well as statues of Dionysus and Aesculapius, collections

Tuscan facade on the dome in the old city.

of coins, jewellery, amphora, goblets and glasses.

The museum authorities are particularly proud of their collection of Early Christian and medieval artefacts, which represent a complete history of the island from its early Christianisation until the end of the *giudicati* period. The exhibition includes ancient inscriptions in Greek from the Early Christian and Byzantine era, Latin epigraphs from the 5th and 6th centuries AD – most of which were found in cemeteries in the vicinity of Cagliari – metal objects (in particular, gold necklaces), jugs, lamps, incense burners, silver and bronze fibulae. In short, it provides a rare opportunity to discover for oneself the culture of the island's early invaders (the Byzantines, Vandals and Arabs) and their lasting influence on the culture of the native inhabitants.

Visitors with the stamina to see more should progress to the museum's comprehensive coin collections – which include specimens from Byzantium, Pisa, Genoa, Aragon, Spain and Savoy – or a number of Afro-Mediterranean clay oil lamps with varied decorations and designs, or valuable fragments of sculptures dating from early Christian to early medieval times.

On the site of the **Royal Palace** (*Palazzo Regio*) near the Castello, nowadays the seat of the prefecture, stood from the 14th to the 18th centuries the palace of the Viceroy sent to rule the island by the King of Aragon. The present building was constructed in the 18th century on the orders of the Kings of Sardinia. Inside, it is worth taking a look at the fine staircase leading up to the bel-étage designed by the military engineer De Guibert, as well as at Bruschi's frescoes, illustrating allegorical and realistic subjects, in the Provincial Assembly Chamber.

Soaring heavenwards not far from the **Palazzo Regio** is the **Cathedral**, the oldest parts of which date from the 13th century. It was remodelled on a number of occasions, finally receiving its Romanesque facade in the style of Pisa and Lucca in 1930. Work began in the 13th century at the behest of Pisa. Of the unadorned original building, the belfry and the supporting beams of the main doorway still remain. When the forces of Aragon conquered the town in 1326, the cathedral was far from finished. It is therefore assumed that the original plans underwent alteration at this stage in their execution. Evidence supporting this thesis can be found in the Catalan Gothic-style chapel in the right transept, the construction of which was begun at about this time. It bears a striking resemblance to the famous basilica on the hillside overlooking the sea at Bonaria.

Palaces: Cagliari contains numerous other buildings of historic and artistic interest. These include, for example, the 18th-century **Town Hall** (*Palazzo di Città*), the **Palazzo Arquer** on the Piazza Carlo Alberto, and the **Bastion**, also known by local residents as the *Terrazza Umberto*, and approached via a magnificent staircase built between 1899–1902. The complex includes the **University** and the **Seminario Tridentino** (Tridentine Seminary),

Phoenician gryphon head in the Cagliari museum.

built in the 18th century after the plans of Saverio Belgrano di Famolesco and housing today the **University Library**.

The finest *Palazzi*, the former homes of the patricians and noblemen of the town, include the **Palazzo Brondo** in what is now the Via Lamarmora – its entrance, dating from 1622, is of particular note – and the **Palazzo Zapata** in the Via Genovesi. Also worth seeking out are the **Palazzo Boyl** by the San Remy Bastion, and the **Palazzo Sanna Cao** and the **Palazzo Cugia** in the Via Genovesi, both dating from the middle of the 19th century.

Churches and saints: Apart from the cathedral, several of the town's other churches are worth visiting: **San Giuseppe** (1649), whose cloister contains an inscription commemorating Charles Albert's visit to Sardinia in 1841; the **Basilica di Santa Croce**, built by the Jesuits on the ruins of an old Jewish synagogue (the Jews were expelled from the island in 1492 by Ferdinand the Catholic); **Santa Lucia** and **Santa Speranza**, both dating from the 16th century; the underground **Cappella di Sant'Agostino**, a reliquary in which the saint's bones were kept before being transferred to Pavia; the **Chiesa di Santa Chiara**, built in 1600, **Sant'Anna** (1700), **Santa Restituta** (1640) and **Sant'Efisio** (1700). The latter is the headquarters of the brotherhood *Gonfalone*, which every year on 1 May organises the colourful *Sagra*, the famous folk festival in honour of Saint Efisio.

The festival of the town's saint: The only festivals to enjoy the same degree of fame and popularity as this *Sagra* are the *Cavalcata Sarda*, the Sardinian cavalcade which takes place during the second half of May in Sassari, and the *Sagra del Redentore* staged in Nuoro at the end of August.

The entire town of Cagliari is involved in the preparations for the festival in honour of its patron saint, who is revered throughout the entire island. The statue of the saint, who is credited with saving Cagliari from the Black Death, is carried in procession from the

town to a tiny church in Pula which stands on the exact spot where St Efisio was martyred.

The saint's effigy is transported in a triumphal march. Garlanded oxen draw the statue through the town on a richly decorated cart, escorted by elegantly costumed riders and followed by a vast crowd. All along the way the sounds of *launeddas*, Sardinian flutes, accompany the party.

Not far from the Roman Amphitheatre, in the Viale S.Ignazio, stands the **Chiesa Conventuale del Carmine**. This Capucin monastery church is a popular place of pilgrimage for visitors who come to worship at the shrine of Sant'Ignazio di Laconi. The present building was constructed after World War II, but it stands on the site of a 16th-century religious complex including a chapel and Carmelite convent. Another church, the **Chiesa dell'Annunziata**, is situated at the end of the Corso Vittorio Emanuele; it houses a large number of monochrome paintings.

The **Quartiere della Marina**, the district around the port, expanded rapidly during the 16th and 17th centuries. In the 19th century it was the most densely populated part of town; consequently, even today it possesses a large number of churches: **Santa Lucia, Sant'Elena, Sant'Eulalia, Santa Teresa, San Francesco del Molo, San Sepolcro, Sant'Antonio, Sant'Agostino, Santa Caterina**, the **Oratorio d'Itria** and **Santa Rosalia**.

Modern Cagliari: Cagliari today has a population of almost 300,000; it is not only the capital of the island and its largest town, but also the seat of the Provincial Assembly (*Consiglio Regionale*) and the Regional Committee (*Giunta Regionale*). Nonetheless, for a long time the district surrounding the Castello and the harbour area were allowed to fall into disrepair – a neglect underlined today by the seemingly never-ending rebuilding work being carried out in the **Via Manno** and the **Via Roma**.

The latter thoroughfare contains the Town Hall (*Palazzo Municipio*), built at the turn of the century, and the Council Chambers (*Palazzo del Consiglio Municipale*) – a hideous building frequently criticised because of its inappropriate style. The only mitigating factor is its fine series of sculptures by the Sardinian artist Costantino Nivola, who recently died in America, his adopted homeland, after a career spanning several decades. Nivola established his international reputation above all in the New World.

During recent years the **Via Manno**, the **Largo Carlo Felice** and some sections of the **Via Roma** have become important shopping streets. The ultra-modern stores and clothes boutiques radiate chic. Those is search of world-famous Italian fashion can expect to find it here.

The **Via Roma** enjoys a sunny position overlooking the sea. By day or night the multitude of little cafés are crowded and lively. The weather is so mild all the year round that the tables on the pavements and squares are left outside even in winter.

The main harbour nearby provides a link with the Italian mainland and other Mediterranean ports, including Tunis, from whence sailed the Carthaginians all those centuries ago. The narrow alleys of the **Quartiere**, the harbour district, are lined with a succession of welcoming little *ristoranti*. Their menus are not restricted to fish but if you are in search of first-class seafood – not, as a rule, easily found on Sardinia – try here.

The **Strada Urbana** continues on from the Via Roma, following the coast most of the way for mile after mile as far as **Poetto**, one of the finest and longest beaches in Italy, with views across to the foothills of the Sella del Diavolo. Looking back, one can see in the distance the old town fortifications with the cathedral, the Spanish bastion and its legacy of the past. Cagliari grew up in prosperity and poverty, in giving and taking, fearful and suspicious of all foreigners who came from across the sea. The local inhabitants could never be quite sure of their friendship, for as they had so often learned to their cost in the past it might all too rapidly change into enmity and bloodshed.

Right, the bastion of St Remy has a fantastic view over the city.

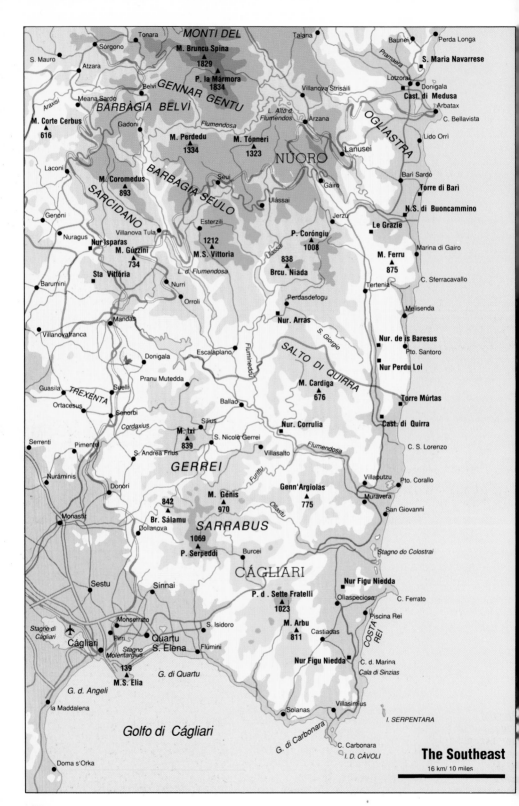

MONTI DEL

Tonara
M. Bruncu Spina
1829
P. la Mármora
1834
Sórgono
S. Mauro
Atzara
Belvi GENNAR GENTU
Talana
Baunei
Perda Longa
S. Maria Navarrese
Pramaera
Lotzorai
Donigala
Cast. di Medusa
Arbatax
C. Bellavista

Araxisi
Meana Sardo
BARBÀGIA BELVÌ
Villanova Strisáili

M. Corte Cerbus
616
Gadoni
Flumendosa
L. Alto d.
Flumendos
Árzana
OGLIASTRA

M. Perdedu
1334
M. Tónneri
1323
Seui
NÚORO
Lanusei
Lido Orri

Laconi
M. Coromedus
893
BARBÀGIA SEULO
Gáiro
Bari Sardo
Torre di Barì

Genoni
SARCIDANO
Ulássai
Jerzu
N.S. di Buoncammino

Nuragus
Villanova Tula
Esterzili
P. Coróngiu
1008
Le Grazie

Nur Isparas
M. Gúzzini
734
1212
M.S. Vittoria
Ulassai
838
Brcu. Niada
M. Ferru
875
Marina di Gairo

Barumini
Sta Vittória
L. d. Flumendosa
Tertenia
C. Sferracavallo

Villanovafranca
Nurri
Orroli
Perdasdefogu
Melisenda

Mandas
Nur. Arras
Nur. de is Baresus
Pto. Santoro

Donigala
Escalaplano
S. Giorgio
SALTO DI QUIRRA
Nur Perdu Loi

Guasila
TREXENTA
Suelli
Pranu Mutedda
Ballaò
M. Cardiga
676
Torre Múrtas

Ortacesus
Senorbi
Cordaxius
Silius
Cast. di Quirra

Serrenti
Pimentel
M. Ixi
839
S. Nicolò Gerrei
Nur. Corrulia
Flumendosa
C. S. Lorenzo

Nuráminis
S. Andrea Frius
Villasalto

Donorí
GERREI
Furittu
Villaputzu
Pto. Corallo

Monastir
842
M. Génis
970
Genn'Argiolas
775
Muravera

Br. Sálamu
Dolianova
SARRABUS
Olliastu
San Giovanni

1069
P. Serpeddi
Burcei
Stagno do Colostrai

Sestu
Sinnai
CÁGLIARI
Nur Figu Niedda

Monserrato
S. Isidoro
P. d. Sette Fratelli
1023
Oliaspeciosa
C. Ferrato

Stagno di
Cágliari
Pirri
Quartu
S. Élena
Flúmini
M. Arbu
811
Castiadas
Piscina Rei
COSTA REI

Cágliari
Stagno
Molentargius
G. di Quartu
Nur Figu Niedda
C. d. Marina
Cala di Sinzias

139
M.S. Elia
G. d. Angeli
la Maddalena
Villasimius
I. SERPENTARA

Solanas
G. di Carbonara

Golfo di Cágliari
C. Carbonara
I. D. CÁVOLI

The Southeast

16 km/ 10 miles

CAGLIARI TO OLBIA

The road from Cagliari to Olbia, the "Eastern Trunk Road" or SS 125, is known as the **Strada Statale Orientale Sarda**. It is one of the main traffic arteries in modern Sardinia, although it is not of quite such a high standard as the SS 131, the **Superstrada Carlo Felice**, which runs from Cagliari to Porto Torres and which has been transformed into a toll-free motorway. Although for many miles it follows the route of the old Roman road linking the two towns, travellers interested in the island's past or simply keen to explore Sardinia's coast need to leave the main highway from time to time.

Setting off from Cagliari via the **Viale del Poetto** in the direction of **Quartu Sant'Elena**, the traveller reaches the first important staging post after approximately 30 miles (50 km). **Villasimius**, a little town with 2,300 inhabitants, lies some 128 ft (40 metres) above sea level. It has enjoyed a remarkable boom during the past few years; it is now dotted with holiday complexes, apartment blocks, hotels and villas which attract large numbers of Italian and foreign tourists during the summer months, when the population expands to three or four times its off-season total. Villasimius and in particular the Albergho Stella d'Oro achieved literary fame through *By The Saracens' Tower*, a novel written by Ernst Jünger.

Villasimius lies in exceptionally lovely countryside; approaching from Cagliari along the road to **Capo Carbonara**, the visitor will be enchanted by breathtaking views of the ocean and a scattering of tiny islands, the largest of which are the **Isola dei Càvoli** and the **Isola di Serpentara**. The coastal margin is overshadowed by granite cliffs polished smooth by the sea over millions of years; the little beaches and bays tucked into their folds are rich hunting-grounds for fossils. It is possible to find chlorite, biotite, orthoclase, muscovite, pyrites, quartz and other rocks. Unfortunately, the lovely setting has been marred by some ugly tourist developments that have failed to respect the natural simplicity of the countryside. To the south of the town, however, some efforts have recently been made to repair environmental damage; for example, new groves of pine trees have been planted.

The *Spiaggia del Riso*, a tract of land covering some 20 sq. miles (55 sq. km), is the site not only of a *domus de janas*, one of the island's typical Neolithic "fairy graves" hewn from the rock (*see page 29*), but also of a number of groups of *nuraghi* and a *tomba dei giganti*, a "giant's grave". The latter is unfortunately in rather poor condition due to weathering and, above all, the destructive attentions of unknown amateur archaeologists.

In Villasimius itself and the surrounding area there are Phoenician remains and Roman necropolises where the dead were interred following cremation. Close to the village of Santa Maria, archaeologists have excavated a small Roman baths complex which includes a

calidarium (room for taking hot water baths) and a *praefurnium*. In ancient times the builders constructed the baths according to the accepted pattern known as *opus vittatum mixtum* – alternating rows of stones and bricks cemented with mortar.

The 17th-century **Fortezza Vecchia** (Old Fortress) rises up above the harbour. Originally built for military purposes and coastal protection, since 1982 it has housed an international centre for experimental art, attracting many European artists of stature. Their works are exhibited in the Town Hall or in the open air.

Villasimius is less well endowed with traditional customs than many others, but worth mentioning is the moving *Sagra* (Folk Festival) held in honour of Our Lady of the Shipwrecks (*Madonna del Naufrago*), celebrated in mid-July in the harbour; it is marked by religious ceremonies, a procession of fishing boats and the scattering of flowers on the sea in commemoration of lost lives.

The Costa Rei and Sarrabus: Rejoining the SS 125, the *Orientale Sarda*, in **San Priamo,** the traveller passes through three important centres of the **Sarrabus**: Muravera, San Vito and Villaputzu. **Muravera**, surrounded by extensive, and in spring wonderfully fragrant orange groves, lies approximately 35 ft (11 metres) above sea level; it has a population of about 5,000 and a modern tourist infrastructure. Hotels, holiday villages, campsites, elegant villas and lodgings in private houses provide accommodation for thousands of visitors every summer. The atmosphere is very relaxing. The seemingly endless beaches of **Costa Rei** reach right up to the foothills of **Capo Ferrato**, the lakes of **Ferraxi** or **Colostrai**, and the saltworks of **Peschiera**.

The flat coastal strip gradually gives way to the mountainous foothills of the Sarrabus, through which, flanked by fields and citrus plantations, meander the **Flumendosa** and the **Pirocca** rivers. Although no larger than 69 sq. miles (179 sq. km) the area includes a range of stunning landscapes, encompassing

Holiday villages are destroying the coastline.

168

plains and ranges of mountains as well as lakes and superb stretches of coast. Instead of ousting agriculture, as has happened in some other regions, tourism has regenerated it by supplying demanding new markets.

Muravera was inhabited at the time of the Nuraghi civilisation; later on, under the Romans, the town must have acquired a certain importance in view of its situation on the Roman road to Olbia. During the Middle Ages, in 1258, Muravera was transferred from the *giudicato* of Cagliari to that of Gallura. In 1324 it fell into the hands of Pisa, and at the end of Pisan sovereignty it was given in fief to Carroz, Count of Quirra, and then to de Centelles and de Osorio.

The community is divided into the three districts of Castiadas, San Pietro and Costa Rei. In the vicinity, near Piscina Rei, there are 22 Neolithic menhirs; six of them are still in their original vertical positions. Their original significance remains unclear. Comparisons with similar ancient structures on other sites in northern Europe seem to

indicate that their purpose was to mark the passage of the seasons. A further 42 menhirs can be seen on the site of the **Nuraghe Scalas**. Here they are arranged in groups of three, four or five. Their height varies between 3 and 6 ft (1.2 and 2 metres) above ground level. Two of the menhirs are noticeably bigger than the others and are roughly human in shape.

Of artistic interest is Muravera's 16th-century **Parish Church of St Nicholas of Bari** (*S. Nicola di Bari*), which was built in a slightly self-conscious Catalan Gothic style. The little town itself has retained numerous folkloric customs. Its cuisine is worthy of mention, and industry is based on good-quality craftsmanship – in particular the local production of sweets, basketwork and musical instruments such as the *launedda*, a sort of flute, traditionally used by shepherds and consisting of a number of pipes, whose origins lie far back in the mists of prehistory.

The village of **San Vito**, northwest of Muravera, has approximately 4,000 in-

Signore Gavino of the Stella d'Oro posing in Villasimius.

habitants and a parish extending over an area of 89 sq. miles (230 sq. km) of mainly mountainous countryside. To the south are woods and oak groves; in the middle rise the peaks of the "Seven Sisters" (*Sette Fratelli*); in the north lie the mountains of the Sarrabus. The entire area is a refuge for wildlife: the Sardinian partridge, ring and turtle doves, wild boar and rabbits, as well as the rare bearded vulture, the hobby and the Sardinian deer all inhabit the area in large numbers. Needless to say, it is a popular centre for hunting.

Mining – for silver, vesuvianite, andalusite and other minerals – was once a major industry of the area. The village enjoyed a remarkable increase in population at the turn of the 17th–18th century; the number of inhabitants rocketed from barely 1,000 to 4,000. The rapid growth was a result of increased mining production, for which large numbers of convicts were used as forced labour.

Since the completion of the **Flumendosa Barrage** the river valley –

previously subject to frequent flooding – has been exploited more intensively for farming, in particular horticulture. Probably most important among the many archaeological finds dating from antiquity are the remains of a Roman temple in the region surrounding **Lake Santa Maria**, and a well-preserved stump of a column some 6 ft (2 metres) tall and carved of monolithic granite. The upper section of the stump bears the Punic symbols *ain* and *aleph*; it is thought that these are probably numbers and that the Phoenicians used the column as a milestone.

In a field near San Vito an ancient grave containing 14 skeletons and a rich store of funeral gifts was unearthed. The collection of gold and silver earrings, bangles, fibulae and pottery dating from the 5th and 4th centuries BC can be seen in the Archaeological Museum in Cagliari. Worth seeing, too, is the **Parish Church**; it has a fine facade, twin belfries, a clock dating from 1840 and a fine crucifix in one of the side chapels. In mid-June the village cel-

Defence towers guard the coastline.

ebrates an interesting religious and traditional festival in honour of St Vitus, the local patron saint.

There is another festival in honour of St Mary on 3 October, when the community gives thanks for the wine harvest. The district has a rich craft tradition and produces some excellent handicrafts – embroidery, basketwork and weaving – and the local cuisine is justly famous. It includes such specialities as roast kid, *is culingionis de patata 'e casu* (a type of ravioli filled with cheese) and *is perdulas cum meli* (pastry cases filled with a delicious mixture of honey, egg and curd cheese).

Villaputzu lies on the SS 125, the *Orientale Sarda*, on a small plain formed by the detritus deposited by the River Flumendosa. It is a small town of 5,000 inhabitants set in a parish district with an area of 73 sq. miles (190 sq. km). Views extend across to the Mediterranean *maquis* on the hills of the Sarrabus, a tangle of wild strawberries, mastic trees, phyllirea, juniper bushes and low-lying holm oaks. A closer look

reveals the remains of two silver mines: **S'Acqua Arrubia** and **Gibbas**, which lies in the middle of the small lake of **Porto Corallo.** These two mines were in operation until the beginning of the 20th century.

In the Middle Ages Villaputzu belonged to the Sarrabus district of the *giudicato* of Cagliari. Its name at the time was *Villa Pupussi* or *Villa Pupia*. Later, together with l'Ogliastra, it was annexed by the *giudicato* of Gallura under Giovanni Maria Visconti. At the end of the 14th century it was the scene of the fierce quarrels between the Sardinian rulers of Arborea and the Aragonese. During the 16th century the **Fortezza Gibas** and the **Porto Corallo** were constructed to protect the town from the increasingly persistent attacks of the Turks operating off the North African coast.

Near **Torre Murta** can be seen the remains of a settlement dating from the 3rd millennium BC, including a *domus de janas*. In 1966, during excavations on the Santa Maria Hills, the archaeolo-

The prehistoric site of Pranu Muteddu.

gist Francesco Barrecca discovered the ruins of a Phoenician settlement. It is likely that the site of the *Acropolis of Sarcopos*, a Phoenician-Carthaginian temple-fortress, must also have stood somewhere near here.

The Latin *Itinerarium* of Antoninus, written at the beginning of the 3rd century BC, refers to the town of Sarcopos as being situated 20 miles from Porticenses (Tertenia) and Ferraria (San Gregorio). North African pottery finds in the area probably date from the 6th and 7th centuries AD; local clay artefacts in the shape of combs and two bronze and clay fibulae indicate that the area was inhabited during Vandal and Byzantine times.

There are two important buildings worth visiting nearby. Some 10 miles (15 km) from the centre, on the SS 125, stands the pretty little church of **San Nicola di Quirra**. And on a broad plateau demarcated by precipitous cliffs perches a grim fortress, the **Castello di Quirra**. The view is breathtaking.

The locals' enthusiasm for folk festivals has not diminished with the passage of time. During the *Sagra di Sant'Antonio del Fuoco* a giant bonfire is lit on the village square in accordance with an ancient pagan rite. The best *launeddas* players from all over the island come to take part in the *Sagra del Ballo con Launeddas* in August. Characteristic local handicrafts include tapestries woven on a loom, blankets and tablecloths, crochet work, mats and wicker baskets.

The Ogliastra: The gateway to the Ogliastra and the Province of Nuoro is **Tertenia**, which lies in the middle of a largely uninhabited region divided into three main districts: **Sapala, Quirra** and **Villamonti**.

There are many springs in the vicinity, as well as a mountain torrent, the Sibirio or Rio Sibi, and a number of mountain peaks such as the San Giovanni. Between the two regions of the Sarrabus and the Ogliastra, at the southern end of the Ierzu district, you may be lucky enough to come across a *Petra Fitta*, a monolith usually in the form of a phallus, or a flat, altar-like *Petra de s'Altari*.

There are a number of well-preserved *nuraghi* in the region surrounding Tertenia, although others have been almost completely destroyed. Some of the best examples are the **Nuraghi** Santu Perdu, De Sa domo de S'orcu, De Luna, De Nuras Solas, De Bacu De S'Ortu, De Bacu de Sa cresia, De su Preidi, De Cana de Tidu, De Fogi manni, De Brebeis, De su Lionaxi, De S'arcu de sa Cannèra, Se Monti Sidduru, De sa Teria.

Travellers interested in churches will enjoy visiting those of the Beata Vergine Assunta, Santa Lucia, San Pietro, Santa Sofia or Santa Teresa. The most colourful festivals include that of the Assumption – Vergine Assunta, and those in honour of St Sebastian (San Sebastiano) and St Sophia (Santa Sofia). The festivities attract visitors from the surrounding villages as well as foreign tourists.

Further to the west, a few miles from the SS 125 between Tertenia and Bari Sardo on a long ridge surrounded by

Farmer from Dorgali.

hilly country, lies the somewhat larger town of **Ierzu**. By sheer determination it seems to survive despite the poor quality of the soil on the surrounding hills. Ierzu's schools – primary, middle and upper – show it to be a modern, progressive place.

A noble *Cannonau* vintage is produced in its vineyards; in former times the farmers themselves would also make the wine, but nowadays this is undertaken almost exclusively by the cooperative wine cellars, which are also responsible for marketing the product at home and abroad. The neighbouring countryside is mostly mountainous. The cone-shaped Monte Corongiu affords a spectacular view of the Tyrrhenian Sea; on clear days one can even see the summits of Villacidro on the other side of the island, towering above the smaller mountain peaks and wooded slopes.

Ierzu's most important festival of the year is held on 13 June in honour of St Anthony of Padua (*Sant'Antonio di Padova*), to whom one of the town's churches is dedicated. Other buildings of note which are worth a quick visit include the churches of St Sebastian and St Erasmus.

Continuing northwards along the *Orientale Sarda*, the SS 125, the traveller arrives in **Bari Sardo**. The origin of the name lies in its *abbari* (marshy ground). Historically the town enjoyed considerable importance, for the jurisdiction of its courts extended as far as Lozzorai, Girasole and Loceri. Today the town derives most of its income from agriculture and cattle breeding; in former times it was also famous for flax and the manufacture of linen. The town boasted 250 looms.

Bari Sardo's best agricultural products are its red and white wine, and various types of fruit: lemons, oranges, pears, plums, apricots etc. An exceptional period of drought in 1833 drastically reduced the stocks of sheep, pigs, goats and cattle, and may have precipitated the change in local farming policy. In the mountains hereabouts are still many species of wild animals: rabbits,

Young beauty in the traditional costume of Oliena.

ring and turtle doves, partridges and wild boar.

Tortolí and Arbatax: Tortolí lies further to the north in a small, fertile plain surrounded by fields. The suburb of **Arbatax** is on the coast a few miles further on. It is a well-known seaside resort with a small harbour used by both commercial and pleasure craft, with connections to the Italian mainland as well as other ports on the island. The nearby paper factory, which produces the lion's share of newsprint for the whole of Italy, has brought the district regular employment, prosperity and increased trade.

Sheltered from the westerly winds by the hills of the Barbagia, Tortolí is equally sheltered from northerlies by Cape Montesanto near Baunei.

In former times the marshes and lakes surrounding Tortolí increased the risk of malaria infection and gave the town a reputation for being an unhealthy place to live in. To the south of Tortolí, which has seen rapid expansion during the past 20 years, flows the river of the same name, fed by a number of smaller tributaries coming from Arzana, Elini, Ilbono and Lanusei. Its banks are a haven for various species of water birds, including cranes and flamingos (*Phoenicopterus Ruber*), whose more usual homes are Andalusia and the South of France.

Tourism, the port, the industry of nearby Arbatax and the fertile surrounding countryside – nowadays no longer plagued by malaria – make Tortolí one of the liveliest towns in the Ogliastra region – a fact evinced by its numerous schools and hotels.

Also characteristic of Tortolí is the absence of *nuraghi* or even the remains of more recent cultures in the surrounding area. The reason for this lies in its long association with malaria, so feared that even the Berbers, Vandals and Saracens were more intent on returning to North Africa than settling here. Tortolí was formerly a bishopric and before that the seat of the margraves of Quirra. It was spared, however, the often cruel and consequently hated forms of feu- **Easter procession in Arbatax.**

174

dalism which prevailed elsewhere on Sardinia.

The little town of **Lanusei** lies away from the coast, perched on the eastern foothills of the Barbagia a few miles from Tortolí. The surroundings are mostly mountainous; the principal peaks are those of Cardiga, Fenurau and Tissidu. Of the many **caves** in the area, the most attractive are Su Mannucone and Sa Grotta de s'Arroli.

General Alfonso La Marmora – geologist, geographer, anthropologist and explorer – travelled the length and breadth of the island, recording his impressions in his *Voyage en Sardaigne*. In 1833 he remarked that the entire Ogliastra region must be rich in copper deposits, for in ancient times local tribes used the metal in the production of their idols and simple artefacts (examples of these are on view in the Archaeological Museum in Cagliari).

Lanusei, now a bishopric and the seat of the local courts, can look back on a long and venerable tradition. It is the proud setting of the first Salesian-Sardinian foundation (established by the followers of St John Bosco); the town also possesses numerous schools and colleges.

Near the **Cathedral of St Mary Magdalene** stand the **Church of the Conception of the Virgin Mary** (*Concezione della Vergine*), the **Church of Ss Cosmas and Damian** (dedicated to two brothers, the patron saints of doctors, who were canonised following their martyrdom in the 4th century) and the **Church of St Lucia**. Contemporary records note that the Church of Ss Cosmas and Damian and the Church of St Lucia were both in poor repair in the 19th century.

The same document, the *Dizionario Geografico Storico-Commerciale*, states that there were four *nuraghi* in the vicinity of Lanusei, "one in the district known as *Genneacili*, another near *Uleé*, a third in *Alaùi*, and the fourth is the one they call *Nuragi-Rubiu*. They have all been destroyed – only the third *nuraghe* mentioned still contains some intact sections."

In the neighbourhood of Lanusei can also be seen a number of towers erected as protection from Berber attack. Examples can be visited at Monteferru, Monte Salina, Dejicuaddus, Porto Corallo, Monte Rosso, Murtas, San Lorenzo, San Gemiliano, Arbatax and Santa Maria Navarrese.

From Baunei to Dorgali: a charming little village by the sea, **Santa Maria Navarrese**, forms part of the community of Baunei. It lies on the southern coast of Montesanto and contains a number of hotels, restaurants and holiday villas. Its environs are wild and untouched and stretch in the east as far as the cliffs overlooking the Tyrrhenian Sea. Even today, goatherds and swineherds lead their animals unhurriedly between the holm oaks, the arbutus and the shrubs of the maquis, where the flocks can feed on the profusion of berries and acorns .

Baunei is famous for its hard-working population. "Leisure is a crime" here and "in the fields, men and women's hands compete for the most calluses", as we learn again from the

Young men carry the Virgin Mary to the *incontro*.

Dizionario. Today, few local residents pursue the area's traditional occupations of woodcutting or weaving; most are employed in jobs associated with the increasing tourism in the region, the manufacture of sweets, or wine production. Tourism has also resulted in a return to the simple cooking methods and traditional fare. It is based on goat, kid and lamb, or occasionally wild boar or other game hunted in the surrounding countryside.

The village's two principal churches are dedicated to **St Peter** and **St Nicholas of Bari**. There is also a number of churches in the surrounding villages, including ones dedicated to St Peter the Apostle, St John the Evangelist, St Lussorio the Sardinian Martyr, and – the most important – St Mary of Navarre. According to legend, this last church was founded by one of the daughters of the King of Navarre in grateful thanks for being saved from shipwreck. The church stands on the site where she reached land.

In the village of Santa Maria Navarrese, local residents still bake acorn bread, at one time prepared all over the island. The local recipe goes like this: soak some clay and wood ash particles in water, decant and pour the water into a large pot. Place the pot on the stove and add some shelled acorns (the ash particles act as a leach and remove the bitter taste from the acorns, whilst the clay softens them). A smooth paste will gradually form. Stir continuously, and cook until it is dark red, almost brown in colour. Allow the mixture to cool and solidify. Place dough in the sun to dry.

Acorn bread can be served with meat, ham, sausages and cheese. The custom of eating acorns is also documented in Spain as well as in Asia, America and Africa, but the recipe for acorn bread is found only on Sardinia.

From Santa Maria Navarrese the main road, the SS 125, continues northwards. The village of **Urzulei** is on the left-hand side, clinging to a wooded hillside and sheltered from northerly and south-westerly winds. It lies at the foot of Mount Pisaneddu, in the midst of

The *nuraghi* village of Serra Orios near Dorgali.

varied terrain where the shepherds allow their flocks to roam wild. Continuing towards Dorgali, beyond Urzulei the road is full of nasty bends but these are more than compensated for by the awe-inspiring views.

Dorgali and Cala Gonone: Barely a mile and a half before the town, there is a newly completed road tunnel through the Monte Bardia. At the far end lies the densely populated suburb of **Cala Gonone**. The views as one exits are magnificent: a gentle limestone hill falls away towards the sea. Juniper, rosemary and other aromatic Mediterranean plants blossom under ancient holm oaks.

Spreading out in the distance, Dorgali is a former fishing village whose original inhabitants were not natives of the island. Nowadays it is a sizeable town with hotels, villas, flats, apartment houses and campsites. It is easy to see why it has boomed. Views extend across glistening emerald waters which every year lure thousands of visitors from mainland Italy and every corner of the globe. Along the coastline visitors can explore a succession of hidden bays such as the famous **Cala Luna**. Here, too, are the caves of the **Bue Marino**, in which a number of rare monk seals (*monachus monachus*) have found refuge. The precipitous cliffs in the direction of Cape Montesanto in the south and Orosei in the north are of unique natural beauty and justify attempts to preserve them.

Dorgali itself seems to welcome the visitor with open arms. The town extends along the foot of the Monte Bardia, which protects the 8,000 inhabitants from the sea breezes. Cattle farming and agriculture have been practised here since earliest times; the vineyards of the nearby community of Oliena to the west are famous for their noble *Cannonau* vintages. Dorgali itself thrives on a flourishing handicrafts industry; cork, wood, wool, gold and silver items are all produced by a variety of medium-sized firms, most of them also involved in local tourism. The rapid increase in the per capita income of

Fairytale bays on the coast of Baunei.

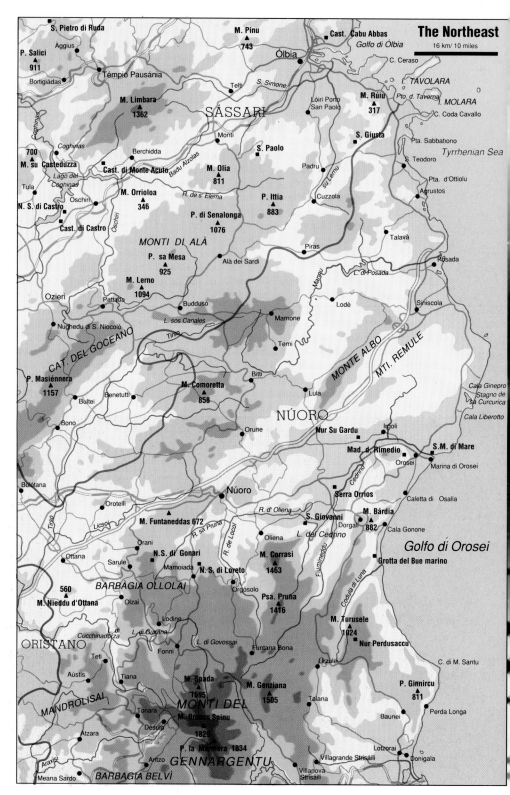

S. Pietro di Ruda

Aggius

P. Salici
911

Bortigiádas

Témpio Pausánia

M. Pinu
743

Ólbia

Cast. Cabu Abbas

Golfo di Ólbia

C. Ceraso

I. TAVOLARA

Telti

S. Simone

Lóiri Porto
San Paolo

M. Rúiu
317

Pto. d. Taverna

I. MOLARA

C. Coda Cavallo

M. Limbara
1362

SÁSSARI

Monti

Berchidda

S. Paolo

S. Giusta

Pta. Sabbationo

Tyrrhenian Sea

S. Teodoro

700
M. su Casteduzza

Coghinas

Cast. di Monte Acuto

Badu Alzolas

M. Olia
811

Padru

su Lerru

Pta. d'Ottiolu

Agrustos

Coghinas

Lago del
Coghinas

Tula

Oschiri

M. Orrioloa
346

R. de s'Elema

P. Ittia
883

Cuzzola

Talavà

N. S. di Castro

Cast. di Castro

Oschiri

P. di Senalonga
1076

MONTI DI ALÀ

Alà dei Sardi

Piras

Magnu

Pósada

L. di Posada

Siniscola

Ozieri

Pattada

P. sa Mesa
925

M. Lerno
1094

Buddusò

L. sos Canales

Tirso

Mamone

Lodè

Temi

MONTE ALBO

MTI. REMULE

Cala Ginepro

Stagno de
sa Curcurica

Cala Liberotto

Núghedu di S. Niocolò

CAT. DEL GOCEANO

P. Masiénnera
1157

Bultei

Benetutti

M. Comoretta
858

Bitti

Lula

NÚORO

Irgoli

Bono

Orune

Nur Su Gardu

Mad. d. Rimedio

Orosei

S.M. di Mare

Marina di Orosei

Bolótana

Orotelli

Núoro

Serra Orrios

Caletta di Osalla

Licsol

M. Funtaneddas 672

R. sa Pruna

R. d' Oliena

S. Giovanni

Cedrino

M. Bárdia
882

Cala Gonone

Ottana

Orani

Sarule

N.S. di Gonari

Mamoiada

N.S. di Loreto

Oliena

L. del Cedrino

Dorgali

Golfo di Orosei

Grotta del Bue marino

M. Corrasi
1463

560
M. Nieddu d'Ottana

Olzai

BARBÁGIA OLLOLAI

Orgósolo

Psa. Pruna
1416

Fiumineddu

Coddu di Luna

Teti

Aústis

ORISTANO

Cucchinadórza

L. di
Gusana

L. di Govossai

Fonni

Funtana Bona

Urzulei

M. Turusele
1024

Nur Perdusaccu

C. di M. Santu

Tiana

MANDROLISAI

Tonara

Désula

M. Spada
1595

MONTI DEL

M. Genziana
1505

Talana

P. Ginnircu
811

Perda Longa

Atzara

M. Bruncu Spinu
1829

Baunei

Araxisi

Aritzo

P. la Marmora 1834

GENNARGENTU

Villagrande Strisáili

Villanova
Strisáili

Donigala

Lotzorai

Meana Sardo

BARBÁGIA BELVÌ

Doragli's inhabitants has earned the town a prominent place in Italy's statistical tables.

The principal sights include the Nuraghi village of **Serra Orrios**, the *nuraghi* at Fuìli, Jorgia, Sortèi, Neulè and Filìne as well as the *tomba di giganti*, the "giant's grave" S'ena 'e Thomes in the Marreri-Isalle Valley.

Also worth visiting is the country church of **San Battista**. Since antiquity it has been the scene of an elaborate folk festival; any visitors arriving in town during the celebrations are automatically invited to participate in the ceremonial feast.

Archaeological finds dating from Palaeolithic times have recently been discovered in the **Cave of Sale Corbeddu**, which during the 19th century served as sanctuary for the bandit of the same name. With the assistance of the community of Oliena and the Principal Office for Archaeological Cultural Remains in the Provinces of Sassari and Nuoro, a group of students from Utrecht has been carrying out excavations which have unearthed plant and animal fossils proving beyond any doubt that the island was inhabited by man during the Old Stone Age, and not merely – as was previously assumed – since the Neolithic Era.

Returning to the SS 125 towards Olbia, a few miles past Dorgali the traveller can turn off towards **Oliena**. The little town lies at the foot of Mount Corrasi, separated from Dorgali by the Lanaittu valley, which is full of holm oaks, juniper bushes and game. At the bottom of a karst crater lie the remains of the prehistoric village of Tiscali. Between the limestone cliffs the untouched valley is a maze of gorges, caves and folds in the earth's crust – amazingly, most of them are as yet totally unexplored.

The most noteworthy sight in Oliena is **Su Gologone**, a spring situated near the hotel and restaurant of the same name. Gushing in a torrent from the limestone cliff, it then flows into the Cedrino mountain stream and thence into the lake. Part of this lake lies within the parish boundary of Galtellìs, an important town in Sardinia in ancient times. After being transferred to the *giudicato* of Gallura, it subsequently became a feudal estate under the name of Baronia; the surrounding area is still called by this name today. Oliena is a centre of apiculture and horticulture, but its main claim to fame within the province of Nuoro is as a producer of olives and wines.

The beauty of the surrounding countryside coupled with the open character and hospitable nature of the inhabitants of Oliena is famous in Sardinia. Many writers – Antonio Bresciani, Tullio Bazzi, Gabriele d'Annunzio, Elio Vittorini and Carlo Levi – described it in glowing terms.

Within Oliena itself and its environs there are numerous late Romanesque and Pisan-style churches, all completed before the 14th century. The town centre is dominated by the **Church of St Mary**; at Easter the forecourt is the scene of one of the most popular and characteristic religious ceremonies in Sardinia: *s'incontru*, marking the meeting between the Virgin Mary and the resurrected Christ. Old but well-preserved are the churches of **Santa Croce** and **San Lussorio**; from 21 August the latter forms the setting for a festival combining both sacred and secular elements, which attracts visitors from miles around.

The Jesuits played a key role in the town's history. They were responsible for the founding of the **Parish Church of St Ignatius Loyola** and the associated boarding school, which previously housed a school of rhetoric. During the 16th and 17th centuries, they painstakingly undertook the development of 39,500 acres (16,000 hectares) of mountainous countryside; some of this was later sold off to local farmers but 9,900 acres (4,000 hectares) are still in the possession of the society today. They nurtured wheat, barley, broad beans and several varieties of fruit trees. Thanks to their skills and their diligence, Oliena is now a thriving agricultural community, more than able to hold its own against all rival agricultural communities in the region.

The visitor is recommended to take the time to see the church offices, where a varied collection of paintings, a number of old manuscripts and some exceptionally well-preserved church utensils are on display. There is also a number of caves, *nuraghi* and giants' graves to be explored in the vicinity. Afterwards you migh like to sample some of the area's specialities in one of the local restaurants.

From Oliena to Olbia: Motorists wishing to join the SS 129 as quickly as possible are recommended to take one of the two short link roads, *norghe* or *su trave*, which join the *nazionale traversale sarda* approximately 6 miles (10 km) before the provincial capital.

The SS 129 to Orosei is a pleasant road, bordered to right and left by pretty hills covered with olive and almond trees. Short lowland stretches occur from time to time, mostly given over to viticulture except when the local livestock farmers use them as grazing for their animals, principally sheep. Now and again the way leads through rough countryside, where the parched clay soil supports oleander, maquis scrubland vegetation, arbutus and the thorny Sardinian gorse, the flowers of which blossom in spring and early summer, covering the landscape in a magnificent carpet of yellow .

The valley of the **River Cedrino** is marked by a mighty dam constructed to prevent the regular destruction caused by flooding when the river bursts its banks. On one occasion, however, not even the dam was able to contain the deluge; the waters devastated the valley and the ancient villages of **Galtelli**, **Loculi**, **Irgoli** and **Onifai**. Of the four settlements, Galtelli lies on the right bank; Loculi, Irgoli and Onifai are all on the left.

In spite of the importance which this valley possessed in the years when it was the diocesan seat of the bishopric of Galtelli (the latter was eventually transferred to Nuoro in 1779), historically speaking the region was a malaria-infested area which offered few work opportunities for its inhabitants; for a

Beach on the southern Costa Rei.

long time, its population lived in extreme poverty.

The houses and churches of the four villages, especially those of Irgoli and Galtellis, bear silent witness to a peasant culture and its religion, displaying fine examples of a formal but modest Mediterranean architectural style: tiled roofs, courtyards, archways, and belfries which – large or small – seem to cling to the ground rather than soar heavenwards.

The small town of **Orosei** is situated on the final section of the SS 129, which joins the SS 1½ miles (2 km) before the coast. The town's coastal margin borders on that of Dorgali and Cala Gonone to the south, and Siniscola and Cape Comino in the North.

Situated on the plains on the right bank of the River Cedrino, the village is overshadowed by the Church of San Gavino on the top of a hill, and by the vantage point **Gollei**, from which there is an idyllic view across the district's fertile flower gardens and orchards. Everywhere in the vicinity of Orosei

you will come across remains of old settlements; the numerous churches in and around the town are a sure sign of former prosperity.

The **Parish Church of St James** (San Giacomo), in January the setting for the festival of Sant'Antonio Abate, dates from 1794. Further celebrations are held in honour of Sant'Isidoro Contadino, San Giacomo (July), Nostra Signora del Mare (Our Lady of the Sea) and, at the pilgrimage place of the same name to the west of the town, the festival of Nostra Signora del Rimedio (Our Lady of the Healing). This last occasion, which takes place in September, was recorded for posterity by the writer Grazia Deledda in her novel *Canne al Vento*; pilgrims come from near and far to take part.

Orosei possesses a large number of *nuraghi*. One or two of them are still in good condition, but the majority are in poor repair or have been completely destroyed due to the practice of using the stones as building material. There are also coastal defensive towers and a

The village of Posada sits in a picturesque mountain.

fortress which it is claimed was constructed on the ruins of a considerably older and more important fortification erected when the *giudicato* was handed over from Gallura to the Visconti family from Milan.

As a town, Orosei is clearly prospering. Its agriculture is sound, and it derives a steady income from its marble and granite quarries. Above all, its seemingly endless beaches (**Cala Liberotto, Cala Ginepro** and several others which are less well known but no less attractive) are gradually being opened up to tourism.

North of Orosei the SS 125 follows the coast. The sea here is as invitingly clear and unpolluted as it looks. After driving for a short while through pine groves and characteristic Mediterranean vegetation, the traveller reaches the twin villages of **Capo Comino** and **Santa Lucia**, before arriving in **Siniscola**, with its coastal suburb, **La Caletta**, which has its own harbour and a pretty beach.

During the past 15 to 20 years, tourism and a number of small industries – including a lime kiln and a cement works – have resulted in a more rapid population growth rate in **Siniscola** than in any of the other towns or villages within the province of Nuoro, apart from the regional capital itself. Today Siniscola has some 10,000 inhabitants; it lies on almost level terrain.

In front, some 3 miles (5 km) further on, is the sea; behind, to the west, lie the parallel mountains **Remule** and **Montalbo**. What these mountains lack in height they more than make up for by their awe-inspiring, strangely shaped limestone cliffs. At dawn they greet the day with a shimmering pale pink hue; by midday they are a dazzling white; and as dusk falls they are suffused in a blaze of crimson.

The region surrounding Siniscola is well known for its numerous healing springs: **Locoi** rising in a limestone cave, **Cordianeddu**, a former spa visited by local gentry, **Fonte del Mare**, not far from the beach at Santa Lucia, **Abba Fritta**, a cold water spring, **Su**

Favourite territory for speculative transactions, the area between San Teodoro and Olbia.

Canturu and Fonte Luittu, which is renowned for its laxative properties.

Many of the *nuraghi* in the vicinity are in rather poor repair or have unfortunately been completely destroyed. Still worth the walk are the **Nuraghi Pizzinu, Mannu** and **Orco** and the numerous *domus de janas* on the Cuccuru de Janas hill.

On a number of occasions Siniscola was the victim of attacks by raiding Turks. In 1512, 150 inhabitants were captured and carried off as spoils of war before being sold into slavery. Later on the citizens built two defensive towers, Santa Lucia and Caletta, which are still in good repair today, as well as constructing a fortified wall around the perimeter of the town.

The **Parish Church of St John** was built in 1766. Apart from visiting the community's oldest **Church of St Lucia** it is well worth seeing some of the other places of worship: the **Church of Sant'Elena Imperatrice** (St Helena the Empress) on the Cuccuru de Janas hill, San Giuseppe Patriarca (St Joseph

the Patriarch) on the Montalbo (built in 1730) and the **Church of San Simplicio Vescovo e Martire** (St Simplicius, Bishop and Martyr), built in 1811 alongside the twisting road from Siniscola to Lodè.

Beaches and bays: In earlier times Siniscola was the seat of the Barons of Montalbo, under whose jurisdiction also lay the towns of Lodè and Torpè in the interior and Posada and San Teodoro on the coast. Nowadays Posada and San Teodoro, together with Budoni, are in the midst of rapid economic and touristic expansion. There are numerous hotels, apartments and rooms in private houses to accommodate the hordes of holidaymakers who every summer come to the beaches between Siniscola and Olbia.

The most beautiful beaches to be found along this stretch of the east coast are **San Giovanni di Posada, Budoni Centro, Ottiolu**, the sandy beach of **Arenile de l'Isuledda** on the peninsula of the same name, **Cala d'Ambra** and the beach of **La Cinta** (with the **Stagno**

Large ferry leaving the basin of Olbia.

San Teodoro), not far from the mighty foothills of Punt'Aldia.

The remaining stretch of road as far as Olbia is some 22 miles (35 km) long and leads through one of the most enchanting regions in the whole of Sardinia, past the **Cala Coda Cavallo** ("Ponytail Bay"), the **Spiaggia di Salinedda** beach, and a succession of bays – **Cala Ruia, Cala Suaraccia** and **Cala Purgatorio** ("Purgatory Bay") to the foothills of **Monte Petrosu** and the picturesque beaches of **Porto Taverna, Porto San Paolo** and **Porto Istana**. In the distance, beyond the pretty villages, can be seen the gently green silhouette of the **Island of Molara** and the forbidding cliffs of **Tavolara**, which can be reached either by private boat (enquire among the local fishermen) or by one of the small ferries which leave from Porto San Paolo.

To the west soar the shimmering red and white granite peaks of the mountains of the interior, whilst in the foreground groves of holm oaks and cork oaks stretch out before them, rising above an undergrowth of myrtle, arbutus and buckthorn. Here and there blackened stretches resembling a lunar landscape are reminders of the consequence of fires. These conflagrations cause enormous ecological damage during the summer months.

Traces of antiquity can be found scattered across the countryside, mostly in the form of decayed remains of *nuraghi*. Relics of a more recent date that are worth a visit include the **Castello della Fava**, an almost impregnable fortress some 64 ft (20 metres) high on the hill above **Posada**. It is maintained that the *giudice* of Gallura lived here until it fell to the forces of Aragon and then, in 1431, to Nicolò Carroz d'Arborea.

Olbia: Thanks to a remarkable expansion of both population and the local economy during the past few years, Olbia has become one of the most forward-looking towns in Sardinia. It has a modern airport and a flourishing port despite the proximity of the harbour at Golfo Aranci, only 9 miles (15 km) away. It is the main arrival point for **Sunset on Costa Rei.**

184

those staying on the Costa Smeralda – at least for those holidaymakers not arriving by yacht.

Having almost doubled between 1951 and 1981, the population of Olbia today is approximately 35,000. The tourist infrastructure is well developed, so that the town can be regarded as the gateway not only to the province of Nuoro, but also to the Costa Smeralda. Its first population boom occurred during the years 1921–31, when a group of foreign industrialists saw the financial possibilities of developing local cheese production and mussel farming; the population rose from 6,595 to almost 13,000.

Despite its Greek name (*Olbius* means "happy"), the town was not founded by the Greeks. There is no doubt that the Carthaginians once lived here; they recognised the advantages of the proximity to the coast of Latium. When the Romans conquered Sardinia (AD 138), Olbia ceased to rely purely on its economic value and acquired military power as well as strategic importance. In those days the town was connected to the rest of the island by three roads; they served as highways for the legions as well as for the transport of goods. Later, during the Christian era, they were a great aid to the Christian missionaries in their progress to convert the islanders.

In Carthaginian times, Olbia extended more or less from the site of the present-day Via Asproni to the Piazza Matteotti. But the town's Golden Age occurred under the Romans, from the last century of the Republic to the end of the first century of the Empire. Supporting the theory about economic expansion in Roman times are the number and varieties of currency found on archaeological sites throughout the town. In 1904 a hoard of money was found stashed in the necropolis; the 871 gold coins bear the portrait of 117 different Roman families and include 312 different currencies.

There are numerous Roman remains dating from a later period: temples and baths, necropolises, tombs with inscriptions, monuments, remains of roads, houses, walls, an aqueduct, wells, amphora (some still intact), and the vestiges of the harbour mole and the quay.

The break-up of the Western Roman Empire during the 5th century BC marked the beginning of a long period of decline for Olbia. The town repeatedly fell prey to Arab raids from the 8th century onwards and many of its inhabitants fled to the interior. It was not until the turn of the millennium that it began to flourish again, initially as the first capital of the *giudicato* of Gallura, and later under Pisa, when it acquired the status of a free city. During this time the town was rechristened Terranova, a name which it bore until 1939.

The kings of Savoy were responsible for the road linking Olbia to what is now the main highway, the **Superstrada Carlo Felice**, the railway link with Chilivani and a marked increase in the trading links with Marseilles, Sicily and the Italian mainland, which, according to the *Dizionario* once more, the island supplied with "Wheat, wine, cheese, hides, wool… oil and mastic trees."

Farmer from Arbatax.

COSTA SMERALDA

If you drive directly north from Olbia Airport you will reach the place where Sardinia is at its most beautiful, the **Costa Smeralda**. Olbia, blighted by urban pollution, bunker-like concrete hotels and endless advertisement hoardings, couldn't be more different from the Emerald Coast. Here the sea shimmers in hundreds of shades of aquamarine, your lips tast of salt, and your hair is tousled by a breeze fragrant with the scent of the *macchia*, a heady mix of forest, aromatic rosemary, lavender and myrtle. According to Sardinian legend, this is where the wind was born.

Costa Smeralda is an enchanted place and every visitor falls prey to its magic. High wind-eroded cliffs, wild mountain terrain; 80 stunning bays and a string of idyllic coves make this 55-km (35-mile) coastal strip in north-west Sardinia one of the most attractive holiday destinations in the world.

It is also one of the most exclusive. It was discovered at the start of the 1960s by His Highness Karim Aga Khan. Although scarcely out of his teens at the time, he was able to see the potential of this demi-paradise at the very heart of Europe's already overcrowded Mediterranean region – before the giants of package tourism. In conjunction with some of his very rich friends, he set about creating a holiday resort for the world's wealthiest people.

Over the next 20 years Karim's plans for a Shangri-La unfolded and one of the most expensive, prestigious and best-cared-for holiday regions in the world took shape. The **Emerald Coast** is now a firm favourite of those who only holiday in the most exclusive places in the world. The emerald colour of the water is to be found nowhere, it is claimed, but on a Bulgari brooch or a Cartier necklace; the pink-tinged beaches look as if they have just been given a dusting with Givenchy powder. The Happy Few who can afford to stay here look as though they have just stepped out of an Antonioni film.

Cardinal rule: Today the Aga Khan, head of the Ishmaeli sect of Moslems, is in his fifties. He still heads the **Consorzio Costa Smeralda**, a non-profit organisation which continues to ensure with utmost strictness that the harmonious relationship between nature and the works of man remains intact. One cardinal rule is that no villa, hotel or apartment block may be visible above the tops of the typically small holm oaks and tamarisks. Top architects have been employed to see to this. Jacques Coelle, architectural genius and member of the *Académie Française*, designed the elegant houses surrounding the Piazza in Porto Cervo. Although only recently built, the facades are endowed with the pastel-coloured patina usually associated with maturity – they even glow authentically at sunset.

Land prices on the Costa Smeralda rose by 600 percent over a period of 10 years. Potential developers must reckon today with prices of US$3,000–4,250 per cubic metre of space. During the peak season, which reaches its climax in July/August, some 12,000 people flock to the Emerald Coast: owners and tenants of the luxury villas, hotel guests, visitors in their private yachts. Of these tourists 50 percent are Italian, 15 percent German, 8 percent American and 10 percent Swiss, with a liberal sprinkling of wealthy Lebanese and the occasional French.

Maintaining a clean and ecologically-sound environment is a priority. Not a single tree may be planted or felled without the permission of the consortium. Most of the houses along the Costa Smeralda were constructed with natural building materials available locally: stone and granite. Their roofs are covered with grass, so that they are hardly noticeable until one is standing before the front door. Even then, they mostly look like oversized kennels rather than houses, although inside they may contain up to 20 rooms.

The regulations and measures prescribed by the *consorzio* go further: all telephone wires and electric cables must run underground, waste water from the villas, the hotels and even the yacht harbour is processed by the most expensive treatment plant in the world.

If a boat-owner is caught emptying his chemical toilet into the harbour or into some lonely bay, he can expect draconian punishment. The fines lie between $2,000 and $5,000; in the case of a second offence, exclusion from the marina and the loss of mooring privileges is the rule.

The Aga Khan's own police enforce these laws, but their role is to provide security as much as to punish misdemeanours. If, for example, a visitor should happen to leave a $1,000 bill lying on a towel on the **Spiaggia di Romazzino** (not as improbable as it may sound) he or she will find it still there on returning after an hour's swim – weighted down with a stone to ensure that it does not blow away.

Mr Olivetti has a private villa on this bay; the beach is watched night and day by his team of private bodyguards, not least because Italy's rich live in permanent fear of being kidnapped. For this reason, the famous names of cinema and the giants of industry love the Costa Smeralda: it is a sanctuary; there are no *paparazzi*, and they can rely on silent discretion and watchful eyes at all times. Where else could an international tycoon and his latest escort enjoy a stroll along the beach without being disturbed by voyeurs, gossip columnists or indeed his wife? If the latter should chance to come round the corner, the industrial magnate will have been warned in good time by a member of the security police.

The arrival of any journalist on the Costa Smeralda is quietly registered by the security forces. Many a photographer, travelling incognito as a camera-toting tourist, has been expelled in a none-too-gentle manner.

The Aga Khan lured many wealthy friends who already possessed every material comfort to his Emerald Coast. What he offered them was becoming increasingly difficult to find in Europe's other Mediterranean hot-spots. They came from Monte Carlo, from Ibiza, from Sylt and from Marbella.

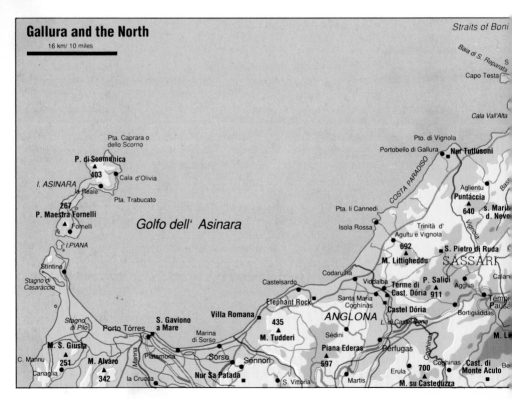

Yachts, boats and skippers: A private yacht is the ultimate status symbol on the Costa Smeralda. People manage without their expensive cars but they are reluctant to hide all evidence of wealth. And so, during their very occasional raids on the yacht harbours of the Emerald Coast, the Italian fraud squad is likely to encounter a number of strange paradoxes: a baker, for instance, whose tax return indicates that he is making only a very modest living, chugging happily around on a million-dollar yacht.

As in the world's other major fashionable yacht harbours, the admiring and the envious throng the landing stages, watching the parade of exotic birds of passage.

Except for *ferragosto* (15 August), when Italian high society swoops in from Milan and Rome, hiring a boat or obtaining a mooring in the harbour should present no problems. The **Marina** was completed in 1975; its wharf is among the best functioning in the world. You can anchor next to the gigantic vessel of Gianni Agnelli (you know, the one with the brown sails!), or beside the largest speedboat in the world (belonging to Bruno Mentasti, the king of mineral waters); the next yacht, bobbing gently on the waves, is perhaps the *Diane*, the floating hotel belonging to Friedrich Karl Flick. The "Sheik" *Atlantis* is more like a floating island; it was once the pride and joy of Stavros Niarchos.

Altogether there are 650 berths for boats between 12 and 55 metres (38–176 ft) in length. There is also a special dry dock. A 12-metre berth costs US$280 a day during high season; a 55-metre berth costs a mere $2,258 a day including electricity and water. During the winter months the yacht basin is scoured by a natural current.

The best skippers in the world, from America and Australia, all converge on the Costa Smeralda. Nowhere else in Europe will yacht owners have so little difficulty finding experienced yachting crews to help them win one of the Costa's many regattas: the *Settimana della bocce* at the end of August, and the competition for the largest yachts in mid-September.

The *Sardegna Club* is an annual event, and the *Premio Offshore* is the race for the fastest motor boats (known as "cigars"). Princess Caroline's husband, Stefano Casiraghi, who died whilst participating in a race of this kind, was a regular competitor here.

Living in style: In spite of its obvious elegance (as His Royal Highness himself said, "This is obviously a place for people with above-average material possessions – I wouldn't even want to have the others here as guests"), the Costa Smeralda is a region where the lifestyle is totally casual. Nobody needs to brag; no-one will gape at the *prominenti*; nobody needs a status symbol. No-one who seeks rest and relaxation here is subject to the trends of fashion which govern the normal world. Dinner jackets and ties are frowned upon; women leave their valuable jewellery in their bank safes in Milan; the Testarossa is left in the garage.

The only essential accessory is a boat

– the means of reaching the finest beaches. A favourite goal for a day trip is, for example, the little island of **Mortorio** (the private property of the Mentastis). Here you can sunbathe or indulge in a nudist champagne picnic. Alternatively, one can sail over to the **Isola Cavallo**, a destination beloved of the Monaco clan and the French clique surrounding Jacques Castel, the owner of the Parisian club of the same name. In the mid-1970s, Castel wanted to join forces with helicopter magnate Conde Agusta and the beer baron Freddy Heinecken in order to create a private island with villas for his friends – a sort of private club. Understandably enough, the Sardinians were against the scheme. You can see the derelict buildings even today.

There are also plenty of uninhabited islands lying within convenient reach of the coast by Zodiac rubber dinghy.

On the mainland you can enjoy diving in style, for example on **Long Beach**. On windy days the sheltered **Petra Manna Beach** is to be recom-mended. Also worth visiting are the **Capriccioli Bays**. The **Romazzino Beach** is highly secure and at lunchtime you can eat well in the **Beach Restaurant** of the hotel of the same name. The loveliest beach is only accessible by boat: the **Spiaggia della Rosa**, the Rose Beach. As the name indicates, the sand is a deep pink colour.

Those whose boat provides sleeping accommodation should include an overnight trip to Corsica. The harbour at Bonifacio is a good place to drop anchor. On the way, you will find enchanting tiny bays tucked away along the latitude of **Caprera** and **Isola Maddalena**. It is supposed to be possible to visit a different beach every day for six whole weeks.

Sporting chances: The sea is not the only attraction of the Costa. International golfers regard the **Pevero Golf Course** as one of the loveliest and most challenging (18 holes, par 72) in the world. It was designed by Robert Trent-Jones on a raised spit of land; from each hole players enjoy spectacular views of

The stage for stars and starlets in Porto Cervo.

the coast and the sea. The setting recalls Palm Beach. At the 19th hole there is an excellent restaurant and a luxurious indoor and outdoor swimming pool.

Those who are not content with the swimming, sailing and golfing facilities can practise striking the other little white ball on one of the nine courts (five of them floodlit) at the **Porto Cervo Tennis Club.** You may even find some professional tenis stars there. It is as least as well equipped as the Monte Carlo Country Club.

Little happens in **Porto Cervo,** the focal point of the Costa Smeralda, before late afternoon. At about 10 o'clock each morning you may see the captains of industry (the Flicks, Sachs, Volkswagen boss Carl Hahn, or Willi Bogner (*Fire and Ice*) dashing to the newspaper kiosk to pick up their personal copy of the *International Herald Tribune* or the *Financial Times*, and in the delicatessen you will probably spot the wives of the yacht skippers purchasing the provisions for their beach picnic. But at sunset the VIPs and the *jeunesse*

dorée and *platinée* flock like exotic birds for a sundowner on the *Piazzetta.* Now is the time for flirting, for friendly banter. The evening breezes stir expectantly, the air is full of a sense of adventure, dates are made for the evening. This is the stage for personalities such as Audrey Hepburn, Laura Antonelli, the Flick brothers, Lo Sachs, the de Balkanys, Leslie Caron, whisky-voiced Paolo Conte, Their Majesties Juan Carlos and Hussein, Jean-Paul Belmondo, bombshell Bo Derek and the Duchess of Kent.

Some of them will take the opportunity to dash into Versace, Tussardi or Krizia to purchase a new dress for the next day's party. But essentially it is a time for socialising. Kisses of greeting are exchanged – everyone knows everyone else. They will all meet again next February at the very latest – for ski or après in St Moritz.

Where the wealthy stay: Most regulars on the Costa Smeralda are the proud owners of their own holiday residences; among them are the Italian media mo-

Cars usually stay in the garage on the Costa.

gul Silvio Berlusconi, Volkswagen boss Carl Hahn, Sachs widow Lo, the sister of Shah Pahlavi, Fiat boss Agnelli, politician Fanfani and the Bogner clan. Universally acknowledged as the Costa's best party-giver is Freddy Horowitz, the director of Bulgari. The loveliest houses are on Romazzino Bay, at **Cala di Volpe**. The finest houses for rental are on Petra Manna Beach.

But it was clear from the beginning, when His Highness discovered the area in 1961, that, as well as the multi-million pound villas, hotel accommodation of an appropriate kind would also be required (the Aga Khan's friends and friends of friends were accustomed to only the very best: silk bed-linen – only from Frette – and butler service).

The Aga Khan now owns five hotels, all of which are among the finest of their kind. Each is intended to cater for a particular taste. There are marked differences as regards architecture, location and clientele.

The **Pitrizza** is the smallest of the big

names, but by far the best. It lies in a rustic and romantic setting on the bay known as **Liscia di Vacca**, a very exclusive mini-resort just a three-minute drive north of Porto Cervo. With only 38 suites in eight chalets – each with private garden and swimming pool – it has no room for the "wrong" types of guests. To this day anyone who stays here can certainly lay claim to being a member of an elite. Those who are not personal friends of the Aga Khan and who are not on their private yachts would stay nowhere else. In this miniature club hotel one notices the luxury only at second glance; Luigi Vietti built it from local granite.

Crowned heads, with or without kingdoms (the King of Jordan), Princess Caroline (who spent both her honeymoons here), and actor Jean-Paul Belmondo are regulars. The manager, Pier Angelo Tondina, greets every guest personally – hardly an arduous task, given the guests. It has a lovely, lonely private beach of white sand, and the finest salt-water swimming pool in

You should shop here…

Europe. Children and dogs are banned; nothing is allowed to disturb the exceptional peace.

Its bar is as well-stocked as Harry's in Venice – when it comes to guests, too. From time to time, regular guest Paolo Conte accompanies the pianist. The restaurant serves what is undoubtedly the best food in Sardinia.

The **Cala di Volpe** looks like a medieval castle. It tends to be filled by wealthy Americans who explore the hotel gardens to shrill cries of "Oh! That's really beautiful!" In fact, only the older part of the hotel, built by Coelle senior (including the bar), is really attractive. It was the setting for the MGM film *The Wizard of Oz*. Coelle junior added a wing like a casbah and a marina like Port Grimaud. The emphasis in the rest of the hotel tends to be on size: the restaurant is as vast as an airport departure lounge; the swimming pool is Olympic-size; the discotheque in the cellar is cavernous. Rolling Stone Mick Jagger loves the Presidential Suite, with its own pool, at $3,000 a

...or here.

night. Others with a taste for the Cala di Yolpe have included Joan Collins and the Trumps.

The **Hotel Cervo** is less expensive than the other establishments, but it is very charming. All rooms have a spectacular view of the harbour, the decor is rustic-elegant, and it is conveninetly situated – you can reach anywhere in Porto Cervo on foot from here. It is a particular favourite of boat owners who want to spent a night on terra firma whilst keeping their boat under close surveillance. The **Terrace Bar**, overlooking the piazza of Porto Cervo, serves as a meeting place for the whole resort. The restaurant is better than at Cala di Volpe, and the view is priceless.

The **Romazzino** directly overlooks the beach, only separated from it by gently sloping, carefully manicured lawns. The hotel, also decorated in rustic elegance, is a favourite of Swiss families with children. It is claimed by those who can judge such things that the hotel's barman, Maria da Como, is the best in Italy. In winter he reigns su-

preme over the bar in the Palace Hotel in St Moritz. He knows everyone and everything. Incidentally, the beach restaurant of the Hotel Cervo serves the best pizza for miles.

Food and nightlife: You can eat and drink quite well on the Costa Smeralda. However, one thing is quite clear: apart from a few notable exceptions it is no mecca for gourmets used to Bocuse. Gourmets may be in for an unpleasant shock. But then, who comes here on a gastronomic spree or with the intention of putting on weight? Specialities always include fish, *spaghetti aragosta*, roast suckling pig from the barbecue and smoked ham of wild boar. Everything is accompanied by warm *pane carasau*, the ultra-thin bread which is seasoned with salt and rosemary and sprinkled with best olive oil, and which "makes music" – a crunching sound – when you bite into it.

The best restaurant is that of the **Pitrizza**, followed by the **Grazia Deledda**. The latter lies some 20 minutes from the "right" coast on the way to Baia Sardegna (a less luxurious copy of the Emerald Coast). The cuisine here has earned a Michelin star and is typically Sardinian-rustic. The fish is exceptionally fine, and so are the pasta dishes. Guests sit on a prettily decorated terrace; the service, conducted under the watchful eye of host Andrea Fronteddú, is impeccable. He invariably advises guests to choose the local suckling lamb, and offers the best wines in the district.

The **Bice** is an offshoot of the Milan and New York establishments; it offers a fine view across the **Piccolo Pevero** bay (the apartment complex of the same name is a favourite haunt of German visitors). The food is excellent, and the restaurant itself is fashionable.

In **La Moula**, one mile further on to the south of Porto Cervo, the same applies: it's very crowded, very "in", and the best items to choose on the menu are the *risotto* (order it in advance by telephone) and *loup de mer* in a salt crust. The elegant **Restaurant Pevero Golf Club** is a favourite venue for dinner

The hotel **Pitrizza**.

invitations. If the conversation at your table begins to pall you can gaze out across the lovely **Cala di Volpe** bay.

The **Piccolo Mondo**, on the **Liscia di Vacca**, lies just before the **Hotel Pitrizza**. It serves excellent fish in a cavern-like atmosphere. Visitors are advised to steer clear of **Il Pescatore** at Porto Cervo harbour; it is a prime example of a tourist trap.

One could be forgiven for thinking Beautiful People never sleep; if they do, even the most observant spectator will fail to gather when. Days are filled with the tiring round of yachting, swimming, golf, cocktail and dinner parties, but everybody still seems to find enough time to enjoy nightlife to the full.

Very chic and always very full is **Sottovento**, a discotheque which looks rather like an elegant barracks located outside the domain of the *consorzio* on the road to Cala di Volpe. It is owned by Carlo and Antonello, natives of Parma who slip down here for the summer months. They are extremely choosy about their guests and only those per-

sonally known by them are guaranteed entrance. Your chances improve considerably if you can arrive in the wake of one of the wealthy regulars: the Crespis, the Sforzas, the Ruspolis, Claudia Cardinale or Duke Luigi Dona della Rosa (also known as the "Godfather" of the yacht harbour), or Ira von Fürstenberg. If you cannot manage this and you really don't want to undergo the ultra-strict face check at the door, eat in the adjacent restaurant beforehand; diners are automatically admitted to the discotheque afterwards. Tip: a drink at a table (should you manage to acquire one) costs at least $35; standing, it costs half as much.

North of Porto Cervo towards Baia Sardegna lies **Ritual**, equally full and the training ground for the children of the Costa's millionaires (anybody over 30 is too old). The discotheque, hewn from solid rock, blasts music from every nook and cranny.

Those who prefer more peace and less stress should take their after-dinner *digestivo* in **Il Portico** on the Piazzetta.

The marina of
Porto Cervo.

The bar is very attractive and decorated in Moroccan style.

Alternatively, one can escape to **Porto Rotondo** (a miniature Porto Cervo), only 20 minutes from Porto Cervo by car, or 10 by boat. Though less attractive architecturally, it is also a stylish resort. It lies in a little bay, with tiny piazzas, a handful of designer boutiques, a little harbour and two white sandy beaches, one known as the **Ira Beach** in honour of Ira von Fürstenberg, who has her house there. Everything here is quieter, more relaxed, with less emphasis on extreme wealth. The entire place is firmly in Italian hands.

Il Sporting, occupying a promontory, is the heart of Porto Rotondo. The complex includes a hotel, bar, restaurant and nightclub. There is also a **Country Club,** located on a hillside, where you can dance on a carefully manicured English lawn.

Shopping: you will find everything you need in Porto Cervo: post office, chemist, travel agent, *Alisarda* agency, car rental, Cartier, Versace, Mila Schoen, Krizia, Gucci and newspaper kiosks. One more reason why the rich and not-as young-as-they-were feel at ease here is the ultra-modern accident hospital in Porto Cervo. It has physicians and heart surgeons, an ambulance and an operating theatre. In short – everything for the bypass and pacemaker brigade.

Nature, of course, is the leading attraction when it comes to sightseeing. You can drive along the *panoramica* between the southern end of Cugnana Bay and the northern tip of the Costa Smeralda. There you can enjoy a breathtaking view out across precipitous cliffs and rolling hills to the sea and the offshore islands.

Those looking for historical or cultural diversions are in the wrong part of Sardinia. The one true sight, the little church at Porto Cervo (there really is one!), looks unremarkable from the outside, but contains some real treasures. Twenty years ago Don Raimundo Fresi, celebrating Mass in what was then the only hotel, the Cervo, found so many

The Costa Smeralda rally attracts thousands of visitors.

patrons among the hotel guests that he was able to have a church built – the **Stella Mares**. It contains a valuable 16th-century organ from Naples, a German altar cross that is just as old, and two outsize shells which serve as baptismal fonts from Polynesia. And what about the **El Greco Madonna**? The sister of Heinrich von Thyssen (he of the Villa Favorita in Lugano) and wife of a Dutch ambassador, once vowed that if her little daughter should recover from an illness she would donate a painting to the church. The miracle happened, the daughter was healed and the Aga Khan, a family friend, accepted the El Greco Madonna on behalf of the church. Here, in Porto Cervo, fairytales do sometimes happen.

Finally, for those who have not yet made their millions, there are ways of cutting costs on Costa Smeralda. Here are a few tips for enjoying this paradise of the well-heeled more cheaply: instead of booking into one of the luxury hotels, try to obtain a room in the Porto Cervo Tennis Club (there are only 16, but they are very attractive, and they cost just $50 a night without breakfast; the only snag is that you must make your reservation six months in advance). Alternatively, you can enjoy the best view of the Cala di Volpe from the **Hotel Valdiola**, where full board costs a very reasonable $120. Or if you belong to a group of at least four people why not choose self-catering and rent an apartment or a villa with maid service? It will be cheaper than a Friesian cottage on Sylt or a villa on the Riviera. When it comes to eating out, dine in the exclusive restaurants mentioned above but order just a plate of pasta and a *vin du pays* and at lunchtime picnic on the beach (that is what the Costa fraternity tend to do anyway). And remember, if you want to remain solvent but don't want to have to stay sober, drinks at the **Sottovento** cost only half as much if you don't sit at a table.

In short, the Costa Smeralda can be enjoyed by those not fabulously rich, whatever the Aga Khan might say – providing they know the tricks.

You need to be a good surfer here.

GALLURA AND THE NORTH

A journey through the Gallura promises the traveller a full and varied programme in every respect. The island's most extensive oak woods surround **Monte Limbara** and the little town of **Tempio Pausania**, and the shores of the **Costa Paradiso** form part of one of its loveliest stretches of coastline. What's more, at **Arzachena** there are two of Sardinia's best-preserved "giants' graves".

The fashionable atmosphere of the Costa Smeralda fades as one drives away from Porto Cervo, but the first place of any size on the **Gulf of Arzachena** is the elegant seaside resort of **Baia Sardinia**, whose string of luxury hotels are almost as expensive as those on the Emerald Coast. Just across the bay, however, **Cannigione** offers the first campsites in the region, and the air of exclusivity quickly becomes a thing of the past.

The steep cliffs surrounding **Arzachena** lend the little town the appearance of a village in the Dolomites rather than one on a Mediterranean island. However, the rapid development of the Costa Smeralda over the past few years has brought economic benefits to these neighbouring regions. The bleak, poverty-stricken Sardinia associated with the Gennargentu has now completely disappeared; the area seems prosperous, without having lost all of its rural character.

Around Arzachena are a number of important remains from the time of the Nuraghi. They have given their name to the civilisation which they represent: the *Li Muri* or Arzachena Culture. Some 3,000 years BC, the Gallura was inhabited by groups of semi-nomads and shepherds.

Witnesses to this epoch are the stone box graves of **Li Muri**, each of which was found to hold a single corpse buried in a squatting position. The graves themselves were surrounded by concentric circles of stones.

More famous, and easier for non-specialists to appreciate, are the two giants' graves near the village on the road to Luogosanto. After a few miles, a signpost indicates the way to the first site, **Lu Coddu Vecchiu**. It is one of the best preserved giants' graves in existence today. A stele, 13 ft (4 metres) high and subdivided into two sections – a square unit and a half-arch – stands sentinel in front of the grave. Through the semicircular opening at ground level, which repeats the contours of the stele, sacrificial offerings could be presented to the dead person. Flat stone slabs positioned vertically form a semicircle demarcating the ceremonial and sacrifical arena.

On a hill a few miles further on, also marked by a signpost on the Luogosanto road, lies the giant's grave of **Li Lolghi.** The form of this grave is very similar to Lu Coddu Vecchiu. The stone box graves of Li Muri are also not far from here.

The traveller approaching the region via the SS 125 from Olbia will find the **Nuraghe Albucciu**, also known as the

Nuraghe Malcchittu. It is signposted about 2 miles (3 km) before Arzachena, but is in any case impossible to miss because of the **Ristorante Nuraghe** nearby. The most interesting feature is the fact that the *nuraghe* itself is not constructed in the familiar tower form. It is one of the very few corridor *nuraghi* in Sardinia. Close by stands the **Temple of Malcchittu**, which formed part of the *Nuraghi* settlement.

The *Fungo* ("Mushroom") is a weathered granite rock near Arzachena. Like the spectacularly-shaped "Elephant Rock" near Castelsardo and the "Bear" near Palau, it frequently features on postcards.

There are a number of excellent – if sometimes expensive – restaurants near Arzachena. Among the best – in fact, one of the top 10 restaurants on the island – is undoubtedly the **Grazia Deledda** in Baia Sardinia. Frank Sinatra once reserved the whole restaurant when he arrived in Porto Cervo in his yacht. Also worth recommending is the **Vecchia Arzachena** in Arzachena

itself, where the food is almost as good as that in the Grazia Deledda, but somewhat less expensive.

Continuing along the SS 125, the traveller passes first through the little port of Palau and then through **Capo d'Orso**, where a weathered cliff formation resembles the eponymous bear. As far as Cannigione the coast road skirting the Golfo d'Arzachena is in excellent condition, but after that the surface is poor until Palau. On the way are a number of pleasant campsites, offering overnight accommodation.

Palau itself is a little coastal town dominated by its harbour, from which ferries leave regularly for La Caprera and La Maddalena. Apart from the ferry port and the "Bear" rock, the town offers visitors few attractions of particular note, although there are two excellent restaurants which merit a stop. The first, **Da Franco**, lies in the centre of the town, on the Via Capo d'Orso. As well as seafood specialities it serves traditional dishes from northern Sardinia. The second, **La Griglia**, lies on the SS

The most beautiful coastline of the north, the Costa Paradiso.

125; it specialises in Sardinian national cuisine. Both restaurants serve, for instance, *Zuppa Cuata*, a bread soup prepared with mutton broth. The prices at both lie in the medium range.

It's easy enough to find boats to take you to any of the offshore islands (just ask around at the quay; the fishermen will advise), but at **Palau Mare** in Palau's Via Nazionale you can hire everything you might need to explore the archipelago independently – from a rubber dinghy to a proper yacht.

The island of **La Maddalena** is formed of granite and porphyry. It has an area of 8 sq. miles (20 sq. km). Lying only a few miles from the mainland, together with the other islands of the archipelago of the same name, it represents what remains of the land link that once existed between Sardinia and the island of Corsica.

Tectonic movements were responsible for the formation of this miniature island chain, consisting today of more than 50 islets. On the largest island, almost 19 sq. miles (50 sq. km) in size,

lies the town of **La Maddalena**. Its fashionable atmosphere underlines the elegance of its architecture, notably its noble *palazzo*.

Also on the island is a most interesting **Maritime Museum,** the *Museo Archeologico Navale Nino Lamboglia*. Apart from the remains of a Roman cargo ship dating from the 2nd century BC, the museum contains the ruins of several Piedmontese forts. Worth a detour is the **La Mistral** restaurant in the Via Santo Stefano.

Thanks to its advantageous strategic position, La Maddalena often played an important military role in the past. Even today, it is the site of bases of both the Italian navy and NATO. Unfortunately, the presence of the latter's nuclear submarines has resulted in a considerable proportion of the island's being declared a prohibited area.

The fame of the other large island, **Isola Caprera** is largely due to its famous resident, Giuseppe Garibaldi, for whom it was for many years home, the refuge to which he always returned, and

One of nature's whims, the mushroom of Arzachena.

the place where he died in 1882. Garibaldi created a model farm on the island; his memorial museum, the *Museo Garibaldo di Caprera*, has the air of a place of pilgrimage. It is worth taking a look inside.

Santa Teresa di Gallura lies at the northernmost tip of Sardinia. Its harbour is the starting point for ferries across to Corsica. The twin approach roads – the SS 133 from Tempio and the SS 200 from Castelsardo – both pass through attractive countryside. The most noteworthy sights here are the bizarre rock formations along the cliffs near **Capo Testa**. From the **Torre Longosardo** there is a spectacular view of the wild, often inaccessible coast of the Gallura, whose waters and sea-beds provide ideal conditions for deep-sea diving. Also in the vicinity of Capo Testa are two quarries dating from Roman times.

Along the coast: The road from Santa Teresa to Castelsardo passes through what is undoubtedly one of the loveliest regions in Sardinia, boasting stretches of outstanding coastline – the most famous of which is the aptly-named Costa Paradiso. The steep precipices typical of the northern coast force the road inland. Running parallel to the coastline, it follows a serpentine course through untouched *macchia;* travellers will discern the reddish peaks of the Monte Pitrighinosu and the Monte Puntaccia on the horizon.

The sparsely populated area between the SS 200 and the SS 133 has a wild charm. Along the lonely stretch of road to Tempio you will see time and again cork oaks, their trunks, with patches of freshly peeled reddish bark, gnarled and misshapen by the wind. An enduring impression of these regions is of the impenetrability of the *macchia*. In places, however, it is dissected by routes to the sea which are welcome to the hot and weary motorist. Some 6 miles (10 km) past Santa Teresa, the **Spiaggia di Rena Maiore** and the **Cala Vall'alta** afford some of the best bathing opportunities.

The situation on the lovely **Costa**

Cork bark dries out in the open for months.

Paradiso, whose turning lies about 16 miles (25 km) from the main road, is quite different. The development consists of an extensive, well-planned holiday park. In fact, it comprises several little *villagi*, hidden away in dense thickets, well protected from the common crowd. Its architects made great efforts to make the complex as unobtrusive as possible. But their aim that the buildings should blend harmoniously with the countryside has been only partially successful. Inevitably, development has meant the destruction of the natural equilibrium of another lovely stretch of coastline.

Critics worrry, believing traditional Sardinia will die in the stranglehold of its *residencias* and *villagi*. It is irrelevant whether a development is constructed in a traditional Sardinian manner, which harmonises more satisfactorily with the countryside, or as a vast concrete hotel complex – or even as a string of sugar-cube-style villas. The choicest land is being snapped up by the tourism industry; the loveliest beaches

are being bought by big, private hotels for the exclusive use of their patrons.

The two smaller beaches of the **Baia Trinità** are open to the public; overlooking them is the **Isola Rossa.** From here there is also a long sandy beach stretching almost as far as the rocky promontory overlooking Castelsardo.

The town of **Castelsardo,** perched on a trachyte cliff, looks as though it might be the very source of Sardinian folklore – and kitsch, to judge by the large number of shops (including a hypermarket) offering souvenirs and handicrafts for sale.

Castelsardo was founded in 1102 by the Genoese Doria family. Known in those days as Castel Genovese, the settlement's name was changed after the Spanish conquest to Castel Aragonese; in 1796 the King of Sardinia gave it its present name of Castelsardo. Nowadays, during the summer months at least, the town is usually too full of tourists to make a visit here entirely pleasurable, but the castle hill has managed to retain its attractive atmosphere

Traditional design in a carpet from Castelsardo.

and it is worth venturing up its steep, narrow alleys. The fortress at its summit houses the Wickerwork Museum, the *Museo dell'Intreccio*. Other attractions in the town include the **Cathedral of Sant'Antonio Abate,** which boasts a 16th-century altarpiece – a so-called *retable* (reredos) by the *Maestro di Castelsardo* – and the **Roccia L'Elefante**, a curiously shaped natural outcrop of rock which resembles a young elephant with its trunk raised; it lies on the twisting road to Perfugas.

Castelsardo is well known for its Easter procession, which takes place on the Monday of Holy Week. Interspersed with ancient rituals and traditional songs, the ceremony has retained all its original medieval character; *Lunissanti* in Castelsardo is generally regarded as one of the finest examples of Easter festivities to be found anywhere on the island.

Continuing south the SS 200 follows the outline of the coast once more. Some 9 miles (15 km) from Castelsardo it arrives at the **Punta Tramontana**. By taking the route via **Sorso** and **Senori**, the traveller can very quickly reach Sassari. The SS 200, however, carries on along the coast through the *pinetta,* beyond which lies the **Platamona Lido,** the favourite beach of the inhabitants of Sassari though not one that can be recommended to visitors with the time and means to go elsewhere.

Over 12 miles (20 km) long, the beach stretches as far as the industrial port of Porto Torres. Its backdrop of pine groves makes for an attractive setting, but the proximity of Sassari has somewhat marred its beauty. The shore itself is littered with refuse and debris, and the shady woods are polluted by the rubbish dumped by picnickers. Campsites alternate with discotheques and beach cafés. However, none of this seems to deter the local residents; the Platamona Lido is to Sassari what the Poetto Beach is to Cagliari.

It makes no difference from which side you approach **Porto Torres**; it is an unattractive little town dominated by vast oil refineries. Since Roman times it

The Romans were the first to ransack Sardinian quarries.

has been famous as the home of seafarers; even in those days the inhabitants conducted lively trade with the mainland. Nowadays container ships and tankers have taken over. The principal port in northern Sardinia, Porto Torres is one of the main gateways to the island, with ferry links to Civitavecchia, Genoa, Bastia and Livorno. Since the 1960s the population has expanded rapidly from 9,000 to today's level of more than 22,000. It is impossible to overlook the main cause of the boom: those vast oil refineries.

The town can still boast impressive remains from its early Roman history – ruins of the original trading post and the former *Turris Libyssonis*. Near what is now the railway station lie the *Terme Centrali*, the former **Roman Baths** with mosaics dating from the 3rd–4th century BC. Also dating from the same time is a seven-arched bridge. The **Basilica of St Gavin** was completed in the year 1111; it houses the tomb of the martyr of the same name and is one of the most important Romanesque buildings to be found on Sardinia.

Following the main highway to Sassari, the SS 131, you will arrive at **Monte d'Accodi**, an early sacrificial terrace dating from approximately 2000 BC and the only one to be found in the entire Mediterranean area. The altar complex was used for sacrifices and fertility rites; it also includes dwelling huts and a number of *domus de janas*, or "fairies' houses".

The most northwesterly point of the island is a small triangle of land bounded by the towns of Porto Torres to the north and Alghero to the south. With the exception of Porto Conte on the Capo Caccia and the little resort of Stintino, the entire area is as yet virtually untouched by tourism. The drive from Porto Torres to Stintino passes through fertile, sparsely populated farmland; unfortunately vast chemical complexes dominate much of the landscape, and as a result, the long expanse of beach between the two towns is not particularly attractive.

Stintino is a small, unaffected place consisting of holiday cottages, a few

hotel complexes and two marinas. The Church of the Immaculate Conception houses art treasures taken from the churches on the island of Asinara.

If one ignores the prospect to the east in the direction of Porto Torres, it is easy to fall prey to the charm of the little peninsula known as **Capo del Falcone**, from which there is a view across the Isola Piana to the prison island of Asinara. The water here looks so shallow that it is tempting to think one could wade across. The **Torre Pelosa**, one of the numerous watch towers built to protect the coast, soars picturesquely above the white inlets of the Spiaggia di Pelosa. Just before Stintino lies the Tonnara Saline, formerly an important tuna fishing station which has now been converted into a well-designed complex of holiday homes.

Industrial developments of the past century possess a certain charm of their own, and travellers who appreciated the unique attractions of the abandoned mines near Sulcis and Iglesiente may also find it worthwhile to drive across to

The closed mine of Argentiera in the Nurra.

Argentiera. Since ceasing to serve their original purpose the little miners' cottages have undergone conversion into comfortable modern homes; additional groups of houses have also sprung up overnight. The main shaft, however, has been retained in its original form, as has the heart of the mining village, which recently gained protected status.

The interior of the Gallura: The little town of **Tempio Pausania** lies at the heart of the **Gallura,** at the foot of the granite peak of **Monte Limbara.** Irrespective of the direction from which you approach this area, you cut through dense oak forests unlike any to be found elsewhere in Sardinia. Tempio Pausania itself lies at an altitude of 1,820 ft (555 metres) giving it the air of a mountain resort – an impression underlined by the town's atmosphere. Lately Tempio (in competition with Olbia) has been campaigning to become the island's fifth provincial capital.

You will notice large numbers of slogans on house walls maintaining that this administrative change should be decided in favour of Tempio. The ancient rivalry between the two towns, dating from the time of the Spanish occupation, is still strong today. Visitors wishing to spend some time in Tempio can visit its 15th-century cathedral and **Museo Bernardo De Muro**, dedicated to the famous tenor who was a native son of the town. Ideal for a rest and refreshment is the **Café Gabriel** in the Via Mannu, which serves excellent Sardinian food: *suppa cuata, ravioli dolci di Tempio, pane frattau* or *cordula* – a popular dish of lamb offal and peas in a tasty sauce.

A short distance from Tempio lies the centre of the Sardinian cork industry. **Calangianus**, some 6 miles (10 km) away, is the cork capital. The town makes a worthwhile detour.

The SS 392 continues with a series of sharp bends through a mountainous area to the **Lago del Coghinas**, the second-largest lake in Sardinia. It was dammed in 1927 and provides one of the island's main supplies of drinking water. The journey is a delightful one for drivers and passengers who do not mind the serpentine nature of the road. Passing through **Oschieri** and taking the SS 199 one finally arrives in **Ozieri**, a prosperous and attractive little town lying on a fertile plain supporting crops and cattle farming. The most impressive feature of the town is its magnificent range of neo-classical houses. They outshine those in many of the other, larger towns on the island.

Not far from Ozieri lies the **Grotta San Michele**, the scene of some of Sardinia's most important archaeological finds. The name of the town was given to the prehistoric period which they represent: the Ozieri Culture.

The nearby town of **Pattada** is the best place to buy a genuine hand-crafted shepherd's knife.

Those who are still not tired of winding roads are recommended to tackle the lonely, sinuous and unforgettable stretch of road from **Buddoso** to **Bitti** and **Nuoro**. Such a journey will appeal in particular to anyone exploring the island by motorbike.

Left, sometimes you have to help yourself. **Right,** winter on the Monte Limbara in the Gallura.

THE SHEPHERD'S KNIFE

Many a Sardinian factory worker or bank employee would not dream of going anywhere without his shepherd's knife. He sees the simple pocket knife with a carved horn handle as not only a proven weapon in his fight with the canteen chop at lunchtime, but also a part of his identity – a potent symbol of a lost pastoral world.

A true Sardinian loves his knife; the poet Montanaru from Desulo immortalised this nostalgic sentiment in verse:

Semper' lughente parias de prata,
Segaias chei su pensamentu
Ispilinde sa pedde in d'unu 'entu
Comente ch'aeres giut
tu fogu in s'ata!
(Perpetually shining, you seemed to be made of silver,
Your blade cut as sharp as a thought
and you shaved my skin as in a flash
As if there were fire in your blade!)

The very best knives are made by true master craftsmen who only work to order. These men need at least two days to make a shepherd's knife in the harmoniously classic form with a pointed blade *a foll'e murta* – "like a myrtle leaf".

Should you toy with the idea of buying a knife, perhaps as a souvenir of your visit, don't be tempted by cheap imitations; they really aren't worth the money. And be sure to to treat any transaction with due respect. The careless remark by a French man of letters who, complaining about the prices of these knives, called them *couteaux de cuisine* (kitchen knives) was tantamount to an assault on Sardinian national pride.

If we wanted to split hairs, we would point out that a "kitchen knife" has a fixed blade; the Latin term, *culter*, is the root of the Sardinian *gulteddu*, the word for a kitchen knife. *Sa resolza* or *sa resordza* (the Sardinian shepherd's knife), on the other hand, comes from the Latin word *rasoria*, knives with a swivelling sheath, and only the very finest knives have their blades protected by a sheath of wood or horn.

You will notice that anyone who brandishes a particularly fine shepherd's knife will be surrounded in a trice by a crowd of Sardinians, all proffering expert advice – and each of them purporting to be a knife specialist!

The knife will be passed from hand to hand, examined and discussed, and opinions exchanged as to whether the alleged ram's horn handle might not, after all, be the latest Japanese imitation of the real thing – a theory which can only be disproved by the smell when it is heated over a naked flame. The proud owner will usually refuse to agree to such an experiment, thus inviting further taunts that in his ignorance he might have bought *i skiffu* – rubbish. The hallmark of one of the recognised master craftsmen stamped on the blade is the only thing likely to silence such conjecture.

The final test of a good knife is to spit on the back of one's hand, rub hard and then check whether the knife will give a close shave. (Onlookers with no hairs on the back of their hands rarely have a place in such a circle anyhow – unless their comments indicate them to be true connoisseurs, therefore compensating for their apparent lack of virility.)

Another means of judging the quality of the knife is by laying the blade at a flat angle across the thumbnail and pulling it very lightly across its entire length, as far as the point. The entire movement must be executed slowly and with a look of intense concentration on the face; the verdict on the "bite" of the blade is invariably restricted to an appropriately intoned, suitably meaningful "hmm" or a withering "pah!".

As recently as 50 years ago such knives were commonly produced in pastoral communities all over the island – Arbus, Guspini, Gavoi, Fonni, Santu Lussurgiu and Pattada, to name a few. Nowadays, however, good quality knives are really only produced in the traditional manner in the last two of these villages.

The inhabitants of Pattada, a peaceful rural village near the town of Ozieri, are most anxious to retain the village's reputation as the "Sheffield" of Sardinia. Knives from Pattada are the ultimate in Sardinian craftsmanship, more esteemed than any of the needlework or jewellery. The very name Pattada has become synonymous with "knife".

THE CORK OAK

Were it not for the droves of Tuscan speculators who during the 19th century turned 2,000 sq. miles (5,000 sq. km) of the island's oak forests into charcoal or railway sleepers, Sardinia might well have become known to travellers as the Island of Oak Trees.

Spread across what remains of the once-magnificent cloak of woodland are three different species of oak tree. Up to an altitude of 3,900 ft (1,200 metres) on the more exposed upper mountain slopes is the down oak (*Quercus pubescens*), which is deciduous; two evergreen species, the holm oak (*quercus ilex*) and the cork oak (*quercus suber*) grow at lower altitudes (up to about 2,240 ft (700 metres) in more sheltered positions.

The holm oak thrives on limestone and karst soils, but the cork oak – which is found only in the Western Mediterranean, from Apulia to Portugal – prefers the earth of slate, granite and volcanic regions. Extensive woods of cork oaks therefore exist primarily on the acid basalt and trachyte uplands of the island, such as the Giara of Gesturi, or on the infertile granite wastelands of the Gallura in northeast Sardinia.

The various dialect names for the cork oak – *suberju, suelzu, suveliu, suergiu, suaru* or *cortigu, ortigu, orteghe* – are derived from the Latin *suber* or *corticulum* – "cork" or "bark". The thick cork bark which is a characteristic of the tree protects it from damage, cold, heat and drying out. Nowadays large specimens – 200 to 300 years old and up to 65 ft (20 metres) tall, with a trunk diameter of as much as 3 ft (1 metre) – are only found in the remotest areas of Sardinia. According to the French traders who introduced industrial cork processing to the island in 1830, a cork oak is classed as "finished" when it is 125 years old.

The peeling of the cork from the trunk requires experience and considerable skill, in order to avoid harming the bright red cambium, the growing surface for the next layer of cork. Indiscriminate stripping of the trees in the late 19th century led to severe damage of the industry. Done prop-

erly, the bark is peeled from a cork oak for the first time when the trunk at a height of 4 ft (1.3 metres) from the ground has achieved a circumference of at least 24 inches (60 cm). This is usually when the tree is about 15 years old. The tree will be peeled a total of about eight times in its life, at intervals of 9 to 12 years, until the quality of the cork declines below an acceptable level.

The sections of bark are transported to the depots in front of the cork factories in the towns of Tempio and Calangianus. Here they are sorted out according to quality. The poorest quality consists primarily of the first peeling of the wild "male" cork oak. It is processed straightaway into cork waste for the building industry, where it is used as isolation material.

The elastic "female" cork from later peelings is left to mature in the open air for at least six months. This open-air storage is essential for the desired "white" and "extra white" qualities, for the alternation of sun and rain, heat and cold removes most of the red powder and other impurities from the cork's pores. The cork is then soaked in enormous vats of hot water for an hour. This removes most of the tannic acid, and the cork swells up and gains the requisite elasticity. The corks are then stamped out from the sheets of bark, which are pressed flat as they dry. Corks for bottles are cut parallel to the annual rings, and barrel corks at right angles.

Although its most common use is as a wine bottle stopper, cork is a remarkably versatile substance. It is used in shoe-making (usually as a lining) and in the building industry, where its heat and sound-isolating properties make it especially useful for lining floors and walls.

A quick trip through the island's numerous souvenir shops, however, reveals to the visitor the depths to which the cork manufacturing industry can sink. Worse examples of kitsch are difficult to find anywhere. Measuring beakers for cereal, cutting boards for meat, drinking vessels and stools made of cork – in other words, the items which until quite recently were laboriously carved by hand and which were examples of useful Sardinian handicrafts – are seldom seen these days, even in the island's most rural areas.

SASSARI

If you arrive in Sassari at the end of a tour of Sardinia, you will probably feel as if you have returned to the Italian mainland without actually crossing the sea. Here there is no trace of the island's rural soul, which is usually evident even in the island's larger towns and cities. **Sassari** wears an urban, worldly countenance. The people in the cafés and restaurants are noisier, more lively, more cheerful; in their attitude towards strangers they seem more open, talkative and curious – and they are much more inclined to irony and humour than elsewhere on the island.

A proud history: In fact, a great deal of mainland blood flows through their veins. In the early 13th century the merchants of Genoa and Pisa – both cities of international importance in medieval times – transformed an insignificant peasant village in the hinterland of Porto Torres into a flourishing commercial town. Even today, the citizens of Sassari are proud of being a "community of shopkeepers". Trade enabled them to free themselves from the dependence on Porto Torres which had dogged their existence since Roman times. Their only regret is that throughout their long history they have never quite managed to oust Cagliari from its position as the most important town on the island.

During the 17th century it was a close-run thing, as Sassari almost managed to overtake its arch-rival in the south. In 1617 the university of Sassari received its charter, three years before that of Cagliari. Such was the town's prosperity that private citizens donated enough money to build or renovate nine churches and monasteries. However, the plague in 1652 and the subsequent fall in population shattered the hopes of Sassari's inhabitants. It seemed that thereafter their town was fated to remain the perpetual runner-up.

But now, with its population having reached 120,000, Sassari is again able to show that it is at least as good as the capital. The three most famous Sardinian politicians of post-war times – the former state president, Antonio Segni, Enrico Berlinguer and the present president of the Republic of Italy, Francesco Cossiga – are all natives of Sassari.

In the sphere of arts, too, Sassari succeeded in finding its own individual style – possibly the only Sardinian town to do so. Many of the churches are the work of local stonemasons, known as *picapedras*, who gave the basic architectural styles imported from the mainland a popular, Sardinian touch. This tendency also applied to the sculptors of Sassari, who during the 17th century adorned the town's numerous new churches and monasteries with countless statues and altars. They also carved the *candelieri*, enormous wooden pillars shaped like candles which every year on 14 August are carried through the old town from the **Piazza Castello** to the **Church of St Mary of Bethlehem** by the members of the various craftsmen's guilds.

The **Feast of Candles**, whose origins seem to lie way back in the 13th century, has remained an authentic folk festival, for which some expatriates even return home from overseas. During the **Cavalcata Sarda**, held on the third Sunday in May, however, the local population prefers to leave the town to foreigners and tourists.

A walk through the town: The spacious **Piazza d'Italia** covers an area of precisely 3 acres (1 hectare); framed by official buildings dating from the 19th century such as the **Palazzo della Provinzia** and the neo-Gothic **Palazzo Giordano**, it is an ideal starting point for a tour of the town. It is a good idea to visit the square during the daily *passeggiata*. This evening stroll is a custom in every Italian town and takes place between business closing time and dinner. The traditional rigid segregation of the sexes, still strictly observed by the older generation, seems to have lost its significance for the youth of the town.

In times past, some 120 to 150 years ago, sheep still grazed on this piazza, in whose numerous banks and administrative buildings the financial and political fate of the town is now decided. Until well into the 19th century there seemed no necessity to expand the urban area beyond the limits set by the 13th-century city walls. For 600 years, under the Spanish and the Piedmontese, the entire area was compressed within an area of some 75 acres (30 hectares).

Providing a link between the **Old Town** and the newer districts is the **Piazza Castello**, which lies next to the Piazza d'Italia. In the1870s, whilst new buildings in the architectural style of the Italian mainland were sprouting up on the Piazza d'Italia, on the Piazza Castello they were demolishing the fortress after which it is named. The castle was built in 1330 by the Aragonese; for centuries afterwards it served as a symbol of foreign rule and oppression on Sardinia. It is a moot point whether the decision to build a military barracks on the site was a particularly diplomatic one; such an edifice might, after all, be interpreted by independently-minded Sardinians as just another symbol of "foreign" domination.

There is one more essential site to see before making a tour of the Old Town: the **G.A. Sanna National Museum**. Its 17 immaculately-ordered galleries present a summary of the most important aspects of Sardinian archaeology and ethnology. The highlight of the museum is the collection of 2,000–3,500-year-old bronze statues of the Nuraghi period; equally fascinating is the gold and silver jewellery. Such pieces are still worn with traditional Sardinian costumes.

Pulsating with life: Through the middle of the Old Town runs the **Corso Vittorio Emanuele II** – invariably busy, but unfortunately polluted by noise and exhaust fumes. The town's long-standing residents, ever conscious of tradition, still call it the *Plath de Codinas* (the "Street of Stone") because the thoroughfare was once lined with elegant *palazzi* and the residences of wealthy merchants.

Apart from the Corso, the citizens of

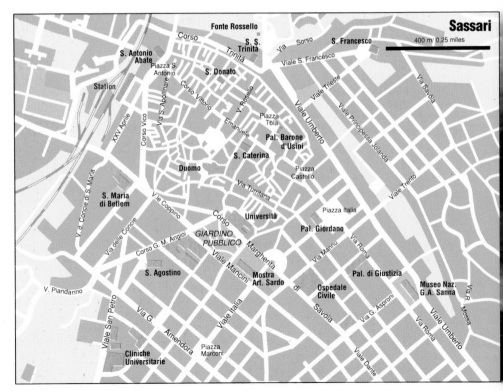

Sassari have given other streets and squares local dialect names. The **Via Lamarmora**, which runs parallel to it, is known to locals as the *Carra Longa*; leading off the Corso is the *Carra Pizzinna* (today's **Via Battisti**), which links up with the *Carra Manna* (the **Piazza Tola**). The dialect names – "little bushel" and "large bushel" – refer to the fact that these measures were once in use here.

Rising above the Piazza Tola, invariably overcrowded with cars and market stalls, is the monument to the historian Pasquale Tola. Today the square has a neglected, down-at-heel look; even the long, winding Via Lamarmora scarcely hints that it has seen better days; the local aristocracy once held court behind the crumbling stucco and seedy-looking facades. But the rather splendid looking **Casa di Maramaldo** at No. 81, dating from the 17th century, at least gives some indication of the noble magnificence which once characterised the street.

The most popular street in the Old Town is the **Via al Rosello**. The silversmiths after whom the alley was named are a rare species today, and most of them have moved into more modern, more elegant quarters. Here and there you'll see the the odd cobbler and carpenter at work, latter-day representatives of a once-thriving craft tradition. In one cheese store, which offers an enormous choice within a very small space, you can be sure of finding genuine Sardinian cheese, sold with a wealth of original cooking tips. It's an excellent place to buy *pecorino romano*, the famous Italian sheep's milk cheese (*see "Food and Drink", pages 140–145*).

The picturesque Via Rosello leads – as the name indicates – to a spring and the **Fontana di Rosello**, the island's most famous monumental fountain. Contemplating the 12 stone lion's heads adorning the Renaissance fountain as they tirelessly spew water, one cannot help a momentary feeling of surprise at the copious supplies of water here compared with the permanent shortage elsewhere on this arid island so parched

So close and yet worlds apart.

that it is annually plagued by a series of forest fires.

The viaduct was erected during Fascist times. Beyond the bridge lie the densely populated districts of town. They provide typical examples of Italian government-financed housing of the pre- and postwar periods.

Here on the outskirts of Sassari, the suburbs are as characterless and monotonous as those of any other town. Your best bet is to return via the **Ponte Rosello** to the **Nuovo Mercato**, the New Market, where fresh fish from the Gulf of Asinara is offered every morning. Continuing along the Via al Rosello and across the Corso, you will arrive at the **Cathedral**. Its ornately carved facade was added to the Gothic building in about 1700; the structure of the latter modified an 11th-century Romanesque church. Its interior shows strong Gothic influences and houses the most valuable painting in town: a **Processional Standard** by an unknown master, dating from the late 15th century.

In the vicinity of the cathedral there is

a church every few yards. It is as if the "Corso" divided the Old Town into two sections – a secular northern district completely devoted to trade, and a nobler, more contemplative southern area where attention was focused entirely on spiritual matters. Opposite the cathedral stands the desecrated Manneristic **Church of St Michael**; on the far side of the broad expanse of the **Piazza Mazzotti**, during the construction of which some 50 years ago a large number of historic houses were demolished, rises the **Church of the Convent of the Capuchin Nuns**. The latter houses a number of carved altars by local artists.

Across the **Corso Vico**, outside the city walls, stands the **Church of St Mary of Bethlehem**. After its consecration in 1106 it was tended first by Benedictines and then by Franciscans. The church is held in high esteem by local residents; it is here that the 10 ft (3 metre) high wooden candle-shaped *candelieri* are stored between festivals.

Passing along the **Via Maddalena** and the **Via Turritana** in the Old Town, where lines of drying washing festoon the way and a succession of modest inns and restaurants invite the guest to gastronomic pleasures and friendly encounters, the visitor arrives in the bustling **Via Brigata Sassari**, whose name recalls the heroic Sardinian brigade which saw action during World War I. Continuing across the **Emiciclo Garibaldi** – planned as a circular piazza but executed as a semicircle, and dominated by the statue of Giuseppe Mazzini (1805–72), the politician instrumental in the unification of Italy – one soon reaches the Municipal Park, a refreshing place to unwind.

The park contains a modern pavilion housing selected Sardinian **handicrafts**. Of better quality than the items offered in many of the island's shops, where the souvenir industry often sinks to the lowest common denominator, the goods offered here provide an insight into the standards reached today by the island's authentic craftsmen and women. A further advantage is the reasonable prices that are asked.

Left, the Corso Vittorio Emanuele. Right, the Fontana di Rosello, the former main well of Sassari.

224

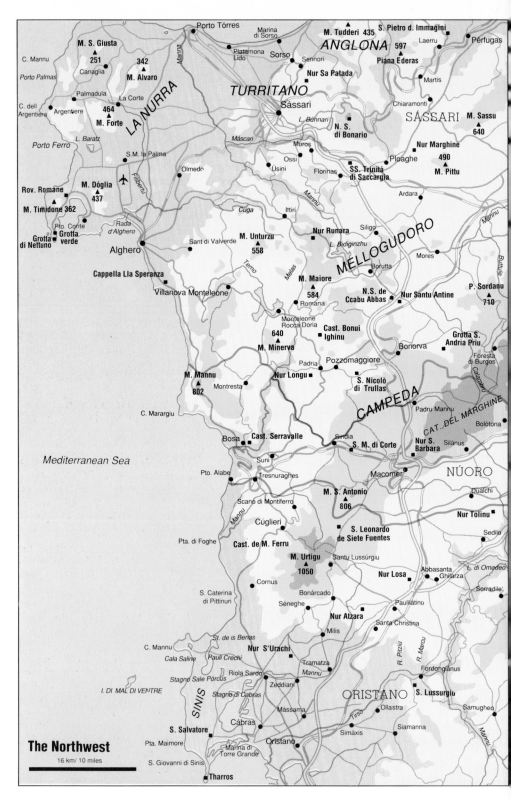

C. Mannu
M. S. Giusta
▲ 251
Canaglia
342 ▲
M. Alvaro
LA NURRA
Porto Palmas
Palmadula
C. dell
Argentiera
Argentiera
La Corte
464 ▲
M. Forte
L. Baratz
Porto Férro
S.M. la Palma
Rov. Romane
M. Dóglia
▲ 437
M. Timidone 362 ▲
Grotta
di Nettuno
Grotta
verde
Pto. Conte
Grotta
verde
Rada
d'Alghero
Alghero
Cappella Lla Speranza
Villanova Monteleone
Sant di Valverde
Cuga
Ittiri
M. Unturzu
558 ▲
Temo
Olmedo
Máscari
Filiberu

Porto Tórres
Marina
di Sorso
Platamona
Lido
Sorso
Sennori
M. Tudderi 435
ANGLONA
S. Pietro d. Immagini
Laerru
597
Piana Ederas
Pérfugas

Nur Sa Patada
Martis
TURRITANO
Sássari
Chiaramonti
L. Bunnari
N. S.
di Bonario
Muros
Ossi
Florinas
SS. Trinità
di Saccargia
Ploaghe
SÁSSARI
M. Sassu
▲ 640
Nur Marghine
490 ▲
M. Pittu
Ardara

Úsini
Siligo
L. Bidiginzhu
MELLOGUDORO
Mores
Borutta
Nur Runara
Mannu
Mannu

M. Maiore
▲ 584
Romana
N.S. de
Ccabu Abbas
Nur Santu Antine
P. Sordanu
▲ 710
Buttule

Monteleone
Rocca Doria
640
M. Minerva
Cast. Bonui
Ighinu
Bonorva
Grotta S.
Andria Priu
Foresta
di Burgos

Padria
Pozzomaggiore
M. Mannu
▲ 802
Nur Longu
Montresta
S. Nicolò
di Trullas
Padru Mannu
CAMPEDA
Bolótona
Catalamnu

C. Marargiu
Bosa
Cast. Serravalle
Sindia
S. M. di Corte
Nur S.
Barbara
Silánus
CAT. DEL MARGHINE

Mediterranean Sea
Suni
Pto. Alabe
Tresnuraghes
Macomer
NÚORO
Dualchi

Scano di Montiferro
M. S. Antonio
▲ 806
Nur Tolinu
Sedilo

Cúglieri
S. Leonardo
de Siete Fuentes

Pta. di Foghe
Cast. de M. Ferru
M. Urtigu
▲ 1050
Santu Lussúrgiu
Abbasanta
Ghilarza
L. di Omodeo
Sorradile

Cornus
Bonárcado
Paulilátino
Santa Christina

C. Mannu
S. Caterina
di Pittinuri
Séneghe
Nur Atzara
Milis
R. Pitziu
R. Marcu

St. de is Benas
Cala Saline
Pauli Crechi
Nur S'Urachi
Tramatza
Mannu
Fordongiánus

Riola Sardo
Mannu
Zeddiani
ORISTANO
S. Lussurgiu

I. DI MAL DI VENTRE
Stagno Sale Pórcus
SINIS
Stagno di Cabras
Mássama
Ollastra
Samugheo

S. Salvatore
Cábras
Oristano
Simáxis
Siamanna
Tirso
Mannu

Pta. Maimore
Marina di
Torre Grande
S. Giovanni di Sinis

The Northwest
16 km/ 10 miles

Tharros

ALGHERO TO ORISTANO

Alghero is generally considered to have been founded in 1102. However, long before the dawn of the Christian era the Phoenicians set up a trading post on this exposed bay in western Sardinia. In the early Middle Ages fleets of marauding Arabs also maintained a base for their fleets here, from which they could set out on their raids on the southern coast of France. Nonetheless, it was not until the beginning of the 12th century that settlers fortified the little peninsula on which the Old Town remains huddled to this day.

Spanish loyalty: It was at this time, too, that the place received its somewhat inauspicious name, Alghero; the meaning, "full of algae", takes on a new significance nowadays when one thinks of the environmental problems plaguing the Adriatic coast. For 250 years the Doria family from Genoa was in power here, but in 1353 they were forced to cede the town to the forces of Aragon. With the arrival of the first Aragonese-Catalan officials came the first Catalan settlers. Following an uprising against harsh Aragon rule, the resident Sardinians and Ligurians were all driven out of Alghero, and were replaced from 1372 by settlers from Barcelona, Valencia and Mallorca.

Alghero was transformed into an "urban fortress" in which only citizens whose loyalty to the regime was proven were allowed to live. The town was closed in on all sides by walls, towers and bulwarks (the fortifications on the landward side were demolished during the 19th century to provide work for the inhabitants of a nearby penal colony). The citizens were not allowed to travel further than about 2 miles (3 km) beyond the city boundaries, in fact as far as a number of churches in the surrounding countryside. The dominant influence in Alghero came not from the mainland but from the sea – or, to be more precise, from the Iberian peninsula. To this day it has remained the most Spanish town in Sardinia.

Although one soon becomes accustomed to the coexistence of two languages on the rest of the island, the situation in Alghero is considerably more complicated. Here one will hear Catalan in addition to Italian, which virtually all Sardinians speak perfectly even if it is not their mother tongue, and the archaic-sounding Sardinian, which is comprehensible only to the initiated. The visitor will often hear local inhabitants using Catalan in conversation, and will notice that it is used with increasing frequency on the streets, in the squares and, for some reason, in relation to buildings of interest to tourists. Perhaps the local inhabitants think *Prassa del Pou Vel, Carrer de Bonaire* and *les Quatre Cantonades* sound more inviting than **Piazza Civica**, **Via Umberto** and **Via Carlo Alberto**.

In the general wake of all stronger minorities the citizens of Alghero have revived an interest in their Catalan roots, founding parties to promote the interests of their minority culture and various folklore groups to breathe new life into their traditional folk music. It is not surprising, therefore, that the town's most famous culinary speciality is "Catalan-style lobster".

A stroll through the town: The Old Town of Alghero covers barely one-tenth of today's total city. It is, however – apart from the beaches and hotels located beyond the city limits – the only part of the town worth exploring. It is surrounded on three sides by towers and fortifications; the best introduction to the town can be gained from a walk along the old **Battlements**.

Setting out from the massive round **Torre dell'Espero Reial** ("The Tower of Royal Ambition"), the visitor can stroll for a mile past the lively **Piazza Sulis** in the southeast, fringed by cafés and trees, to the half-ruined but still impressive Forte de la Magdalena lying right beside the harbour in the north. En route is the octagonal **Torre de Sant Jaume** (St James's Tower) and the circular **Torre de la Polvorera**, which is situated on the north-westerly tip of the peninsula. From the fortifications along the **Lungomare Marco Polo** there are spectacular views across the Bay of Alghero as far as Capo Caccia. Finally, via a narrow battlement walk, you reach **Forte de la Magdalena**, which dates from the 16th century. It loses none of its impressiveness from the fact that the town's fishermen now use its base as a workshop where they repair their boats.

The local inhabitants enjoy taking a walk along the three-sided seafront promenade, especially the **Lungomare Colombo** to the south; during the height of the holiday season it is as busy here as on any metropolitan boulevard. The fascinating alleys of the Old Town, tall and narrow like dark mountain gorges, finger off the promenade. The Old Town itself is best entered through the **Porta a Mare**, the "Sea Gate", on the north side.

The **Cathedral of Our Lady** is reached by crossing the long, funnel-shaped main square – the **Piazza Civica**. Its style evolved over 200 years, from the mid-16th to the mid-18th century; unsurprisingly, in most observers' opinion, the result, a late Baroque-Manneristic superstructure on top of the late Gothic main building, lacks unity.

In front of the cathedral, on either side of the **Via Sant'Erasmo**, lies the former Jewish quarter; the Jews formed an essential part of the community in every trading centre of international importance during the Middle Ages and often rose to positions of influence. In the middle of the 15th century, with the necessary permission of the King of Aragon, Alghero's Jews raised the necessary finance for the construction of the **Torre des Hebreus**, the Jewish Gate. It provided a second point of access to the town on the landward side; until well into the 19th century it was closed every evening at dusk with the traditional cry "All those outside must stay outside!"

Fanning out behind the cathedral are the most elegant streets of the Old Town: the dignified **Via Umberto**, in which the aristocracy and clergy resided under the rule of Spain and Savoy, and the **Via Carlo Alberto** (*Carrer Major*), where today the visitor will find the finest and most expensive shops in town. Domi-

Motorcyclists just love the roads on Sardinia.

nating the end of the street is the Baroque **Church of St Michael**, sumptuously fitted out by the Jesuits. Its coloured majolica dome rises above the exquisitely restored monastery complex of **St Francis** (built during the 14th and 16th to 17th centuries); during the summer months the Romanesque cloisters form the atmospheric setting for classical music concerts.

Some of the alleys of the Old Town have a distinctly southern flair; here, unlike in other, more restrained towns on the island, one is sometimes struck by resemblances to Naples. For centuries Alghero, as the capital of the "Coral Riviera", has attracted fishermen from the Naples area, especially from Ponza and Torre del Greco. They have traditionally specialised in the hazardous business of fishing for coral.

The combination of this influx from Campania, linked to the Catalan influence already mentioned, has given the townspeople their characteristically cheerful temperament. As far as the coral is concerned, despite being promoted as the town's emblem by the tourist industry, nowadays only a small proportion of the coral used in the decorative items in the local shop windows actually originate off the Sardinian coast. The coral reefs have long been depleted.

Excursions: For the traveller wishing to get to know the northwest of the island there is no better starting point than Alghero, with its excellent tourist infrastructure. Taking the road through Sassari, one soon reaches the **Via Carlo Felice**, the SS 131, which passes through a region full of historical interest. In this area there are several of the 20-odd Romanesque churches founded on the island between the 12th and 14th centuries. The majority of them were constructed by master craftsmen summoned from Tuscany – often at the behest of the wealthy mainland merchants who imported large quantities of minerals, coral, hides, cattle, cheese, salt and cereals from Sardinia.

One of the finest and best preserved churches is the **Santissima Trinità di Saccargia**, "Church of the Trinity of the

A brass band accompanies the Easter procession.

Spotted Cow". It stands near the village of Codrongianus, some 9 miles (15 km) from Sassari. According to local legend: a gentle, pious cow played a significant role in the church's foundation – though, with its distinctive walls of alternating layers of dark-coloured basalt and light-coloured limestone, it actually looks more like a zebra than a cow. In reality, the construction of these religious buildings on Sardinia was nearly always politically inspired. The ruling families from the mainland hoped that the influence of the church on the island, boosted by impressive decorative arts, would secure and strengthen their political influence.

But whatever the reason underlying the foundation of the "Spotted Cow" church, there is no denying the splendour of its position. Inside, the apse contains the only extant cycle of 13th-century frescoes on Sardinia.

Only 2 miles (3 km) from the Church of the Santissima Trinità di Saccargia stands the **Church of San Michele di Salvènero**. Although it also dates from the 12th century, its design seems less elaborate, more traditional.

Some 8 miles (14 km) further along the road is the village of **Ardara**, an interesting stop for all admirers of the Hohenstaufen dynasty. Here, in 1239, in the so-called "Black Cathedral" – built of black basalt in about 1100 – Enzo, the son of Emperor Frederick II of Hohenstaufen celebrated what was to prove a short-lived marriage to Adelaida. Since his good wife's dowry included a sizeable proportion of the island in the form of the *giudicati* of Torres and Gallura, Enzo proclaimed himself "King of Sardinia".

He soon abandoned both his wife and the island (the son of the emperor seems to have been unable to stand life on this rough and lonely island for any length of time); but he didn't relinquish his royal title until his death in a dungeon in Bologna, where his enemies held him prisoner for 23 years.

Twelve miles (20 km) after the tranquil village of Ardara, with its sad memories of the Hohenstaufens, the **Frutta di mare.**

232

highway rejoins the Carlo Felice Superstrada at the farming village of **Bonnànaro**. The effects of the steady migration from the land during the past decades have been particularly noticeable here – witness the advanced ages of most of the farm labourers.

The settlement was the centre of an advanced culture during the time of the Nuraghi, between 1800 and 1200 BC. It must have been an austere civilisation based on the bare essentials of life – in keeping with the harsh, unyielding nature of the island interior – and yet, according to archaeological evidence, it was sufficiently sophisticated for the performance of complicated surgical operations such as trepanation, the drilling of the skull.

Another Romanesque church lies in the vicinity of Bonnànaro. **San Pietro di Sòrres**, in the village of **Borutta**, stands perched at a height of 1,665 ft (520 metres) on a little plateau. Its location amidst the bleak limestone landscape is breathtaking. Situated on a another limestone plateau nearby is a largish village, **Thiesi**, whose inhabitants make their living from arable and livestock farming.

A mural in the local middle school illustrates the part played by chauvinism and exploitation in Sardinian history. Those of the island's politicians who support Sardinian autonomy accuse the Italian nation-state of the same attitudes. The mural, by Aligi Sassu, a famous Italian artist of Sardinian extraction, represents the "Year of the Attack". He was referring to 1800, the year of the attack by the Duke of Asinara on the villagers who refused to deliver his feudal dues.

Along the "Carlo Felice": From Thiesi, a road crossing pretty countryside passes under the Carlo Felice Superstrada and leads into the **Valley of the Nuraghi** near **Torralba**. The name sounds as though it is a slogan coined by the tourist office, but it is no exaggeration: the hollow contains a large number of these mysterious megalithic constructions. The finest, the **Nuraghe Santu Antine**, stands in a dominant position on a hill.

Deck of a fishing vessel.

Its main tower, now some 56 ft (17.5 metres) high, may well have measured as much as 68 ft (20 metres) before the top courses of stones were dismantled during the 19th century to build the village well in Torralba. The *nuraghe* is of a highly complex construction; built of layers of basalt blocks, it includes – apart from the 3,000-year-old main tower – three lower and less ancient subsidiary towers arranged in a clover-leaf shape. In later times, the local population was so impressed by the *nuraghe* that it called it *Sa Domu de Su Rei*, the "Royal Palace". Strangely enough, the king referred to was actually the Roman emperor Constantine, who is revered throughout the island as a courageous fighter of holy wars and a protector of the Sardinian people.

The visitor wishing to discover more about the Nuraghe Santu Antine (St Constantine) – its labyrinthine interior structure of walls, corridors and rooms as well as the remarkable construction of the main tower, which consists of 28 courses of stone blocks, mounted upon

each other without the use of mortar – should not fail to visit the **Museo della Valle dei Nuraghi** in Torralba. He will find displays of excavated items and other interesting exhibits.

Also famous for its *nuraghi*, as well as its attractively coloured hand-woven carpets, is **Bonorva**, a small agricultural market town lying further to the south on the Carlo Felice. The ancient ruins lie at an altitude of approximately 2,080 ft (650 metres) on the **Su Monte** plateau; they can best be reached on foot with a guide hired from the village; the walk takes about an hour. Here the Nuraghi must have made their last, desperate stand against the incursions of the Carthaginians.

In 1478 yet another Sardinian dream of maintaining the island's independence was shattered near the little town of Macomer, which lies some 10 miles (15 km) further southwards. The soldiers of Leonardo Alagon, Margrave of Arborea, were defeated by a vast army sent by the new rulers from Aragon. It was this Spanish victory that broke the last remaining pocket of resistance on the island.

Macomer lies on a trachyte ledge which slopes away to the south. The panorama from the town sums up the island's geological history. It stretches from the basalt plateau in the foreground to the granite and limestone mountains of the interior on the horizon. The town itself has a gentle and lively atmosphere in which the visitor will feel instantly relaxed and at home: as an ancient trading centre and road junction, Macomer has a long tradition of expending hospitality to strangers of every kind.

The area was settled in ancient times by the Nuraghi, who were followed by the Carthaginians and the Romans. They found it an agreeable site, especially compared with the rough, often inaccessible land that characterises much of the interior. The roads radiating from Macomer follow tracks used since time immemorial: through the village of **Silanus**, with the Byzantine-Romanesque **Church of Santa Sabina** and the *nuraghe* of the same name, and through **Sindia** with its nearby Romanesque-

Left, former royal palace turned luxury hotel, the Las Tronas in Alghero. **Right**, the rocky coast between Alghero and Bosa is the last resort for vultures.

234

Burgundian **Cistercian Abbey Church** to Bosa, which lies on the Carlo Felice on the way to Abbasanta. Alternatively one can take the road to **Lussúrgiu**, which runs through the hills to the southwest of Macomer; after 10 miles (15 km) of lonely countryside one reaches the hamlet of **San Leonardo di Siete Fuentes**, whose *siete fuentes* (seven springs) rise in a shady park. In summer people come to take the waters – which have a diuretic effect. The **Parish Church of St Leonard**, built of dark-coloured trachyte rock, dates from the 12th century. It was originally constructed in the Romanesque style, but extensive Gothic additions were built at a later date.

Along the barren rocky cliffs of the Monte Ferru, the traveller passes an extinct volcano. The region's topology shows the traces of past eruptions. The little market town of **Santu Lussúrgiu** spreads out across a former crater. Livestock farming is the main source of livelihood for the inhabitants, and its handicrafts are closely linked with sheep rearing: the women weave rugs and blankets from the wool, and the men produce the sharp knives which they need for shearing in the spring. The town also has a reputation for excellent wood-carving, a skill which in days gone by occupied the shepherds in the long days and weeks as they grazed their flocks.

From Santu Lussúrgiu to Abbasanta the road descends the barren slopes of the Monte Ferru and then passes between an endless succession of *tancas*. These plots of land demarcated by stone walls are an essential characteristic of the Sardinian countryside, giving it a geometric chequerboard appearance. When the land was parcelled out during the 19th century to enable more peasants to become landowners, the construction of these walls marked a revolution in land use. For thousands of years – since the earliest days in the island's history – the Sardinians enjoyed common land which was worked by the community as a whole. From this point on, however, this almost communist concept of property ceased to exist.

In the tiny village of **Sant'Agostino,** modest cottages and guest houses for pilgrims, known as *muristenes*, are clustered round a basalt church. The same dark stone was used for the buildings forming the heart – the oldest part – of **Abbasanta**. This village possesses a pseudo-Renaissance parish church which lends it a certain dignity, but it remains merely a simple, sprawling community of farmhouses and shepherds' cottages. **Ghilarza**, which today forms part of the Abbasanta built-up area, appears to have a much more urban air, an impression due in part to the large number of churches within the town limits. They include **San Palmerio, San Giorgio**, **Santa Lucia** and the **Carmelo**. In addition there are several picturesque medieval country churches.

There is the small **Gramsci Museum** on the Corso Umberto, which provides an insight into the life of the Marxist writer, philosopher and politician. He was born in 1891 in the Sardinian village of **Ales**, attended the school here in Ghilarza for 10 years and died in 1937

Tuscan zebra pattern on the Santa Trinità di Saccargia.

after enduring a lengthy prison sentence for his anti-Fascist views.

From Ghilarza it is only a stone's throw to the tiny hamlet of **Tadasuni**. The local priest, Don Giovanni Dore, founded its **Sardinian Musical Instrument Collection**. It is perhaps the most instructive and interesting museum on the island, and contains one of the most complete Italian collections of traditional musical instruments.

Housed in rather cramped conditions in the priest's house, the collection stands and falls with its founder, whose indefatigable enthusiasm has led him to make a study of the sophisticated construction techniques employed in the seemingly primitive musical instruments of Sardinia – above all, the *launedda* shepherd's flute, the *serraggia* fiddle and the *tumbarinu* drum. Don Dore's authoritative explanations and demonstrations provide the best possible introduction to the island's musical tradition. Although traditional music is still frequently performed at folk festivals, the archaic tone patterns make it largely inaccessible to the uninitiated. If you want to understand it, this is the place to learn.

The village of **Zuri**, near Tadasuni, is also worth visiting. During the 1920s, when the Omodeo Dam was under construction, the entire settlement was moved to its present site. Not only the inhabitants but also the lovely parish church of San Pietró was relocated: the pink trachyte blocks were painstakingly dismantled, one by one, and then reconstructed here. Today it resembles an authentic 1925 replica of a Romanesque-Gothic building.

Water temples and nuraghi: Before leaving this densely populated region on the edge of the basalt plateau of Abbasanta, it is worth making a detour to view the well-preserved **Nuraghe Losa**, some 2 miles (3 km) southwest of Abbasanta.

The ivy-clad ruins exude a nostalgic air; naturally enough, in this volcanic area, the walls are constructed of dark basalt blocks. The main tower is estimated to be approximately 3,000 years old; the subsidiary towers and exterior

walls were built a few centuries later. Even visitors whose main purpose in coming to Sardinia is not to see the *nuraghi* should include this megalithic construction near Abbasanta in their tour of the island.

The Nuraghe Losa, the *nuraghe* fortress of Santu Antine near Torralba and the *nuraghe* settlement Su Nuraxi near Barumini are each constructed according to a different plan, but they represent excellent examples of the total of some 7,000 *nuraghi* which are still a characteristic of the Sardinian countryside today. Many of this total are, of course, decayed almost beyond recognition.

The *nuraghi* lend the landscape an aura of archaic melancholy, in which all attempts at progress seem out of place. All the more powerful, therefore, is the impact of the Nuraghe Losa, standing in peaceful timelessness on a small rocky eminence just a few dozen yards from the noise and frenzy of the traffic ploughing up and down the Carlo Felice superstrada.

One is frequently surprised by the obvious parallels between the religious rites of the Nuraghi and those of present-day Christianity. Three thousand years ago, the Nuraghi used to gather to celebrate their festivals around the **Water Temple of Santa Cristina**, which lies a few miles south of **Paulilatino** on the stretch of *Carlo Felice* between Abbasanta and Oristano. The elegantly constructed well shaft of the ancient sacred spa is surrounded by walls which archaeologists believe to be the remains of former pilgrims' huts. The rural **Church of Santa Cristina**, which is situated not far from the ruins of the *nuraghe* spa temple, is similarly encircled by simple dwellings for worshippers. Here, as so often on Sardinia, there is no clear distinction between the pagan and the Christian. Anyone who comes here in May or October, when the local inhabitants gather to celebrate their festivals, which are a potent mixture of the secular and the sacred, will have plenty of opportunity to experience genuine Sardinian hospitality.

On the road to Oristano, one more

San Salvatore, known for many a spaghetti-western.

detour remains – a short side-trip to **Milis**. On the edge of the village stands the Romanesque **St Paul's Church,** dating from the 12th–13th century. The houses are surrounded by the citrus orchards which the French poet Paul Valéry described with fascination in his *Sardinian Journey.*

Small capital: Regardless of the direction from which you approach the town of **Oristano**, you will find it hard to dispel the impression that you are entering an overgrown village of peasants' homes rather than the (smallest) capital of the (smallest) Sardinian province. Too little time has elapsed since 1974, when Oristano was made the capital of the island's fourth province, and the community hasn't yet adapted to its new-found importance. Awaking like Sleeping Beauty from 500 years of oblivion, Oristano has once more become the focal point of western Sardinia, the region it governed during the period of the medieval *giudicati.*

Until well into the 15th century the town was the capital of the judicature of Arborea, which was subjugated by the rulers of Aragon later than the other three *giudicati.* It is possible that the Aragonese were in no particular hurry when it came to conquering this province – the ruling family of Arborea was itself originally of Catalan descent, although they had been resident on Sardinia for many years.

The dominant personality of the house of Arborea was the *giudicata*, Eleonora, who died in 1404. Her seat of government is commemorated by the name of the main square; during the 19th century it was also decided that a somewhat pompous statue should add to the tribute. Surrounded by figures of lions, the lovely Eleonora strikes an elegant attitude. The descendants of her subjects love to meet at her feet, especially in the evening, to meet their friends and lovers, lick ice creams, exchange gossip or just to see and be seen.

Dominating the **Piazza Eleonora** is the **Palazzo Comunale**, the Town Hall. It is a former Piarist monastery, whose (desecrated) church, with an unusual

oval ground plan, now serves as the council chamber. The churches and two remaining towers of the former perimeter wall are virtually the only sights worth seeing in this rather colourless provincial town.

Despite the increase in population to a present total of over 30,000 over the past 30 years, Oristano has none of the sophisticated flair of Cagliari, Sassari or even Alghero. The **Cathedral** was built in a mixture of styles; of the original complex, dating from the 13th century, only the Gothic **Cappella di Rimedio** in the right aisle remains. The fragments of a Romanesque *ambon*, created by Pisan craftsmen during the 11th century, serves today as the chapel balustrade. Nino Pisano, whose name indicates that he, too, was a native of Pisa, carved the coloured Gothic wooden statue of *The Annunciation* in the Cathedral, as well as a statue of St Basil standing in the nearby Church of St Francis. Nino Pisano was a craftsman who lived and worked during the 14th century, when Pisa was still anxious to

maintain its links with the *giudicato* of Arborea and its capital.

Over a century later the Church of St Francis received the colourful wooden crucifix of Nico-demus, which is generally considered to be one of the finest examples of Spanish sculpture. Following in the footsteps of the Pisans and other Tuscans, who had been instrumental in bringing about a unique blossoming of the skills of Romanesque church builders on the island, the new Spanish colonial rulers began to show their determination to excel in the realm of the arts as well. The best way of establishing contact with the people and buying their loyalty was undoubtedly via the churches and the art treasures they contained; they enabled them to impress and surreptitiously influence the masses.

Also clearly of Spanish origin is the *Sartiglia*, a spectacular competition for mounted riders which takes place on the last Sunday before Lent and on Shrove Tuesday. Cervantes describes a *Sortija* of this kind (even the name is identical)

Flock of sheep near Macomer.

in his world-famous picaresque novel *Don Quixote*.

The event is a riding competition between two leading riders and their attendants, masked and wearing typical Spanish dress, with lace mantilla and top hat. Lances at the ready, they are required to gallop at and pierce a hanging star. Magical powers are ascribed to the two leading riders, who are known as *componidoris*. It is said that the success of the next harvest can be predicted from the number of times they manage to strike the star.

The **Church of Santa Giusta,** 2 miles (3 km) south of Oristano, was built when influence on the region was at its zenith, not only in politics but also in the arts. Standing on an eminence, the 12th-century sandstone basilica served as a model for many Romanesque-style churches in Sardinia. The interior, with its triple nave, is supported by granite and marble columns which are far older than the church itself: they were filched from the Carthaginian-Roman settlements of Tharros and Othoca (a com-

mon practice at the time). Latest archaeological investigations indicate that Othoca, once a prosperous town, must have been located on the site of the present village of Santa Giusta.

A bird paradise: The village of **Santa Giusta** lies between two lakes which are havens for island wildlife. The first, the **Stagno di Santa Giusta**, covers an area of some 2,225 acres (900 hectares) and is well-stocked with fish; there are, however, plans to reduce its size by half – which would mean a death sentence for much of its wildlife – to create room for industrial plant.

The second lake, the **Stagno Pauli Majori** ("Big Swamp") is smaller (though still very large) and lies to the east. Its dense reeds, interspersed with tamarisk, provide a home for mallards, coots and marsh harriers, bitterns and the rare purple heron. Ruddy shelduck, which are already extinct in mainland Italy, can still be spotted in the **Stagno di Cabras**, a lake lying to the west of Oristano. Its vast size – 5,000 acres (2,000 hectares) – helps to make it one

of the most fascinating ecological wet areas in the whole of Europe.

Although it is directly linked to the sea, the lake displays a relatively low level of salinity; for this reason, the flamingos prefer the saltier waters of the **Stagno di Mistras**. In autumn they settle in their hundreds – even thousands – when they migrate from the Camargue in the South of France to spend the winter months in Sardinia.

A wealth of unexpected discoveries awaits nature-lovers in the region surrounding Oristano. They should try to hire a local guide for a tour of the Stagno di Cabras. If one sets off early enough in the morning it will seem like a trip into a faraway, foreign world. The fishermen here use long, narrow one-man boats made of reeds similar to those that are still used on parts of the Nile and Lake Titicaca.

Those heading from Cabras to **San Salvatore** will also feel themselves transported into another world as they approach the village across a stretch of desolate moorland. Standing incongruously in the centre is a replica of a Wild West saloon – a relic of the early days of the Spaghetti Western film industry. In fact, the atmosphere of the whole place has an aura of the unreal. For most of the year it is utterly deserted and only comes to life at the beginning of September, when pilgrims from the surrounding villages come to take part in the nine-day Festival of the Redeemer. During the festival they live in the simple pilgrims' houses known as *Cumbessias* which are typical of the island – praying, eating and sleeping in the company of the other visitors over a period of several days.

Elsewhere in the world, folk festivals of this kind which have not yet been corrupted by tourism, have long since lost their significance. Here on Sardinia, however, they have managed to retain their important role in the social life of the island. The statue of Christ is borne in procession from Cabras to the church of San Salvatore, accompanied by youths attired in white robes and running barefoot.

No welcome for the photographer in Sedilo.

It is noteworthy that here, too – as in Santa Cristina near Paulilatino – a Christian place of pilgrimage coincides with a pagan holy site. Beneath the present building lies a *hypogaeum* (ancient burial chamber) constructed by the first inhabitants of the area, the Nuraghi, as a water temple.

Carthaginians used the three underground cellars as storerooms for their wares (the flourishing trading centre of Tharros lay only 3 miles/5 km away); the Romans used them as a dungeon, and from the 4th century AD the Christians turned them into a catacomb church, which they decorated with monochrome wall paintings.

Not far from San Salvatore, the **Church of St John of Sinis** also has a long history. A simple 6th-century building was extended into a triple-naved edifice during the 13th century, or possibly even earlier; the barrel vaulting of the roof rests on short, massive pillars. The stone blocks needed for the conversion were brought from nearby Tharros. *Portant de Tharros sa perda a carros* is an old Sardinian proverb, "They carry stones away from Tharros", for from the 11th century onwards the once-magnificent Phoenician and Carthaginian trading city served only as a quarry – not only for the extension of San Giovanni in Sinis, but also for **Christano**. Here magnificent medieval buildings were constructed using marble and stone blocks already hewn into the appropriate shapes and often decorated with splendid carvings.

Tharros: The town, which was founded by the Carthaginians during the 8th century BC, soon achieved incomparable prosperity. In the 3rd century BC it came under the rule of the Romans, who extended it considerably. During the 8th and 9th centuries the inhabitants started to leave the town – possibly because of the Saracen raids, which were an almost daily occurrence, but conceivably also because of the malaria which had reached epidemic proportions in a marshy district of the peninsula. Later, during the 11th century, when an attempt to resettle Tharros ended in complete failure, the new and rapidly growing town of Oristano finally wrested supremacy from its declining neighbour.

It was a Punic custom to bury the dead with rich funeral gifts: exquisite gold jewellery, precious stones, valuable glasses and fine pottery. Many such items can be seen in the principal archaeological museums of the island, especially in Cagliari and Sassari. Since, however, organised excavations did not begin until recent times, in many cases not until the 20th century, some archaeological treasures fell into the hands of anonymous or even well-known plunderers.

An English aristocrat, Lord Vernon, removed the contents of 14 graves during the 19th century; and neither the King of Sardinia and the Piedmont, Charles Albert, nor the French novelist Honoré de Balzac could resist the temptation to take a few precious "souvenirs" home with them. Of the magnificence of former days, only ruins and the remains of walls are left – the best-preserved dating from Roman times.

One of the last fish trap weavers in Bosa.

Visitors with little experience of archaeological sites may find it difficult when confronted with these abandoned ruins to imagine a living town with residential districts, temples, public baths, streets, shops and a colourfully mixed population. But even non-experts can apreciate the magnificent setting of the ruined city on its narrow peninsula jutting out into the Gulf of Oristano, and of the Phoenician-Carthaginian *tophet*, in which until the 2nd century BC first-born children were sacrificed to the gods in times of war and pestilence.

The **Sinis Peninsula** lies far from the island's well-trodden tourist track and is familiar to few native Sardinians. The lonely beach of **Is Arutas**, northwest of San Salvatore, has only recently become accessible, thanks to the construction of a new road. It consists of glittering round grains of quartz, some of which have a diameter of up to half an inch. It is hardly surprising that glass factories are considering how they can best turn to industrial advantage this remarkable natural phenomenon. Futher to the north, by the **Campo sa Sturaggia**, the coast becomes steeper as it plunges seawards down yellowish-brown cliffs. Here the flocks of cormorants reign supreme, building their nests on the rocky crags.

A short distance further on, **Putzu Idu** is well on the way to becoming a new centre of tourism on the island, expanding without a properly coordinated plan, though the realisation of the **Sinis Peninsula National Park**, a long-cherished project, may put a stop to such building proposals.

Not all well-meaning attempts to conserve nature have the desired effect, however. **Is Arenas**, south of Santa Caterina di Pittinuri, is a case in point. Several years ago, an expanse of sand 5 miles (8 km) long and 1 mile wide, with a coastline marked by dunes of up to 160 ft (50 metres) piled up by the strong onshore winds, was cleared and transformed into a magnificent grove of pine trees – an admirable achievement on an island as poor in tree cover as Sardinia.

San Pietro di Bosa in the beautiful surroundings outside the town.

What was lost forever, unfortunately, was a strip of true African-type desert landscape.

Santa Caterina di Pittinuri is an unpretentious modern seaside resort situated on a very charming rocky inlet, near which interesting examples of coastal erosion, such as the rock arch **S'Archittu**, are in evidence. Near the town lie the ruins of **Cornus**, probably founded by the Carthaginians during the 5th century BC at the latest. During the First Punic War the native Sardinians and the Carthaginian immigrants, between whom relations had not always been convivial, joined together in an anti-Roman alliance – but this did not prevent their being defeated by the legions of Rome.

Cornus remained a town of some importance even in Roman times; in about AD 1000 it was nonetheless abandoned by its inhabitants, who probably found a new place to live in Cuglieri, 10 miles (15 km) away.

In days gone by there were no fewer than three monasteries in **Cuglieri**, a farming village with an attractive location, and nearby **Scano di Moniferro**. The region also boasts other remains bearing witness to even older civilisations: giants' graves and the ubiquitous *nuraghi*, of which there must have been three (hence the name) in **Tresnuraghe**. From here it is worthwhile climbing down to the crystal-clear sea, where an enchanting coastal strip is protected from ruin by developers by strict protective regulations.

The leafy branches invariably lying on the village streets of **Flussio** and **Tinnura tend to** remind visitors of preparations for Palm Sunday. In fact, they are fronds of bog asphodel grass, spread out to dry before being woven into attractive basketwork, which is then offered for sale in the doorways of the houses along the main street. Passing through **Suni**, with its characteristically squat houses, the road continues downhill into Bosa.

Bosa: This little town on the Temo, the only navigable river in Sardinia, was built according to an unusual plan. Dur-

Las conzas, tanning houses by the lake of Temo.

ing the late 15th century two smaller towns were amalgamated after having existed side by side for many years. The upper town was subject to the lord who lived in the castle, whilst the other was a "free town" subject only to the king. The district of the town known as **Sa Costa** clings with a succession of parallel rows of houses to the side of an 260-ft (80-metre) high hill, the summit of which is crowned by **Serravalle Castle**, which was built by the Malaspina family in 1112 and later extended by the rulers of Aragon.

This miniature town has no church of its own, since the residents were dependent on the castle in religious as in other affairs. They were permitted to use the castle chapel **Nostra Signora di Regnos Altos**, where in recent years a cycle of frescoes of the Spanish school was discovered.

Beneath the maze of alleys and stairs which make up the streets of Sa Costa, the former free town of **Sa Piatta** sprawls across the plain by the river. This has an imposing **Cathedral** and elegant patrician houses along the **Corso Emanuele II**. Later on, a residential area grew up and formed a link between the two towns; the main characteristic of Sa Pitta is that the buildings are rather higher and the alleys narrower than in any other town on the island.

There is a small, picturesque river port by the bridge over the Temo; beyond the bridge extend the unusual terraced houses of **Sas Concas** – former dyers' workshops which today present an interesting example of industrial architecture of a bygone age. In idyllic isolation on the left bank of the Temo, 1 mile from the town centre, stands the Romanesque-Gothic **Church of St Peter**. Constructed in the 11th century, the church formerly served as the cathedral of Bosa. As the presence of the necropolis indicates, it occupies the site of the Roman town.

Thanks to its attractive urban architecture and the gentle greenness of the surrounding countryside, Bosa is one of the most attractive towns in Sardinia. Be sure to take a gentle stroll up to the fortress – wandering aimlessly through the Sa Costa district before climbing a further 111 steps between olive, fig and almond trees to the summit of the castle hill. In the alleys of Sa Costa it is tempting to accept the invitation of the black-clad elderly women who produce beautiful **network embroidery**, offering it for sale at what is effectively a "black market" price. They are supposed to sell all their needlework to the cooperatives, which buy up their exquisite handiwork in order to sell it at astronomic prices in the luxury boutiques of the main towns.

Along with gold and silver filigree work, coral jewellery and wood carving, this so-called *Filet de Bosa* is eloquent proof of the craftwork tradition still practised here.

The nearby seaside resort of **Bosa Marina** has a beach of dark, radioactive sand which contains a high proportion of iron. It has been proved to possess healing properties in the case of rheumatic illnesses.

From Bosa, a road leads northwards in the direction of Alghero. It passes through an austere landscape with eroded slopes and strangely formed trachyte rocks. Skirting round the villages of **Montresta** and **Villanova Monteleone**, it then descends to the plain of Alghero via a series of vertiginous bends and switchbacks.

For the past few years Bosa and Alghero have also been linked by a new coastal road. Environmental lobbyists have been vociferous in their criticism of this new traffic artery, since they fear its impact on what has been until now a lonely and untouched stretch of countryside, which has served as nesting territory and sanctuary for many species of coastal and sea birds.

They fear, too, that increased numbers of tourists will drive away the huge but rare griffon vulture from this habitat, thus possibly condemning it to extinction. Nonetheless, the stretch of coastline made accessible by this new road, the "Lobster Coast", arouses in the visitor a wonderful sense of solitude more intense than almost any other place on the island; driving or hiking through the region is a real pleasure.

Right, excited arrival in the courtyard of the pilgrims' chapel of Sedilo.

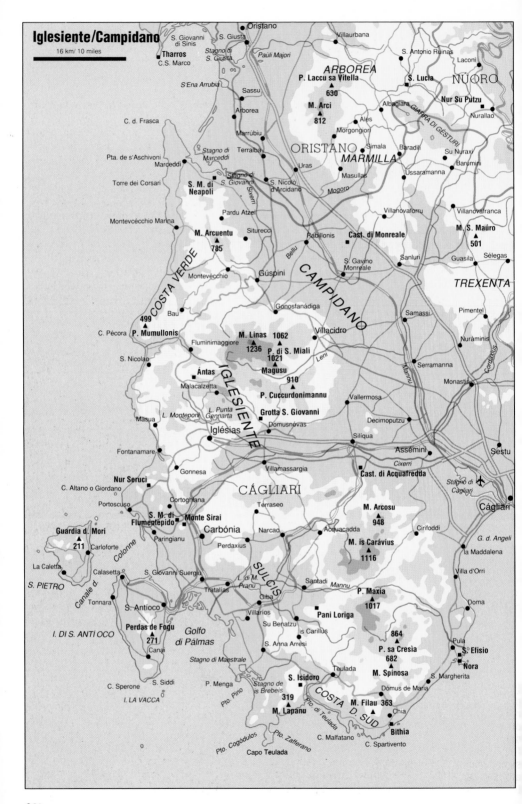

Iglesiente/Campidano

16 km/ 10 miles

Oristano
S. Giovanni di Sinis
S. Giusta
Tharros
C.S. Marco
Stagno di S. Giusta
Pàuli Majori
Villaurbana
S. Antonio Ruinas
Laconi
ARBOREA
P. Laccu sa Vitella ▲ 630
S. Lucia
NÙORO
Nur Su Putzu
S'Ena Arrúbia
Sassu
M. Arci ▲ 812
Albagiara
GIARRA DI GÉSTURI
Nurallao
Arborea
Alés
Morgongiori
C. d. Frasca
Marrúbiu
ORISTANO
Simala
Baradili
Su Nuraxi
Terralba
Su Nuraxi
MARMILLA
Barumini
Pta. de s'Aschivoni
Stagno di Marceddi
Marceddi
Uras
Masullas
Ussaramanna
Torre dei Corsari
S. M. di Neapoli
Stagno di S. Giovanni
S. Nicolò d'Arcidano
Mogoro
Montevécchio Marina
Pardu Atzei
Villanovaforru
Villanovafranca
M. S. Maúro ▲ 501
M. Arcuentu ▲ 785
Siturecci
Fabillonis
Cast. di Monreale
Guasila
Sélegas
COSTA VERDE
Montevecchio
Gúspini
Bellu
CAMPIDANO
S. Gavino Monreale
Sanluri
TREXENTA
Bau
Gonosfanádiga
Samassi
Pimentel
P. Mumullonis ▲ 499
C. Pécora
Fluminimaggiore
M. Linas 1062 ▲ 1236
Villacidro
Nuràminis
S. Nicolao
Ántas
P. di S. Miali 1021
Leni
Serramanna
Magusu ▲ 910
Mannu
Malacalzetta
P. Cuccurdonimannu
Vallermosa
Monastir
Masua
L. Montepori
L. Punta Gennarta
Grotta S. Giovanni
Decimoputzu
Iglésias
Domusnóvas
Silíqua
Fontanamare
Assémini
Cixerri
Sestu
Gonnesa
Villamassargia
Cast. di Acquafredda
Stagno di Cágliari
Nur Seruci
CÁGLIARI
Cágliari
C. Altano o Giordano
Cortoghiana
Terraseo
M. Arcosu ▲ 948
Cirifoddi
G. d. Angeli
Portoscuso
la Maddalena
Guárdia d. Mori ▲ 211
S. M. di Flumentepido
Monte Sirai
Narcao
Acquacadda
Villa d'Orri
Carloforte
Paringianu
Carbónia
Perdaxius
M. is Carávius ▲ 1116
La Caletta
Calasetta
S. Giovanni Suergiu
L. di M. Pranu
Santadi
Mannu
P. Maxia ▲ 1017
Doma
S. PIETRO
Tonnara
Tratalias
Giba
Pula
Canale d.
S. Antioco
Villarios
Pani Loriga
S. Efisio
Perdas de Fogu ▲ 271
Golfo di Pálmas
Su Benatzu
is Carillùs
P. sa Cresia ▲ 682
Nora
I. DI S. ANTÍOCO
Canai
S. Anna Arrési
M. Spinosa
S. Margherita
C. Sperone
S. Siddi
Stagno di Maestrale
Teulada
Dòmus de Maria
I. LA VACCA
P. Menga
Stagno de is Brebeis
S. Isidoro ▲ 319
COSTA D. SUD
M. Filau 363
Chia
Pto. Pino
M. Lapánu
Pto. di Teulada
Bithia
Pto. Cogódulos
Pto. Zafferano
C. Malfatano
C. Spartivento
Capo Teulada

250

THE SOUTHWEST

A tour of the southwest takes the traveller through attractive countryside, crossing the former mining regions of the Sulcis and the Iglesiente. The stretch of coastline along the Costa Verde is as yet still largely untouched, and the two islands of Sant'Antioco and Isola di San Pietro each possesses a charm of its own. The alluvial plains known as the Campidano, which sometimes call to mind the valley of the Po, divide the Southwest from the rest of the island. The most important north-south highway in Sardinia, the Carlo Felice, which links Cagliari with Sassari, runs across the plain. Nowadays it is thus possible to cross the region in a few hours instead of one-and-a-half days.

The coastal route: Leaving Cagliari on the SS 195, the well-maintained road leads southwards towards the **Capo Malfatano**. To the north lies the **Stagno di Cagliari**, a miniature biotope which has managed to survive despite the surrounding industry, aircraft noise and other unfavourable conditions. In the **Golfo di Cagliari**, particularly here in the **Golfo degli Angeli**, the traveller is made aware of the damage done to nature and the environment during the past few years. The petrochemical depots in **Sarroch** and **Macchiareddu** are distressing examples. Sardinia had to undergo a rapid process of industrialisation, regardless of the costs involved, even though this was not always to the advantage of land and people. Large-scale industry was imported – refineries and factories – and the entire bay presents as tragic a picture as Porto Torres in the North.

One saving grace for the traveller is the **Ristorante Cadiga e su Schironi** by the turning to Capoterra; it is considered to be one of the finest places to eat on the island.

About 12 miles (20 km) from Cagliari you will notice the *Domu 'es' orcu*, a twin-towered *nuraghe*. Thereafter the drive continues through the **Caputerra**. The range of mountains on the horizon reaches an altitude of 3,230 ft (1,010 metres).

Near the town of **Pula**, perched on a small peninsula, lies the Roman town of **Nora**. It was here that the oldest Phoenician inscription was found, dating from approximately 1000 BC. In 238 BC Nora was chosen as the capital of the Roman province of Sardinia, largely due to its favourable location and a fine natural harbour. From the 5th century AD the town sank into insignificance, to be reawakened after centuries of oblivion by archaeological excavations during the 1950s. They revealed what is thought to be a Phoenician temple to the fertility goddess Tanit, a 2nd-century Roman temple, a theatre and on the *sa punta 'e su coloru*, the "Cape of Snakes", a Phoenician-Carthaginian holy place.

In contrast to the north of the island, the south coast of Sardinia has not yet been properly opened up to tourism. The five-star hotel **Is Molas** offers luxurious recreation facilities including an 18-hole golf course. Between **Santa**

Margherita and **Bithia** stretch 6 miles (10 km) of sandy beach, La Pinetta. The sandy bays of the adjoining **Costa del Sud** are as yet largely unspoilt.

The next port of call along the coast is **Bithia**, accessible via the nearby village of **Chia**. In addition to the watch-tower, a so-called **Saracen Tower** built in the 17th century to defend the island against the Turks, there is also the site of a **Phoenician-Roman Township** with a temple complex where a likeness of the archaic deity *Bes*, originating in Egypt, was discovered.

The coast road now becomes a *Strada Panoramica* as it leads past the **Capo Spartivento**, through a sparsely populated area to the lighthouse on the **Capo Malfatano**. The rocky headlands are emphasised by additional watch-towers, such as the 17th-century **Torre Piscinni**. Near the little hamlet of **Porto di Teulada** the street leaves the coast, skirting the **Monte S. Impeddu** (855 ft/ 265 metres) on the inland side. Near **S. Anna** a little side road leads back towards the coast, to the seaside resort of **Punta Menga**. Perhaps more interesting than these little villages are the many lakes hereabouts: the **Stagno de is Brebéis, Stagno di Maestrale, Stagno Baiocca,** and the **Stagno di Santa Caterina** shortly before you hit Sant'Antioco. For bird-lovers, there are plenty of possibilities to observe flamingos, herons and cormorants.

The Isola di Sant'Antioco: Its area of 42 sq. miles (109 sq. km) makes the volcanic island of Sant'Antioco the largest of those lying off the coast of Sardinia, and the fourth-largest in Italy. The island can be reached by means of a causeway; just before entering the village of Sant'Antioco itself you can see the remains of an old **Roman Bridge**. The semicircular arch looks somewhat lost beside the main road, but it proves that in former times the offshore island was linked to Sardinia. Sant'Antioco is a bustling little port with a picturesque old town centre. Its main street, the **Corso Vittorio Emanuele**, is sheltered from the searing sunshine by a dense avenue of pine trees.

During the Phoenician era, in the 9th and 8th centuries BC, the former town of **Sulcis** was one of the most important cities in the Mediterranean. It was the port of dispatch for the ores mined in what is now the Iglesiente region. The town covered a much larger area than its present-day successor. The **Antiquarium**, a small museum, provides a glimpse of the glorious past of what today is just a remote island. Nearby lies the **Tophet**, the ritual ground of the Phoenicians where their child sacrifices were carried out. Countless urns containing children's ashes stand on the archaeological site close to the vast **Necropolis**.

Additional relics of the past are the catacombs underneath the Parish Church. During the First Punic War, Sulcis acted as a Carthaginian naval base, which in turn led to harsh retaliatory measures by the forces of the Roman Empire. Under the emperors the town regained much of its former importance, but it was plundered on several occasions by the Saracen hordes. During the 16th century virtually all the inhabitants abandoned the city. Only in the 19th century did it rise again from oblivion, a trend which has continued as a result of the local tourist industry.

More attractive is the little port of **Calasetta**, which lies on the northernmost tip of the island. The chequerboard street layout and the low houses recall the Arab influence during the 18th century. The local popularity of couscous is a culinary relic of this time. Any tour of the island should include the **Tonnara** on the **Punta Maggiore**. During the *Matanza* – which takes place in about May, depending on when the schools of tuna pass by the island – a complicated system of nets is erected in order to lure the fish into the *camere del morte*, in which the sea turns crimson with blood as the tuna are killed. Processing takes place in the *tonnara* itself. The entire procedure attracts large crowds of onlookers every year.

Calasetta is also the starting point for the crossing to the **Isola di San Pietro**. Its area of 20 sq. miles (50 sq. km) makes it the third-largest of the offshore islands. The only place of any significance is **Carloforte**, founded in 1738 under the King of the House of Savoy, Charles Emmanuel III. As in the case of Sant'Antioco, the island was settled by Ligurians; during the 16th century many of them were kidnapped and borne off to Tunisia, but were later set free. The island is a nature paradise, with precipitous rock formations and pillars such as the **Punta delle Colonne** and myriad species of birds. For years Sardinian conservationists have been lobbying to have the island declared a national park. Apart from a **Grotta** in the south, San Pietro can also offer the visitor a *Tonnara* in the north of the island.The **Ristorante Da Nicolo** on the **Corso Cavour in Carloforte** is to be recommended.

The inland route: Leaving Cagliari in a northwesterly direction on the SS 131, the traveller passes **Elmas Airport** and continues towards Iglésias and Sant'Antioco. About 20 miles (30 km) from the capital lies the village of **Uta**, which is worth a detour. Some way outside the village itself lies the **Church of St Mary** (AD 1140), which is without doubt the loveliest Romanesque country church in the whole of southern Sardinia.

A few miles from Siliqua stands the **Castello di Acquafredda** on a volcanic outcrop overlooking the **River Cixerri**. The castle is a picturesque fortress dating from the 13th century. A particularly scenic route is the winding SS 293 as it passes over the **Colle della Campanasissa** and beyond to **Villapéruccio** and the **Monte Pranu**. The abandoned stations and marked-out route of the erstwhile **Narrow Gauge Railway** criss-crossing this mining region of the **Sulcis** recall the long-since uneconomic industry. Visitors wanting to enjoy a stroll through the oak woods of the *macchia* are recommended to park by one of the stations and walk along the routes of the former tracks.

Not far from the village of Villaperrúccio is the site of the most important rock necropolis in Sardinia. Dating from prehistoric times, it contains almost 40 *domus de janas*, the so-called

Disused railway in the area of Iglesiente.

"homes of the fairies". The gravel turning to the site is not very easy to find; the best method is to follow the road from Villaperrúccio to Narcao as far as the junction. Then one can drive up to the vast rocky plateau of **Monte Essu**, on which is situated the extensive Ozieri Culture complex.

Miners' towns: At the centre of the Sulcis region is the town of **Carbónia**, planned during the Fascist era. Following the international boycott of Italy as a result of the 1936 Abyssinian Campaign Mussolini instigated the building of the mining town of Carbónia. Within just two years it was completed. The sulphurous "Sulcis coal" subsequently produced was virtually useless but was supposed to ensure self-sufficiency as far as Italy's energy was concerned.

The monotonous Fascist architecture of the blocks of flats and the monumental central square, the **Piazza Roma**, still dominate the town today. And yet one senses that the town is determined to prove itself more than merely another of Mussolini's crazy notions; some

attempts are being made to bring new life to this municipal and economic hydrocephalus.

Inifinitely more interesting than Carbónia itself is **Monte Sirai**, which lies directly outside the town and which is the setting for one of the most important archaeological sites in the whole of Sardinia. The former Nuraghe settlement was destroyed during the 7th century by Phoenicians from Sulcis (Sant'-Antioco), who then constructed a fortress here. Today the complex includes the remains of an **Acropolis**, houses and a **Necropolis**. From the summit one has an undisturbed view of the havoc wrought throughout the countryside by the nearby industrial complexes – one of the less attractive aspects of Monte Sirai. From the nearby harbour of **Portoscuso** one can set sail for the Isola di San Pietro.

Continuing along the road in a northerly direction, one should strike off westwards towards **Fontanamare** soon after the **Gonenesa** turning. Driving through the district surrounding the

Children's urns at the *tophet* **near the Phoenician town of Sulcis.**

reedy estuary of the **Torre Gonnesa**, the road eventually reaches the sea. Of the former coal port very little remains today; only the buildings still standing serve as reminders. Nowadays the coast here is an extensive bathing beach. And yet, it is hard to escape the relics of the region's mining past; the few intact quarries and slag heaps take on the appearance of prehistoric ruins. From Fontanamare there is a breathtakingly beautiful corniche leading to the mining villages of **Nebida** and **Masua**. One drives directly towards the **Scoglio Pan di Zúcchero**, a vast rocky outcrop rising suddenly from the sea.

The mountains of the Sulcis and the Iglesiente show the scars of centuries of exploitation: huge craters dug into the mountainside, the removal of half an entire mountain and ruined 19th-century mines. Further to the north, on the **Monte Vecchio** and in the little settlements such as **Ingortosu**, or **Argentiera** at the island's most northeasterly point there are countless ruined complexes such as these. To a greater extent than the other towns, villages and tourist sights, these mineworks provide an eloquent record of Sardinian economic and social history.

The most important town in the southeast of the island is the mining town of **Iglésias**, situated at the heart of the zinc quarrying district. The town's name is derived from its local church (Latin: *ecclesia*, church). Founded in the 13th century, it was a significant silver mining centre; the community was even awarded the right to mint its own coins. One should not be deterred by the somewhat desolate outskirts, but should head immediately for the historic town centre.

The Old Town was built according to a chequerboard plan; it is clustered around the Romanesque **Church of Santa Chiara** on the **Piazza Municipio**. Also on the same square stands the **Ristorante Villa di Chiesa**, named after the town's original name and serving good Italian food at an acceptable price. Also worth seeing are the pretty little townhouses of the Old Town,

Miners' memorial in the mining town of Carbónia.

many with wrought-iron balconies. The **Museo Mineralogico** displays over 8,000 rare stones and fossils discovered during the excavations throughout the Iglesiente.

The **Grotta di San Giovanni** near **Domusnovas** is the only cave in Italy into which one can drive by car. An asphalt road, some 2,950 ft (900 metres) long, follows the course of the river through the picturesque grotto.

Iglésias–Costa Verde–Oristano: Before embarking upon the trip from Iglésias to Oristano one should consider whether one can allow enough time not to have to hurry, and whether one's stomach is strong enough for the hairpin bends. Immediately after leaving Iglésias, from **Gúspini** the SS 126 climbs up the mountain in an endless series of tight curves. It passes through acres of oak forests which can compete with those of the Barbagia in terms of both remoteness and beauty. The region itself is virtually unpopulated, allowing the visitor to appreciate Sardinia's famous timeless charm.

At the top of the pass, the **Arcu Genna Bogai**, marked by a small convent, the view of the valley below suddenly opens up to include the pillared temple of *Sardus Pater*. A Roman place of worship during the 2nd century, it was built on the site of a much earlier Punic temple.

According to Sardinian mythology, *Sardus pater* is the orginal ancestor of the island's inhabitants. He reputedly came from Africa to populate the island, but the origins of the deity can be traced back to a Punic god. Today, remains of pillars and the partially restored floor plan of the temple remain; its undeniable attraction is derived primarily from its unique site.

Following the course of the **Rio Antas**, we pass the **Grotta de su Mannu** and the secluded **Fluminamaggiore**. The SS 126 winds on its way, climbing from the level of the river to the next eminence before entering the village of **Arbus**. Shortly before doing so it passes a small side turning which leads down to the mining communities of **Ingortosu** and **Naracáuli**. The in-

dustrial ruins are worth seeing. **San Cosimo** is a well preserved giant's grave by a little road leading from Arbus to **Gonnosfanadiga**; it lies immediately before the bridge over the stream running down into the valley.

On the Costa Verde: A small, winding road leads from Gúspini along the ridge of the **Monte Vecchio** and then down to the **Costa Verde**, the "green coast". The name refers more to the hinterland than to the coastal margin itself, for its massive sand dunes recall a desert rather than a green and pleasant land. From **Marina di Arbus** the coastal strip is open to vehicles in both directions. The sand dunes near **Torre del Corsari** are particularly magnificent. But even this maritime landscape, as yet largely untouched, seems to be endangered by the speculators.

The few fishing villages are already beginning to sprout holiday complexes, most of which are sadly being built without much concern for nature and countryside – and this is despite a law passed in 1900 forbidding development

ardinian
itrus fruit,
oo pricey
or export.

of this particular coastal strip. An alternative means of exploring the coast is on horseback; mounts to suit all ages are available for hire in the villages of Torre del Corsari.

After negotiating an arduous series of bends the traveller arrives some 20 miles (30 km) later at the **Golfo di Oristano**, behind which lie the **Stagno di Marceddi** and the **Stagno di San Giovanni**. After rejoining the SS 126, your next town along the route is **Arborea**, also built during the Fascist era and originally christened "Mussolinia" in honour of Il Duce. Arborea was laid out along new-town principles in 1928 in order to populate the plain of Oristano, which had been made agriculturally viable by the construction of irrigation canals. It was decided to introduce settlers from Venetia and the plain of the Po; they defied the endemic malaria and transformed the region into fertile land.

The little town possesses a few fine Art Nouveau houses as well as a well-run hotel and restaurant – the **Hotel Ala Bidi,** which serves as the equestrian sports centre for the surrounding area, and the **Ristorante Al Pavone**.

The present-day name of Arborea recalls the old *giudicati* of Gallura, Torres, Cagliari and Arborea. It also serves as a reminder of Eleonora d'Arborea, the former *giudicata*, who refused to acknowledge the sovereignty of the Aragonese, uniting virtually the whole of the island in her resistance. Today she is celebrated as a national heroine. In 1392 she was responsible for the famous *Carta de Logu*, a comprehensive legal code which governed the lives of the islanders and which prevailed until the 19th century.

Cagliari–Oristano: The most important traffic artery on Sardinia is the SS 131 Carlo Felice, which runs from Cagliari to Sassari and Porto Torres. By Sardinian standards the quality of the highway permits remarkably rapid progress. But don't be tempted to drive too fast; along the route lie a number of interesting places worth a stopover. The road crosses an intensively cultivated

The coast close to Calasetta on Sant'Antioco.

alluvial plain, the **Campidano**; on the eastern horizon rise the mountains of the Barbagia.

Su Naraxi: Following the SS 131, the **Villasanta** exit leads to the most important archaeological site of the Nuraghi civilisation – **Su Nuraxi** near **Barumini**. It consists of a large Nuraghe fortress dating from the 13th to the 6th century BC, surrounding a massive round defensive tower with a well. The layout of the complex is still clearly visible today; it is easy to recognise the different phases of construction.The main central tower was built between the 15th and 13th centuries BC, and the further fortifications with four round towers were constructed about 300 years later. The connecting walls, of massive lumps of solid rock, as well as five further towers, date from the period leading up to the 7th century BC.

Outside the fortified walls arose a village of more than 50 circular huts; during their construction in the course of the 7th century BC the main complex itself was destroyed. During a fourth phase it was rebuilt, before being abandoned by all inhabitants during the 5th century BC. Walking through the village of round huts, the visitor is struck by the cramped and self-contained style of building. The entire complex was excavated as recently as 1949.

South of Su Naraxi, the appropriately named *Mamella* ("Bosom") rises out of the plain. Perched on top is an ancient fortress marking the frontier where the territory of the former *giudicato* of Arborea met the *giudicato* of Cagliari. The ruins of the castle of **Las Plasas** date from the 12th century. Further along the road, it is worth making a short detour to visit **Sanluri** with its 13th-century castle.

Sardinia has a number of springs which have been exploited for thermal cures. The town of **Sardara** was famous in Roman times for its healing spas, and even today they are used in the treatment of rheumatic illnesses. Sardara also contains an important sacred spa from the era of the Nuraghi; it rises near the **Church of St Anastasia**.

Column in the Phoenician own of Nora near Pula.

MINING

Even in the days when Sardinia was regarded as a "forgotten" island, geologists and mineralogists were interested in its ancient and remarkably varied rock formations. Specimens of Sardinian geology were prize exhibits in all major museum collections. Extensive areas of the island, especially the Southwest (Sulcis and Iglesiente), the Southeast (Gerrei and Sarrabus) and Nurra in the Northwest consist of limestones and slates from the earliest periods of the earth's existence (Cambrian and Silurian eras).

These areas are considerably older than the other principal mountain formations in the Mediterranean; their rich mineral deposits, especially lead, zinc, silver, copper and iron, made Sardinia the first and largest mining region in Italy. Over 4,500 years ago the island's early settlers began to extract and smelt metals (copper, lead and silver). There seems little doubt that the Bronze-Age civilisation of the Nuraghi flowered 3,500 to 2,500 years ago largely as a result of their trading links and metalworking skills. Evidence of the degree of mining activity in Phoenician, Carthaginian and Roman times can be found in the tools and oil lamps discovered within the shafts, as well as in the vast slag heaps such as the one at Campo Romano near Iglésias.

During the Roman Empire, Christians were often exiled to the mining areas of the Iglesiente. Under Pisan rule, silver casting around Iglésias (Monteponi, Campo Pisano) soon rose to great fame. During the 13th century Iglésias, the former city of Uilla Ecclesiae, received its charter as a "silver town" with exemplary mining regulations and municipal rights under Pisan law, including that of minting its own coins. An episode described in records recently discovered in a Spanish archive illustrates the leading role of the Sardinian mining industry under the Pisans. In 1343, 20 years after their conquest of Sardinia, the rulers of Aragon imported Sardinian mineworkers to Spain in order to improve the state of the silver mining industry on the Iberian peninsula.

Sardinian mining enjoyed a further upturn in the 19th century – thanks to increased mechanisation and the use of explosives, and also to the introduction of the Piedmontese Mining Laws of 1848, which permitted foreign investors to circumvent the property rights of Sardinian landowners (ownership of the land was restricted to the earth's surface, and did not include the mineral deposits lying underground).

The year 1871 saw the foundation of the College for Mining Engineers in Iglésias, which is still in existence today. Sardinian mining operations were amongst the most up-to-date of their time; on a number of occasions machines which were subsequently manufactured under licence by Krupp were in fact invented in Monteponi, where ore extraction proved progressively more difficult.

The four main Sardinian mining concerns – the concessionaries of Malfidano near Buggerru, Montevecchio, Monteponi and Iglésias – took part in the World Exhibition in Paris in 1900.

With falling prices on the world market and the declining productivity of the Sardinian mineral seams, the heyday of the island's mining concerns scarcely survived the turn of the century. Under the dictatorship of Mussolini an artifical boom was created with the intention of making Italy strong and independent. It was one of the many over-enthusiastic, stubborn acts so typical of Fascism, culminating in the foundation of the "Coal Town" of Carbónia and the sulphurous lignite (with a combustion rate scarcely above that of peat) which was elevated to the title of "Sulcis coal" for propaganda purposes.

Iglésias, once a wealthy town, with its charming historic centre and Pisan city walls, is well worth a visit. The traveller arriving in Buggerru will have difficulty imagining that only 100 years ago this mining community, complete with hospital, schools, library, concert hall and a little theatre, was the first town on Sardinia to boast electric light – before both Cagliari and Sassari. Even outside the town limits, in the workers' housing estates and the opencast mines of Malfidano, there will soon be no trace left of the living and working conditions which in 1904 led to bloody unrest and the first general strike in Italy's history.

THE BARBAGIA

The Barbagia, which runs almost parallel to the mountain range of the Gennargentu, is the highest of the sub-regions of Sardinia. The name is of Roman origin and is derived from the Latin *Barbaria* or Barbaricum. The Roman conquerors described all peoples as "Barbarians" whose culture was based neither on the Roman nor the Greek civilisations, and whose social order and lifestyle were markedly different from their own (the people here resisted Roman colonisation for longer than any other Sardinian region). For this reason, the Romans called the inhabitants of the region *Barbaricini*. It was probably a *giudice* from the *giudicato* of Arborea who first subdivided the region into three sections: **Barbagia Superiore**, **Barbagia Centrale** (including the districts of Belvì and Mandrolisai) and **Barbagia Inferiore**.

Prehistory and history: Remains of antiquity, bearing witness to the early settlement of the area, can be found here as elsewhere in the form of the *nuraghi*, which date from the 8th to the 2nd centuries BC. Estimates put the total number on the island between 7,000–8,000; some 200 to 250 of these are situated in the Barbagia. Unlike those to be found elsewhere on Sardinia, where human hand or inclement weather has wrought extensive damage or even removed them from the landscape altogether, most of the *nuraghi* in this area are remarkably well preserved.

Some of the *nuraghi* in the Barbagia still have exterior walls standing, linking several towers or small cone-shaped buildings by means of corridors which were designed to provide a means of internal communication. A wall some 7 to 20 or 30 ft (10 metres) high surrounded the earth bulwark at the height of the living accommodation of the main *nuraghe*.

The entrance was almost always very low; it was – and still is – only possible to pass under the architrave on all fours.

One then entered an oval room connected by means of a spiral staircase with the two upper-floor rooms and eventually with the terrace on top of the flat-roofed cone.

The existence of the **Nuraghe Longu** in the Samugheo district and the **Nuraghe Monte Norza** in the vicinity of Meana was known even during the 19th century. Archaeologists are still unable to agree as to the original purpose of these buildings. The hypotheses range from simple clan dwellings or fortifications to burial grounds for important members of society or combined burial grounds and sacred places.

Further evidence of the region's early history can be found here, as in other districts of Sardinia, in the shape of *Sas pedras fittas* or *Sas pedras longas* – massive standing or lying tetrahedral stone pyramids which are firmly anchored in the ground. Remains of these pyramids exist in the vicinity of Gavoi-Lodine, not far from the original Byzantine cemetery of Nostra Signora d'Itria, as well as in the Grillu district (near Fonni), or in the mountainous forests of Ovodda. They may be sacred stones which were worshipped as late as the 6th century AD, before local inhabitants and their chieftain Ospiton were converted to Christianity by Pope Gregory I.

Also dating from prehistoric times are the giants' graves, the *sepoltu ras de gigantes* (also known as *gigantìnos, pedras ladas, tomba di giganti* or *altares*). They are to be found scattered across the entire island as well as here in the Barbagia. These graves – which, according to legend contain men of enormous stature, the mythical first inhabitants of Sardinia – are often situated remarkably close to *nuraghi* or on the outskirts of a Nuraghi village.

The giants' graves are rectangular constructions of unworked stone about 26 ft (8 metres) long and 3 ft (1 metre) deep. Characteristic of these tombs is the vertical *pedra lada* (stele), whose size is proportional to that of the grave. The smallest measure 30 sq. ft (3 sq. metres) and are 20 inches (50 cm) thick. Above the rectangular stone covering the tomb there is often a semicircular slab, though some other *sepolturas de gigantes* are only sealed by a single stone. In this case the lower square half of the slab is shaped on its upper side into a half-oval or a semicircle. One of the best-known giants' graves in the Baragia region is the *S'Altare de Lògula* near Sarule. It was discovered during the 19th century by General Alfonso La Marmora; the interest it aroused prompted the search for further sites.

Also worth visiting are the *domus de janas*, also known as *domus de ajànas* or *bajànas*. Again local tradition ascribes a supernatural origin. Legend maintains that they were inhabited by fairies or virgins; they took the form of small houses or caves hewn from the bedrock and measured 3 to 5 ft (1 to 2 metres) in height. So far, it has not proved possible to date the *domus de janas* with any degree of accuracy.

Fact and fable: Ancient scientific and historical texts describe the inhabitants of the Barbagia as "the people from Ilion" or "the descendants of Iolaos", who bravely fought against the Carthaginian and Roman hordes in an attempt to preserve their freedom and independence. One derivation of the name indicates a link with Troy ("Ilion"), and refers to a maritime people originally from Asia Minor who had come to Sardinia in order to found their own colony. The other harks back to Iolaos, the legendary Greek hero who is purported to have reigned over a Greek colony with the assistance of the sons of Hercules.

Pausanias, an early chronicler, confirms that in the interior of the island and in the mountains of the Barbagia there are many place names which are derived from the Iolaos of antiquity. Two examples are the villages Ollolai and Artilei; according to the historian Angius the latter stems from *Arx Jolai*.

It is claimed that the Carthaginians attempted to subjugate the inhabitants of the Barbagia on several occasions, but that they were never able to achieve a clear-cut and therefore final victory.

When the island came under Roman rule in 238 BC, the new conquerors,

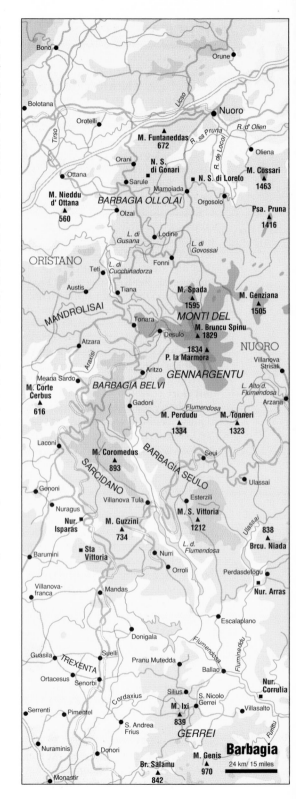

whilst trying to bring the entire island under their sway, encountered determined resistance in the Barbagia. In view of this, the Roman government sent men of the stature of Publius Cornelius, Marcus Pomponius, Tiberius or Sempronius Gracchus with instructions to subjugate the Barbagia in order to bring the entire country under the control of the Empire.

Under the rule of the Emperor Tiberius a large number of exiled Romans, possibly as many as 4,000, were dispatched to Sardinia. They were sent to prevent the attacks by the *Barbaricini* on other regions of the island which had already been pacified and brought under Roman rule. Under the Emperor Justinian they started up their raids once more, and the emperor was forced to give orders for the Roman legions to set up camp at the foot of the rough mountains of the Barbagia. It was during this period that the name of the Barbaricini occurred for the first time.

Scarcely 50 years after Justinian, the Sardinian tribe at last found a leader and general in King Ospiton, whose reputation owes as much to legend as it does to historical veracity. He possessed the ability to guide his proud people with a firm hand. By all accounts they were a nomadic tribe whose only interest lay in tending their flocks, and who exhibited no interest in the arduous tasks associated with agriculture, although it is possible that the large numbers of discontented refugees from the Roman province of Sardinia may have taught them the rudiments of farming and other manual skills.

During the 6th century AD the Barbaricini were converted to Christianity. Pope Gregory I sent Felix and Cyriacus to the Barbagia to spread the gospel throughout Sardinia. Under the influence of the commander-in-chief of the army, Zabarda, King Ospiton became a follower of the new faith. From this point on he tried to win the tribes under his sovereignty over to Christianity and to discourage them from the worship of pagan idols, the practice of superstitious rites and pagan customs.

The Barbaricini embraced the new faith with fervour. It seems possible that their passionate enthusiasm for the new beliefs encouraged them to desecrate the symbols of their former religion, as other Sardinian tribes before them had done. There is some evidence to support the theory that at this time they began to overturn and in some cases to destroy the *pedras fittas*, or to tear apart the holy places of their pagan gods.

During the Saracen invasion many Sardinians fled deep into the interior of the island in the face of the brutality of the advancing foe, finding refuge with the Barbaricini and thus augmenting their numbers. Although contemporary sources provide no information on the matter, it seems possible that the inhabitants of the Barbagia, true to their reputation as indomitable warriors, may have played a decisive part in the crushing defeat of the Saracen Prince of Mogeid-al-Amiri, referred to in ancient chronicles as Museto.

After the victory over Museto (AD 1015–16), the history of the Barbagia becomes progressively more integrated into that of the island itself. It passed through the period of the *giudicati*, became the scene of violent struggles and was ruled in turn by the Genoese, Pisans, Aragonese and Spanish. In the face of the frequent unjust tricks played on them, the people of the region never abandoned their guard and maintained a rebellious attitude. This can be witnessed in an episode dating from 1719, when a sudden doubling of taxes prompted the Barbaricini, and in particular the citizens of Olzài, to revolt against Spanish rule.

Mountains, flora and fauna: The Barbagia consists almost entirely of mountainous and hilly country, which rises towards the east as it approaches the massive ranges of the Gennargentu. Some of it is very bleak. Its highest peak is named after General Alfonso La Marmora, who travelled the length and breadth of the island during the 19th century, exploring the mountain as he did so. He recorded his impressions in his *Voyage en Sardaigne*.

The summit of **La Marmora** reaches 6,030 ft (1,885 metres) above sea level;

the neighbouring peaks of **Bruncu Spina** and **Orisa**, which for several months each year are capped with snow, are both more than 5,840 ft (1,825 metres). On a fine day, the view from the highest peaks of the Gennargentu is overwhelming and confounds the sense of bleakness that the region so often inspires. It extends across the mountains, which imperceptibly fall away towards gently rolling hills; in their folds lie densely wooded valleys snaked by streams that become transformed into rushing torrents in times of flood. In particularly clear conditions one can see as far as the Tyrrhenian Sea on the distant horizon, where the Straits of Sardinia and the Sardinian Sea are broken up by countless islands.

The peak of **Monte Spada** lies in the region known as **Barbagia Superiore** or **Barbagia di Ollolai**. It marks the end of an extensive mountain range which stretches eastwards as far as the **Corru'e boi** ("Cattle horn") gorge and the pass of the same name on the main Nuoro-Lanusei–Ogliastra road. Then

the highland area winds on further to Montenuovo S. Giovanni in the district of Orgoloso, where the River Cedrino rises, and on as far as the limestone escarpment by Oliena and the Lanaitto Valley, which marks the boundary between the administrative districts of Oliena and Dorgali.

The highest peaks of the **Barbagia Superiore** – Upper Barbagia – are the **Tiddòcoro**, the **Foddis** and the **Tiliddai** near Ovodda, the **Gúlana** near Ollolai and **Sa serra de Millu** near Lodine. In the **Barbagia Centrale**, which extends from the Mandrolisai district as far as the Belvì, the principal mountains are the **Monte Iscudu** in the Dósulo district, the **Monte Floris, Serra Longa, Sa Costa,** the **Accòro, Monte S. Elia, Serra Toppài** with the lovely Laurèntulus overhang and the famous "locked spring", the **Funtana Cungiada**.

Even in the **Barbagia Inferiore** ("Lower Barbagia", also known as the **Barbagia di Sèulo**), there are a number of peaks worth mentioning: **Monte Pedrèdu** near Sèulo, **L'Arcuèri** near Ussàssai and the **Montalbo** near Seui.

In the vicinity of the previously mentioned Corru'e boi gorge visitors are recommended to take a look at the narrow mountain valleys of **Pibinàri, Litipòri, Genna è Argentu** ("The Silver Gate") and, south of Aritzo and Belvì, the "Gate of the Winds", **Genna de Ventu.**

Throughout the region there are springs fed by the mountain snows. Their fresh water is popular all over the island; healing powers are even attributed to some of them, such as the springs of **S'Abba Medica** near Gavoi, or the spring water from the **Guppunnìo** spa and the **Regina Fontium** ("Queen of the Springs") in Ollolai. The most famous healing spas are those of **Monte Spada** and **Campu Majore** in Ortueri. People come to sample them from all over the island.

There are only three rivers of any significance: the **Flumendosa**, the **Talòro** and the **Aráscisi**. The Flumendosa rises in the southern glacial gorges of the Corru'e boi, collecting the water

Whitsun preparations.

of the eastern Gennargentu and numerous smaller tributaries from the Mountains of the Ogliastra before flowing into the Tyrrhenian Sea. The Taloro, a tributary of the Tirso – the island's biggest river – has its source in the Barbagia Superiore, expanding between the districts of Gavoi, Ovodda and Olzai to become the lake of the same name, after which it flows across the Plain of Ottana and the central Tirso Valley before joining the main river.

The Barbagia still retains a part of the luxuriant vegetation, especially the forests, which at one time made Sardinia one of the greenest spots in the entire Mediterranean.

In the mountains, acorn-bearing oak trees still grow up to an altitude of 3,800–4,200 ft (1,200–1,300 metres) above sea level. By far the most common species is the holm oak, followed by pedunculate and cork oaks. The latter supply the cork industry, an important factor in the Sardinian economy since the 19th century. The cork, stripped from each tree every seven to eight years, is exported in a raw and processed state. The numerous forest fires which plague the region in the hottest summer months and uncontrolled overfelling have led to a drastic reduction in the tree stocks. At the beginning of the 19th century they were estimated at 66 million.

Apart from the incalculable ecological and aesthetic damage, the fires have a deforesting effect which has led to a shortage of food for livestock. Pigs, in particular, produce excellent meat for the manufacture of ham and sausages when fed on acorns.

Visitors who appreciate the natural wealth of the coastal regions of Sardinia will be further delighted by an excursion into the woods and meadows of the Barbagia. They will discover, apart from areas of natural or specially-planted new forests, specimens of holm oaks which have stood there for several centuries – if not millennia.

As far as flora is concerned, the Barbagia is especially well-endowed: broom, oleaster, yew, ash, tamarisk,

The mountain village of Tonara in the western part of the mountainside.

willow, elder, alder, poplar, holly, laurel grow in abundance. *Maquis* shrubs – blackthorn, myrtle, arbutus and numerous other species – enchant nature-loving tourists and especially scientists from home and abroad.

Many of the plants bear berries or wild fruits with a slightly bitter taste, for instance, the sloe. Others, such as the arbutus, produce delicious fruits; it is from the blossoms of the arbutus that bees collect nectar for the famous, pungent-tasting Sardinian honey. The fruits are red and are about the size of a morello cherry. They are eaten raw or made into jam, and are known for their laxative effect. In former times it was common for locals to distil them to make schnapps.

Chestnut woods and hazelnut bushes are chiefly found around Desulo, Tonara, Aritzo and Belvì. The inhabitants of these districts include the fruits of the forest in their diet to some extent, albeit less than in days gone by. Nowadays much of the produce is exported to other regions of the island.

Almonds and hazelnuts are the principal raw ingredient required by the confectionery industry for the production of *torrone* (nougat with nuts and candied fruits), eaten in great quantities during festivals. For generations it has been manufactured in Tonara, Aritzo and Belvì. The chestnut trees used to supply (and still do to some extent) excellent wood for a variety of purposes. In the old days (and occasionally still today) craftsmen use it to make items for everyday use, such as doors or windows. More stylised objects, too, are produced – also functional, but requiring a greater degree of artistry – such as benches with built-in storage chests (the front panel of which is almost always decorated with stylised illustrations of birds, flowers, leaves or the landscape of the place of manufacture), looms, spindles, distaffs and other items for the processing of wool. Tables, plate racks, kitchen furniture and beds were usually made of a softer wood, in particular that of the pear tree.

Among Sardinia's plants and herbs

Shepherds often don't come home for days.

are thyme and rosemary – both of them common in the South of France and Spain – as well as wild lavender, gorse with its characteristic yellow flowers and sharp thorns, brambles (laden with blackberries during September), pink and red rock roses, heathers and a wide variety of forest ferns.

Unforgettable in spring and early summer are the seemingly endless fields of daisies, corn poppies and bog asphodel. The latter is one of the typical plants of the maquis; it produces long, thin stems with small white flowers in late summer.

The island possesses a relatively varied fauna. Eagles, falcons, vultures, red kites, partridges, ring doves, thrushes, magpies, quail, turtle doves, snipe, blackbirds and buzzards all live and breed here.

On the mountain slopes, where acorns and berries are plentiful, or even near vineyards and vegetable gardens, one will often encounter wild boar – a robust species which breeds easily in spite of environmental damage, in contrast to many others whose numbers have declined or which are even threatened with extinction. In recent years they have become a popular addition to the Sardinian menu.

The most common wild animal on Sardinia and in the Barbagia used to be the mouflon, a wild short-fleeced mountain sheep. In former times it wandered the mountains in herds, but sadly today it is becoming increasingly rare. Only those walkers crossing the crests of the Supramonte near Oliena and Orgoloso, or wandering through the heart of the Gennargentu are likely to be fortunate enough to see this magnificent creature. It looks like a ram, but has the coat of a deer.

Also of interest are the beehives. Apiculture was once more widespread than it is today, but the increased number of uninhabited areas given over to protected flowering plants has led to a revival of the ancient occupation of bee-keeping. As in the old days, walkers can once again delight in the unexpected discovery of a honeycomb

Goat in the mountains.

CAVES AND CAVING

Sardinia's rocks are the oldest in the whole of Italy. Karst formations cover a relatively small area of the island compared with the more extensively occurring metaliferous rocks and granite – only about 6 percent of the island, i.e. some 600 sq. miles (1,500 sq. km) of a total of more than 1,200 sq. miles (24,000 sq. km), most of it along the coast. The quality and exciting variety of forms, however, serves to compensate for the relatively small size of the area involved.

The underground world of grottoes and caves that characterise Sardinia's karst limestone was created almost 500,000 years ago, during the epoch of prehistory known as the Palaeozoic Era. Ever-new shapes were formed during the geological periods which followed: the Mesozoic, Tertiary and Quaternary Eras. The result is a truly remarkable variety of forms.

The inroads made by the sea also lends the grottoes a completely individual character, making them doubly attractive to geohydrologists, palaeoclimatologists, biologists and, of course, the island's many tourists. A trip to one of the island's numerous grottoes is a standard excursion.

The study of Sardinia's caves didn't start until the 1950s. In 1954 a British team of explorers discovered and investigated the Grotta di Nettuno, a picturesque cave not far from Alghero on the Capo Caccia, a formation of red limestone rising 600 ft (180 metres) above the sea. During the same year the grotto was made accessible to visitors by land. Today, over 100,000 people clamber into the bowels of the earth via the Escala Cabirol, the so-called Deer's Steps, each year. Many more, including those who can't make the 650 very steep steps, visit this fairytale world by fishing boat from Alghero harbour.

The cave contains a small lake (La Marmora), which – like the lake in the Grotta del Bue Marino in Calagonone (Dorgali) – provides a perfect miniature example of the vast underground lakes of Europe. It is thought that these, along with other caves on the island, had magico-religious significance during the Ozieri period. More recently, but sadly no longer, the two caves were the undisputed territory of a colony of rare monk seals (Latin: *monachus monachus*; Italian: *bue marino*), a remnant from the last Ice Age. They were the last colony of seals to be found on the whole of the Mediterranean.

Quite apart from their scientific importance, the sections of the Grotta di Nettuno which have been explored and opened up to the public enchant all comers by virtue of their extraordinary beauty. Passing through the "Hall of Ruins" (*Sala delle Rovine*) into the "Palace Hall" (*Sala della Reggia*), the visitor ascends the "Music Tribune" (*Tribuna della Musica*) from which there is a view into the "Organ Hall" (*Sala dell'Organo*) and the "Domed Hall" (*Sala della Cupola*).

In some of the caves stalactites and stalagmites have assumed the most bizarre shapes over the course of millions of years; they shimmer in colours ranging from brown, grey and cream to shades of green.

Sardinia's caves were more frequently discovered by accident than as the result of specific exploration. On many occasions, archaeologists were led to explore them in their search for prehistoric bronze statues and jewellery or human or animal remains (the ancient cultures often used caves for important burials); others were discovered by engineers searching for karst springs to increase the island's scarce water supplies, or by workers collecting guano – the dried excrement of seabirds, used in fertilisers – and miners involved in the extraction of lead or zinc.

During the 19th century, General Alfonso La Marmora was one of the first to make a detailed study of the island's caves – their formation, their geomorphology and their exploitation. Scientifically based speleology as such has only been applied to Sardinia since World War II.

Only a small proportion of Sardinia's caves have been studied to date. *Pro Loco* and other societies, some of them well-established, have made it their aim to encourage the opening up of further caves and grottoes within the various local districts on the island. While makeing it their priority to preserve the grottoes and caves, they also hope to make the caves more accessible to everyone, from scientists to schoolchildren.

tucked away in a tree hollow which one of the many swarms of wild bees has converted into a hive.

A journey into the Barbagia: An expedition into the Barbagia is recommended to every foreign visitor; it is a truly wild spot which even many Sardinians haven't explored.This region, which forms the very heart of the island, has neither airport nor seaport. It is accessible only by road, by public or by private transport. In general, the road network and the public transport available are adequate, but one obviously enjoys a greater degree of independence when travelling by private car. The Superstrada has been improved and is now of motorway standard, but has remained toll-free; by taking it, the visitor can soon reach Nuoro, one of the possible starting points for a tour of the Barbagia. The following route, using the island capital, Cagliari – with the largest harbour and the principal airport – as the point of departure, is only one of the many possibilities available.

After leaving the town on the Superstrada Carlo Felice (SS 131), one soon arrives at the right-hand turning of the Strada Statale 197 between **Sorrenti** and **Sanluri**. Here a detour is recommended to the remarkable *nuraghi* complex of **Barumini** and the **Giara di Gesturi**, a vast table mountain of basalt which is as geologically interesting as it is picturesque, and which is the home of the world-famous Sardinian horses. After about 6 miles (10 km) on the Statale 126 one reaches the village of Laconi, which is still in the **Sardicano**, but which lies on the edge of the Barbagia.

Laconi, the largest town in the Sardicano, enjoys an attractive situation. It is the birthplace of St Ignatius of Laconi; the saint's meagre possessions are preserved in the house where he was born (open to visitors). Apart from the 16th-century bell tower, one can also visit **Aymerich Castle**; its magnificent park contains not only flowers native to Sardinia but bay trees, horse chestnuts, pedunculate oaks, beeches and cedars from the Himalaya and the Lebanon.

In the grotto of Ispingoli near Dorgali.

The route continues northwards from Laconi. Passing through **Gadoni**, and **Aritzo**, the traveller arrives at **Tonara** and **Desulo** nestling in the western foothills of the Gennargentu massif. Alternatively, following the Statale 128, one can reach **Samugheo** via **Atzara, Sorgono** and then a number of minor roads should you want to get off the beaten track. Here there is a large site with a number of Nuraghi villages between which grape vines for wine and fruit are cultivated. Here orchards reach as far as the eye can see: cherry and almond trees; plum fig and pomegranate trees, olives, hazelnuts, walnuts and chestnuts. On the way to **Meana** (Statale 128) there is an interesting cave, the **Corona de su Taccu**, in the village of the same name.

From here one can either continue cross-country along minor roads or retrace one's route for a short distance along the Statale 128 and the Statale 198 (which links the Sardicano with the Barbagia di Seulo and, before Lanusei, with the Ogliastra). Whichever alternative is chosen, one soon reaches the twin lakes lying in the south and the east and known as the **Lago di Flumendosa** (via Villanova Tulo) and the **Lago Alto del Flumendosa** (southeast of Villanova Strisalli). Both expanses of water are important not only for the tourism of the region but also for its ecology, since they supply drinking water and generate electricity.

To the northeast of the Lago Alto del Flumendosa rise the mountain peaks of the **Punta La Marmora** and **Monte Terralba** (4,965 ft/1,550 metres above sea level), whilst to the south can be seen the **Monte Tonneri** (4,230 ft/ 1,320 metres above sea level).

This section of the Barbagia is characterised by the *Solitudini*, lonely, uninhabited expanses of land. The average population density in this region is less than 150 per sq. mile (60 per sq. km); sometimes it sinks to as little as a third or even a sixth of that figure.

For several months every year large quantities of snow fall on the summits and gorges of the Gennargentu, where it

Embroidery from Oliena, valuable art.

continues to lie for some period. In former times some villages used to gather the snow and ice and send it to the capital of the kingdom of Sardinia-Piedmont. Most of those behind the operation were not natives of the villages; they were outsiders who earned large sums of money from the business and gave the local residents work collecting and delivering the ice and snow.

Nowadays winter sports complexes and hotels are being built in the area in an attempt to market the snow in keeping with modern needs. There is no suggestion that the Gennargentu can compete wih the better endowed, more famous ski resorts of the Alps or the Appenines, nor is it likely to be able to in the future; nonetheless, it is to be recommended for a skiing holiday with a difference or, for those who have time, as an interesting place to spend an extra week after a stay on the coast.

Changing times: In Sardinia, the past few decades have seen rapid changes in the customs and lifestyle not only of individuals but also of entire communities. Contrary to first impressions, this is as true of the Barbagia as it is of other regions of the island. Only the shepherds with their flocks have remained true to themselves. They are the symbol for the nomadic lifestyle which was once typical of the land.

Pasture land is not always available in ample supply, but the grass and wild herbs available contribute to the taste – even the consistency – of the meat and the milk products. Gone are the days when every shepherd wandered the countryside on foot. Today most shepherds use a car or a jeep when they have errands in the village or want to visit their sheep. Their vehicles also enable them to transport wood or food for their livestock, to deliver the milk to the cheese factory and lambs, kids or pigs to the butcher.

One still occasionally sees a mule or a donkey. At high altitude, in the remotest, most inaccessible places in the mountains, they are still irreplaceable. However, for everyday transport purposes over long distances they have been superseded by vehicles.

Modern times are invading even the farthest corners of the Barbagia, as the inhabitants demand their right to share in the comfort of the present day with its achievements and new products. Most of the one and two-storey houses are still of the traditional variety, with ancient moss-covered tile roofs. In some places they have been renovated with much imagination and personal effort, enabling them to meet modern requirements. Sometimes, however, they have been demolished to make way for brand-new houses. More often than not, these are completely out of keeping with the traditional appearance of the town or village.

Migrant workers and traders who sought employment in the more prosperous regions of the island, such as Nuoro, Cagliari or Sassari, often return eventually to their native mountains, where they invest part of their savings in the construction of a new house or the renovation of an old building.

Today, in the agricultural estates of the parishes of the Barbagia, vegetable

fields, vineyards and orchards which had been allowed to lie fallow since the 1960s are increasingly being revived by owners who wished to take advantage of the steady income offered by a job in the service industries or in one of the factories in the faraway towns.

The future also looks increasingly rosy for the groves of oak and chestnut trees and the large areas planted with hazelnut bushes, which have retained their original charm despite the recurring fire hazard which lays waste vast tracts of land: oak and pine woods, groves of cork oaks and the maquis, where heathers, rosemary, thyme, rock roses, arbutus trees with their red berries, mastic shrubs and black-berried myrtle flourish.

The mastic shrub is the principal source of food for both goats and pigs; it is also used to yield an oil for household use. Myrtle berries and juniper are used to distil *mirto*, a schnapps. At the beginning of the century there were entire woods of juniper bushes several hundred years old. Today the stands are much younger, although in the valleys of the Barbagia one may still come across an ancient specimen which is as big as a tree.

From **Fonni** it is only 22 miles (35 km) to Nuoro via **Mamoiada** along the Statale 389. The road meanders between long rows of vineyards, orchards of fruit trees, past newly planted groves of cork and holm oaks and flowering maquis. Flocks of sheep and herds of cattle graze between fragrant violets and heather; the rich supply of wild mushrooms are a welcome treat for the wild boar – which, however, remain largely unseen.

If one so wishes, one can continue from Fonni to Nuoro by means of an alternative route. The road passes first of all the **Lago di Gusana** (4½ miles/7 km). Shortly before reaching the lake one joins the Statale 128, an attractive route skirting the right-hand shore before passing through **Gavoi, Sarule, Orani** and **Oniferi** and linking up with the Superstrada 131 from Abbasanta to Nuoro. Not far from the junction several

Many villages in the Gennargentu are run-down.

domus de janas are set into the hillside. Partly square and partly concave, some of the individual chambers are linked to one another by means of low doorways or windows.

The pilgrimage church of **Nostra Signora di Gonare** lies between **Sarule** and **Orani** on an unmistakable wooded cone-shaped hill from which talc is quarried. The building is unadorned and dates from the time of the *giudicati*. The festival of dedication, which is celebrated in appropriate style, falls on 8 September. During the Roman occupation Orani itself may well have been one of the most densely populated *villae* in the Barbagia. Many of Sardinia's artists, including the well-known contemporary painter Costatino Nivola, have hailed from Orani.

Nuoro, heart of the Barbagia: Nuoro lies under the same spell of enchantment as the Barbagia itself, the region in which – more than anywhere else – Sardinia has clung most tangibly to its past: caught between reality and myth, a passive witness to history and to the fate of its shepherds, peasants and poets. D. H. Lawrence reckoned there was nothing to see in Nuoro, though he did admit: "I am not Baedeker."

Today Nuoro has put on the guise of modernity. On every corner public and privately owned buildings have sprung up; new schools have been built. An expanding services industry and tourism have led to the town's rapid growth over the past 20 years.

Since 1926 Nuoro has been the provincial capital again, as it was under the Sardinian monarchy. At the beginning of the 19th century approximately 3,500 people lived here; by the end of the century this number had increased to over 6,000 and during the early years of the 20th century there were not quite 8,000. Now the population lies between 35,000 and 40,000, and the upward trend continues. No other town within the province can compete on a cultural level, although the economy, work situation, tourism and trade have resulted in greater fluctuations than were the rule in the not-so-distant past, when small

Political messages and social tension expressed in murals.

independent businesses flourished by making and selling only the essential requisites of life.

Traces of vanished peoples in the form of remains from the Nuraghi era and later epochs are to be found not only in the surrounding district but also close at hand: towards **Monte Ortobene** or in the direction of **Valverde** and **Badde Manna** ("The Big Valley"), from which one can see in the distance the delightful plains and the mountains of Oliena and Orgoloso.

Nuoro's position as the centre and symbol of the entire Barbagia is of relatively recent date; the region itself extends considerably beyond the boundaries laid down over the years, encompassing such places as **Orotelli, Orune, Bitti, Onanì** and **Lula** to the north. The town assumed its present key role at the turn of the century.

Famous sons and daughters of Nuoro, such as the poet Sebastiano Satta, the Nobel Prize-winning novelist Grazia Deledda and many others are responsible for the town's amazingly rapid rise to cultural and social prominence. Nowadays one can visit the final resting place of Grazia Deledda in the eastern district of town, on the way to L'Ortobene: the **Tempio della Solitudine** ("the memorial hall in which one finds solitude"). The leading citizens of the town have erected a museum in the house where the famous woman of letters was born.

In the **Museum of Folk Costumes**, recently rechristened the *Istituto Etnografico*, visitors can examine a varied and well-chosen collection of folklore items from all over the island: men's and women's traditional costumes from various towns and villages, matching jewellery – valuable filigree work in gold or silver or of coral, and works of art by skilled goldsmiths whose families in many cases have plied the trade for generations.

Apart from costumes, the museum displays a large number of exhibits illustrating the ancient craftsmanship of the island, which even today produces magnificent rugs and wall hangings,

Only the intrepid know this side of Sardinia…

exquisite shawls, scarfs and linen and silk embroidery. Such skills are the result of a continuously evolving tradition going back many hundreds of years. Traditional skills and craft forms were constantly adapted to include those of the succession of foreign powers to colonise Sardinia.

Nuoro possesses in addition an **Archaeological Museum** (*Museo Archeologico*) which also merits attention for the number and fine quality of its exhibits.

Further sights in the town centre include the **Cathedral of Our Lady of the Snows**, erected during the 19th century on the foundations of a considerably older, smaller place of worship. It houses a large number of valuable art treasures of interest to the visitor. Then there is the **San Pietro** district of town, where the birthplaces of Grazia Deledda and Francesco Ciusa are situated, and the **Church of the Graces** (*Chiesa delle Grazie*) – both the old and new buildings – which owns a boarding school run by the Brothers of the Order

...but it has a certain beauty in winter.

of Giuseppini d'Asti. The monks also take care of the pilgrimage chapel which attracts large numbers of faithful from surrounding districts, especially during the *Novene* which is held in November each year.

Two of the rural churches in the vicinity are worth an excursion: the **Church of Our Lady of Valverde** on the wooded northern slopes of the Ortobene, from which there is a magnificent panoramic view right across to **Orune** and the lovely **Valle di Marreri**, and the **Chapel of Our Lady of the Monte Ortobene**, lying about 5 miles (8 km) from Nuoro at an altitude of some 3,200 ft (1,000 metres) above sea level. It is accessible by car, public transport and on foot via a long and twisting road which climbs some 1,280 ft (400 metres) above the town.

From the **Belvedere**, the observation platform on the Monte Ortobene, there is a breathtaking view in all directions. There are also hotels, restaurants and bars (although fewer than in Nuoro itself) and a massive bronze Statue of the

Redeemer (the work of the sculptor Vincenzo Jerace and dated 1901). During the last few days of August (26–30) each year, the *Sagra del Redentore* is celebrated in its honour. The festival is one of the most famous and impressive on the entire island as it demonstrates not only the colourful costumes, the traditional dances and music, but also the deep and sincere piety of the Sardinian people.

Nuoro is a good base for excursions into the surrounding countryside – to the towns and villages of Orotelli, Orune, Bitti, Siniscola, Orosei, Dorgali, Irgoli, Galtellì – all of which are described elsewhere in this book.

Oliena and **Orgosolo** in particular, which lie 6 miles (10 km) and 10 miles (16 km) respectively from Nuoro, are worthy of a more extended visit. Each of the little towns has both cultural and historic attractions as well as strong traditions of hospitality. Both lie on the Supramonte, the first limestone mountain range within the Gennargentu southeast of Nuoro.

The murals (political wall paintings) in Orgosolo are famous. Nowadays the original political message concerning the struggle against powerful landowners and government repression are played down by the villagers. Instead, the cliché image of the bandits of Orgoloso has been sensationalised and turned to financial advantage by the tourist industry.

Mountain walks: The **Supramonte**, which contains the communities of Oliena, Dorgali, Orgoloso and Urzulei, can be approached from a number of directions – albeit in general only by foot, on horseback or in a cross-country vehicle. In each of the four villages, but in particular in Oliena and Orgoloso, walkers will find good accommodation and well-run guided tours – in short, everything to meet a trekker's needs. The tourist information office in Nuoro has produced a free touring map for trekkers and walkers detailing 10 alternative routes.

The Supramonte is clad in unspoiled holm oak woodland. Broom grows be-

Sardinian sweets are delicious.

tween giant tree trunks felled by age or lightning, but from which fresh shoots are already beginning to grow. Others have been transformed into pillars of charcoal by some long-past or more recent forest fire. In the half-shade of day or on bright moonlit nights they stand there like secret beings, monsters or devils from Dante's Inferno. Walkers be warned: grottoes and gullies open up without warning (across the millennia they may have swallowed up animals or even men); today speleologists are discovering their secrets. The mountain itself is not high; its loftiest peaks scarcely reach 4,800 ft (1,500 metres): **Monte Corrasi** (4,681 ft/1,463 metres) and **Monte Ortu** (4,288 ft/1,340 metres). They lie on the northern boundary of the Supramonte, between Oliena and Orgoloso.

In the southwest, within the district of Orgoloso, rise a number of ridges. They, too, are not particularly high, but, like the **Montenovo San Giovanni**, they are steep and picturesque. Changing light conditions and the natural tex-

ture of the rock make the limestone shimmer – sometimes blue-grey or green, then silver, copper-coloured or chalky-white.

The way into the secret, enchanted world of this part of the Barbagia is via ancient footpaths or old, unmarked tracks made originally by the wild boar, mouflons, goats and pigs who even today roam through the dense undergrowth of woods and clearings in search of food. The further one goes, the more overwhelming is the feeling that time has stood still.

The impressions which the visitor takes home with him from the Supramonte are of relics from an Arcadian past: the cottages (*su pinnettu*), built of largely untreated, massive trunks of oak, yew or buckthorn, the stalls for livestock and goats, the pigsties (*s'edìle*), and the few square *nuraghi* constructed of white blocks (**Nuraghe Mereu**), defying decay. And then there are the innumerable underground springs and rivers, crystal-clear especially in the caves, disappearing

underground only to resurface either in **Su Gologone** in the Oliena Valley, or else in the heart of the Supramonte, maybe in the **Gorroppu**, the wild gorge of the same name.

Food and drink: Even the food is natural and simple in the Barbagia: roast suckling pig, wild boar, goat, sheep and goat's milk cheese, ham – perhaps from the local pigs which are often crossed with wild boar and fed on acorns. Since time immemorial every meal has been accompanied by one of the traditional breads such as *pane carasau* (a flat crisp bread consisting of two wafer-thin layers); to drink there is fresh spring water from one of the many caves, or a powerful wine from Oliena, Orgoloso, Dorgali or Mamoiada. Those wishing to experience such typical Sardinian specialities are recommended to visit the **Hotel and Restaurant Su Gologone**, which is situated directly next to the spring of the same name in Oliena. Without being too expensive, the attractive hotel provides its guests with good food and the feeling at times of being in a living museum at the very heart of Sardinia.

In the shadow of a holm oak or a rocky outcrop, by the light of the moon or a camp fire lit to provide warmth, with meat to roast on the spit and one's gaze focused on a *nuraghe* which may have been standing there since 2,000– 1,500 BC, the traveller can indulge in daydreams, building a few castles in the air, or send up a prayer and maybe revise his or her priorities in the pursuit of wealth, power and success.

In the Supramonte, surrounded by nature, one can perhaps assume some of the confidence in the future which led the early islanders to build their *nuraghi*, overcoming their fears of death and natural forces.

Festivals: and song: After a meagre harvest or a year with too little rain, after a seemingly endless period of breathless anticipation, tensions are released in a festival. As well as being celebrations they expresses confidence in the future and faith in a deity. In this traditionally poor country, a concentrated

Nature at its best: *macchia* in full blossom.

284

effort was required to wrest from the soil the bare essentials of life. It was an existence made doubly difficult by the island's long history of foreign rulers. Festivals were a means of expressing – at least for a short while – all the plans, ideals and dreams conjured up by human fantasy and limitless imagination. A festival also provided an opportunity to give vent to a basic melancholy within a circle of friends.

A people like the *Barbaricini*, living amidst the noble silence of mountain, hill and valley, where every stone is a witness to ancient times and forgotten secrets, are a people which often prefers to communicate by gestures rather than words, a tendency that has often led to them being described as taciturn. Feelings and attitude to life are expressed by a look, perhaps by a smile or a scarcely articulated word.

But one of the festivals particularly loved by the inhabitants of the Barbagia is the so-called Poetry Contest. To the universal delight of their audience, two or three speakers supply an impromptu commentary on life in general or aspects of Sardinian history in particular; the delight of the listeners increases in proportion to the elaborateness of the performance.

Dance is an essential component of every celebration in the Barbagia. Indeed, dance formerly held an even more important role than it does today. It is governed by strict rules, which may vary from one village to the next. The musical accompaniment is provided by a single instrument, the accordion. The young men begin and are followed by the girls.

Traditionally, the dancing takes place in front of a church or at country places of pilgrimage, or on the village square. Nowadays performances for Italian and foreign visitors are held in amphitheatres and theatres, and the individual communities include dancing as part of the principal *Sagre* (folk festival). Sometimes the musicians may strike up spontaneously during a wedding or carnival celebration. When they hear the strains of a familiar melody, men and

Acorn bread is still made in some areas.

women seize each other's hands and form a circle, the size of which depends on the number of dancers and the rhythm of the music.

Church festivals assume a particular religious and social value in the Barbagia. The celebrations, which are part of the region's traditional folklore, take place either at places of pilgrimage dedicated to the saint in question or to the Mother of God, or else in the villages themselves. The festival is held in honour of the local patron saint, or another saint, or the Madonna, who is particularly revered in Sardinia.

In some churches or country places of pilgrimage the pilgrims, some of whom may have travelled great distances, recite their prayers in novenae, in a cycle of nine consecutive days. By this means they fulfil a vow or thank God for His mercy. The faithful usually sleep in *pergolas* or little huts (*cumbessias* and *muristenes*), which are built in an arc around the church or in a circle at a discreet distance.

Village and country festivals are ob-served with great ceremony, sometimes even with pageantry. Wealthy men and women of good reputation assist the priest. Sometimes these helpers are known by the title of prior or prioress; more commonly, however, they become the president or member of a committee. Priors and committees alike are invariably determined to do everything better than their predecessors. Sometimes the limits of friendly competition are overstepped, and the event degenerates into an image-building exercise for the organising families or clans.

The festive meal: As in days gone by, vast quantities of meat, wine and food are stockpiled for such occasions. It is considered vital that every guest, be he an invited neighbour, a traveller from further afield, or a chance tourist, should have more than enough to eat and drink. The entire contents of kitchen and cellar will be wheeled out as hosts try to outdo each other in their hospitality, pressing the visitor with genuine warmth to taste all the dishes on offer. If he is lucky, he may even be

Many farmhouses are miles away from the nearest village.

invited to visit the home of one of the local families.

The young people of the community organise entertainments. The *Morra* is a game in which two players have to stretch out simultaneously some of the fingers on one hand, calling out a number between two and ten. The player who guesses the number wins. And then there are the *Ballu Tundu*, the "national" dance of Sardinia, poetry competitions, guitar competitions and horse racing.

At every place of pilgrimage, usually immediately in front, you will find a little market, a tradition which dates from the Middle Ages. The shepherds and farmers, and above all the craftsmen, sell their goods or exchange them for others. Thus the festival acquires the character of a fairground, where *Torrone* or *Sapa* (cider) can be purchased, along with cow bells and a variety of small kitchen utensils of wood, copper or bog asphodel leaves manufactured in Tonara, Desulo, Aritzo, Belvì, Isili, Ovodda or Ollolai.

The **Festival of Our Lady of the Martyrs** is one of the best known, not least because Grazia Deledda described it so well in her most famous novel, *Canne al Vento*. It is held in the little town of **Fonni** on Whit Monday. Visitors from the surrounding countryside join local inhabitants in pious tribute to the Virgin Mary .

Another major festival is in honour of Ss. Cosmas and Damian. It takes place in the little country church of the same name; it stands on a fertile upland plain near Mamoiada, directly opposite the picturesque Gennargentu Massif. Not far from the pilgrimage church, near Di **Gavoi-Lodine**, it is worth making a detour to see the Christian-Byzantine church of Our Lady of Itria.

In **Mamoiada**, a predominantly agricultural village producing vegetables, wine and fruit, one of the most original, fascinating and famous carnival processions in Sardinia takes place.

The protagonists of the drama are the *Mamuthones*. As frequently happens elsewhere, the villagers don special dis-

guises for the occasion (in Orotelli they become *Thùrpos*, in Ottana they are known as *Boes* and *Merdùles*). Their faces are hidden behind wooden masks, and they wear untanned sheepskins or occasionally goatskins, with the fleece to the outside, reaching to their knees. Their costumes are completed by breeches of coarse velvet and knee-high leather gaiters of the type worn by almost every shepherd of the Barbagia until about 30 years ago.

The *Mamuthones* hang a bunch of cowbells weighing up to 110 lb (50 kg) over their shoulders. They walk in procession behind an ox harnessed by its hooves, followed by a youthful escort in bright costumes and carrying a leather shoulder strap, which they use to capture astonished spectators or – better still – their beloved.

The most attractive festivals in the Barbagia Centrale are the *Feste-Fiere* (the church dedication festivals) in Samugheo, Ortueri and Sorgono. The first festival is that of St Basil; the second is the Birth of the Virgin Mary, the *Natività della Vergine*, on 8 September; the third is the festival of St Maurus Abate (1 June), held in the church of the same name, a squat building with a single nave and situated some distance from the village.

In Sorgono the *Assunzione della Barbagia Vergine* (the Assumption of the Virgin Mary) and the Festival of the Redeemer (*Salvatore*) on 9 November are celebrated with due style. On St Maurus's Day the religious ceremony is accompanied by a fair at which handicrafts and produce are offered for sale as in days gone by: iron, copper, leather or terracotta goods, agricultural products – walnuts, hazelnuts, dried chestnuts and honey as well as sweetmeats of all kinds. During the 19th century the fair also provided an opportunity to purchase foreign goods: linen, woollen and leather items, silk, majolica, china, fashion accessories, spirits and thoroughbred horses.

Among the many festivals (*sagre*) celebrated in the rural areas or the towns of the **Barbagia Inferiore** (Barbagia

Tarmac is hardly ever used in the hinterland...

"di Seulo"), the following are particularly worth catching: the Festivals of St Mary Magdalene, patron saint of the parish church of the same name, and that of Corpus Christi and St John the Baptist. The festivals provide an excuse for a huge common feast for villagers and visitors, further evidence of the importance the Sardinians attach to hospitality and community spirit.

In the past, the more isolated churches of the Barbagia have often offered sanctuary to bandits, who were as pious and affable as they were cruel and bloodthirsty. This sometimes resulted in clashes with church authorities. For example, a decree issued in 1832 forbade the celebration of Mass in the Church of St Christopher near Seuila, since it had been desecrated by bandits and turned it into their home.

Magnificent festivals are celebrated in **Esterzili** in honour of the patron of church buildings: St Michael the Archangel in the village and St Sebastian, the Assumption of the Virgin and St Anthony of Padua outside the gates.

Apart from Christmas, a festival observed with special attention everywhere on the island, the festivals are scattered at random throughout the year. A disproportionate number occur in spring, when the shepherds and their flocks return from the plains of the Campidano or the Nurra, and in summer, when the expatriate workers from the Italian mainland come home to see their families. The inhabitants of the Barbagia love to celebrate their delight at seeing them again. Shared memories are revived, and for the duration of a short summer or festival day the melancholy and the loneliness of the too-cold or too-dry winter are dispelled, along with worries about the livestock and the success of the harvest or the problems of economic exile.

Visitors will not be excluded from these festivities, but they should possess the gift of being good listeners to really get the most out of them. Then they may even gain an insight into subtle, deeply felt and inexplicable *Mal de Sardegna*, the very soul of the island.

..many a ourney is hus turned nto a very lusty xperience. ollowing ages: pause or a reather; nurals with olitical and raditional hemes.

MURALS

One of the less-expected aspects of the Sardinian landscape is its number of vividly-coloured murals. They crop up in the most unlikely spots, dazzling the motorist or bus passenger with their colours and causing pause for thought.

It was in about 1970 that Sardinian artists first began to paint murals, wall paintings usually on the exterior of a building, carried out by one or more painters and depicting key scenes from everyday social or political life. It was a new form of art as far as the islanders were concerned, sometimes intended to convey political messages, at other times simply to arouse a nostalgic pride in traditional folk art.

Artists took up a number of themes commenting on the social reality of the times, illustrating the crass contradictions within their country and expressing the sense of alienation felt by many of their compatriots.

A recurring theme is the migration from the land: the consequences for rural communities and the effects upon the men who leave them. Many of the works are by well-established artists of international stature, such as Aligi Sassu, or by younger but no less talented painters, including Pinuccio Sciola, Liliana Cano, Francesco del Casino and, Diego Aspron. Often the artists are also teachers at one of the local schools. The wall paintings are team efforts completed with the assistance of colleagues or pupils; very few are the work of a single individual.

In Orgosolo, Ozieri, Alghero, Serramanna, Villamar, Oliena, Nuoro and many other villages the new art form particularly flourished, but not without disputes with the authorities which at times were decidedly violent. Supporters of the avant-garde style feel an affinity with the Mexican tradition, in which important political subjects are embraced. Many other artists support a more "natural", less traumatic revival of Sardinian traditions and customs.

The murals possess an implicit, sometimes even an explicit link to sung poetry. These wall paintings aim their message directly at their audience; their location – along the roadside or on the village square – make the messages immediately accessible to the man-in-the-street, and passers-by are often invited to make their own personal contribution. Groups of children and young people are encouraged to paint side by side with adult artists and learn from them. They, too, are expected to understand the essential messages of their native land and the times in which they live, and be able to translate them for the community.

In Mexico, the country which has produced masters of the stature of Siqueiros, Orozco and Rivera, whose work follows the established Aztec and Maya traditions, the murals have unfortunately degenerated into mere organs of the political regime. The risk of reducing a picture's message to a political slogan is, of course, also a danger on Sardinia, as is the tendency of some villages to devalue their murals by viewing them as merely another attraction to bait tourists.

Thanks to the dedication of Pinuccio Sciola, a highly successful painter and sculptor, a museum village was created in the province of Cagliari. After only a few years its reputation spread beyond national boundaries. Its success helped Sciola to fire the enthusiasm of the inhabitants of a little hamlet in the Campidano for his new project. He encouraged them to articulate their positive feelings about their lives as peasants, shepherds and villagers and express them through painting.

Sciola has fostered a remarkable flowering of artistic talent within the village. Today it is not only a museum but also a contemporary art gallery where children and established artists, students and unemployed workers feel they can breathe more freely and make a valid contribution to the world in which they live. On occasion the paintings and mottoes present matters in a very drastic light, but this is their strength. They succeed in arousing long-forgotten memories.

TRAVEL TIPS

GETTING THERE

BY AIR

There are no direct scheduled flights into Sardinia from outside Italy. From most European capitals the national flag-carrier, Alitalia (London reservations, tel: 081 745 8286), offers the best connections and usually the best fares, with a change of flight at either Milan or Rome. The domestic leg of the journey is either with ATI – Alitalia's sister company – or Alisarda, the Sardinian airline, with what usually amounts to a 1–2 hour connection time. At certain times of the year and in certain conditions it can be cheaper to buy the ticket for the Milan-Sardinia or Rome-Sardinia leg of the journey when you arrive in Italy; these discounted fares are not available outside the country.

Direct flights to the island (approximately 2½ hours) are with charter airlines only. From the UK, Britannia flies to Alghero and Cagliari, while Monarch flies to Olbia, both departures being once a week. Charter flight tickets are cheaper than scheduled tickets, but there is less flexibility of date of return. Tickets are not available from the airlines themselves, but via travel agents.

In the summer months Alisarda operates direct charter flights from Frankfurt and Munich to Sardinia, and Lufthansa has a flight into the Costa Smeralda airport at Olbia. Within Sardinia there are regular air services between Cagliari, Olbia, Alghero and Tortoli.

BY LAND & FERRY

Getting to Sardinia after travelling across Europe is quite a task of co-ordination between train and ferry or motorway travel and ferry. Motorists are advised to travel down through Europe across Switzerland rather than through France, where the motorway tolls are higher and the roads busier. Petrol coupons which allow the purchase of fuel at 15 percent discount within Italy are available for foreign motorists.

The key ferry points to Sardinia are Civitavecchia, Genoa and Livorno, with some ports having up to three departures per day (much depleted in the winter) and crossing times of up to 20 hours (*see below*). All ferries carry cars.

The most popular sailings are the night-time departures, and overnight cabins on these crossings are booked up months in advance. From London, ferry bookings are best made with Via Mare Travel, tel: 081 452 8231, or Serena Holidays, tel: 071 373 6548. Bookings are not always reliable at congested times; keep evidence of your booking and evidence of the unavailability of your cabin so that you can eventually claim a refund from the ferry agency with whom you made the original booking. Navarma Lines operate a daily crossing between the Corsica (Bonifacio) and Sardinia (Santa Teresa di Gallura).

Carriers are as follows:
Tirrenia Line: the biggest operator to the island, with sailings from Genoa and Civitavecchia to Porto Torres (daily), Olbia (daily), Cagliari (daily) and Arbatax. Ferries also connect Sardinia with Naples and Palermo.
Sardinia ferries: operate between Livorno and Olbia, twice weekly.
Italian Railways: run four crossings daily between Civitavecchia and Golfo Aranci.

Train travellers from Northern Europe should aim to catch the Napoli Express which leaves Paris every evening at 8.56 p.m. (the connection from London leaves at 11.30 in the morning) and arrives in Livorno at 11.05 a.m. the following day. Train travel on Sardinia itself is very slow, but beautiful.

WITH YOUR OWN BOAT

Whether you arrive with your own boat or charter a boat when you get there, you'll find a vast variety of marinas and ports along the coast between Porto Cervo and Villasimius. The most detailed information on their respective merits is best obtained from nautical almanacs. In addition, the Sardinian government produces a useful free booklet *Ma-*

With **Insight Guides** you can make the whole world your home. From Bali to the Balearic Islands, from Munich to Moscow, from Thailand to Texas, from Zurich to Zaire.

With **Insight Guides** the journey begins even before you leave home. With stunning photographs that put you in the picture, journalistic stories and features that give insight, valuable practical information and maps that map out your journey for you.

Insight Guides enrich the travel experience. They can be used before, during and after a journey — as a travel planner, as an indispensable companion and as a way of reliving memorable sights and moments.

We now have over 100 titles in print in various languages. Thanks to our extensive distribution channels your bookseller will have them available. Nevertheless, should you have problems purchasing certain titles, feel free to contact us:

"SEE YOU SOON!"

**Höfer Communications
38 Joo Koon Road
Singapore 2262
Fax: (65) 8612755**

A P A
INSIGHT
GUIDES

*Mediterranean beauty and zest for life have attracted travellers from all over the world for centuries. Peoples, cultures and continents meet at the Mediterranean Sea. Italy, Spain, Greece, Yugoslavia, Portugal... the Mediterranean area reads like a "Who's Who" of popular travel destinations. And **Insight Guides** are indispensable travel companions.*

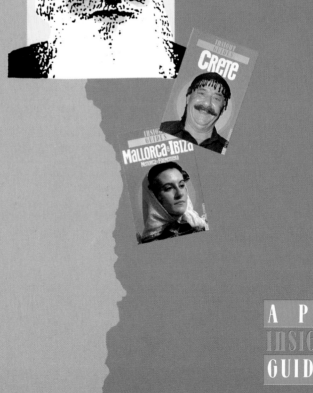

Andalusia/Costa del Sol
Athens
Barcelona
Catalonia/Costa Brava
Corsica
Crete
Greece
Greek Islands
Gulf of Naples
Israel
Istanbul
Italy
Jerusalem
Madeira
Madrid
Mallorca & Ibiza
Malta
Provence
Rome
Sardinia
Southern Spain
Spain
Turkey
Turkish Coast
Tuscany
Umbria
Venice
Yugoslavia

A P A
INSIGHT
GUIDES

rinas in Sardinia, with maps and photographs, which is available from overseas tourist offices.

Travel Essentials

VISAS

Citizens of European Community (EC) countries, the US and Canada are permitted entry with a valid passport or identity card. As Sardinia belongs to Italy, there are no additional requirements that need to be met. Visitors entering either via direct flights or from Corsica must proceed through international customs and passport formalities.

Tourists accompanied by cats or dogs must present proof of their pets' inoculation against rabies at the border. Vaccinations must be obtained at least 20 days prior to arrival.

MONEY MATTERS

As everywhere else in Italy, the unit of currency in Sardinia is the Lira (Lit.). It is possible to cash Eurocheques in practically every bank, often even without first presenting your passport! The maximum amount you can get for one Eurocheque is 300,000 Lit. If your Eurocheques or cheque card are stolen, alert your local bank **immediately** and have the cheques blocked. That way, if someone does cash one of them, you are only obligated to pay 10 percent of the sum, as opposed to being liable for the entire amount if you haven't reported the loss.

As a rule, banks are usually open in the mornings: Monday–Friday, from 8.30 a.m.– 1.30 p.m.

Cash and traveller's cheques can also be changed at the train station in Cagliari.

Many banks are now equipped with the Europe-wide cash machines that operate with four-digit code numbers. Instructions for the use of these cash machines are often given in four different languages.

HEALTH

No particular vaccinations are required for a visit to Sardinia. Nevertheless, there are a few points to consider as well as a few precautions to take. If you have any concern regarding your health, consult your physician before departing. Take care in the summertime and especially at the beginning of your holiday not to underestimate the power of the sun's rays. It's advisable to drink plenty of fluids, including mineral water. During the summer months pay particular attention to any sorts of food that easily become contaminated.

CUSTOMS

As Sardinia is a member of the EC, the usual EC customs regulations apply. Travellers from other EC countries are allowed to bring in or take out duty-free the customary 300 cigarettes, 1.5 litres high-proof or 3 litres lower-percentage alcohol, and 5 litres of wine. In addition to these, goods totalling not more than £250 are also free of duty. For those visitors from countries outside the EC, duty-free items include 200 cigarettes, 1 litre high-proof or 2 litres lower-percentage alcohol and 3 litres of wine.

TIPPING

Choosing to leave a tip, *mancia*, or not depends pretty much on your own judgement, the service and whether you're satisfied with it. Leaving a stingy tip is as inappropriate as leaving an overly excessive one. As soon as you sit down in a restaurant, each person is charged about 3,000 Lit. for *pane e coperto* (bread and silverware), regardless of how much you end up eating. This small sum doesn't take the place of a tip however, so if you've enjoyed your meal, tip accordingly.

While driving through larger cities and halting at traffic lights, don't be surprised if occasionally children offering various services – such as cleaning your windscreen – descend on your car. If you're not interested in paying for what they're offering, make sure you wave them away before they've already started.

GETTING ACQUAINTED

GEOGRAPHY & POPULATION

Sardinia is the second largest island in the Mediterranean Sea. It belongs to Italy, even if there are some native Sardinians who would rather not be reminded of this fact. The total land area encompasses 9,309 sq miles (24,090 sq km), being about 168 miles (270 km) long and about 90 miles (145 km) across. The distance between Sardinia and mainland Italy is almost the same as that between Sardinia and the continent of Africa (Tunisia) – 112 miles (180 km) measured between the closest points. Taking the larger offshore islands into account, the coastline runs for 1,150 miles (1,850 km).

Approximately 1.6 million people live on Sardinia. In the city of Cagliari there are about 235,000 inhabitants, in Sassari 120,000, in Alghero 38,000, in Nuoro 36,000, and in Oristano and Olbia 30,000 apiece. The island is divided into four provinces which are named after their respective capitals: Cagliari (CA), Sassari (SS), Olbia (OL), Oristano (OR) and Nuoro (NU).

Recurrent economic difficulties keep the island busy. Almost all the previously planned industrialisation projects have not come to pass because production costs are about one-third more expensive on the island than on the mainland. The average income, however, is about 25 percent lower than in other areas in Italy. So it is still the approximately 25,000 shepherds herding about 3.5 million sheep – from which the world famous *pecorino* cheese is produced – that lend character to the island today.

Sardinia, referred to as "Africa's Europe" due to its distance from the European continent, was discovered in the 1960s as a holiday paradise. A decisive factor in this development was the transformation of the Costa Smeralda into a luxurious holiday ghetto. Today more than 3 million visitors come to the island annually, thereby making tourism a significant contributor to the island's economy. It is no secret that most of the money invested in this business has come from outside sources, and that the lion's share of the profits return to these sources. *Residencias* have been built often with little regard for nature or the environment. These holiday housing developments are situated right on the coast, and, with the exception of a few summer weeks, remain empty for the most part of the year.

Even today Sardinia cannot get rid of its "bandit island" reputation, despite the fact that many other areas in Italy – for instance Calabria – could easily claim this title. In the meantime however, the "Bandits of Orgosolo" have learned that easier money can be made in the form of "legalised ripoffs": the sale of tacky, printed T-shirts to tourists.

TIME ZONES

As elsewhere in Europe, Sardinia distinguishes between regular and daylight saving time. From the last weekend in March until the end of September clocks are set an hour ahead. Other than this, usual Middle European Time (one hour ahead of GMT) holds.

CLIMATE

Thanks to its relatively southern location and due to the fact that it's an island, the climate in Sardinia is quite pleasant. Summers are hot and dry, lasting from May to September or even October. In the winter, particularly in the south, temperatures remain mild, although periodic heavy rainfalls are very frequent. Spring is generally a time of sunshine and warm temperatures, but can also be subject to incessant and strong winds in March and April. However, late winter and spring constitute ideal seasons for visiting; the entire land is green and blooming and temperatures make travelling pleasant.

Average temperatures

	May	July	Sept	Dec	
Alghero	52–73	61–84	64–86	55–77	°F
	11–23	16–29	18–30	13–25	°C
Cagliari	55–73	57–79	64–79	57–73	°F
	13–23	14–26	18–26	14–23	°C
Mountains	35–54	59–72	59–77	32–43	°F
	2–12	15–22	15–25	0–6	°C

Water temperatures

April	June	Aug	Sept	Oct	
57	68	73	75	68	°F
14	20	23	24	20	°C

On the northern side of the island a strong wind from the northwest called the *maestrale* (mistral) blows frequently. It's easy to see from which direction the wind usually comes by looking at the holm and cork oak trees. And what the raw *maestrale* is to the north, the warm, moist *libeccio* blowing in from the west and the *scirocco*, coming from the southeast are to the south.

ELECTRICITY

The electrical current is 220 volts. British visitors should equip themselves with European plug adapters.

BUSINESS HOURS

With the exception of a few change offices, regular and savings banks are open Mondays–Fridays from 8.30 a.m.–1.30 p.m.

Generally speaking, shops are open from 9 a.m.–1 p.m. and from 5 p.m.–8 p.m. Grocery stores usually open earlier, at 8 a.m. Especially in smaller towns, many shops are closed on Wednesday afternoons; they compensate by being open on Sundays. When exactly a shop closes for the day is still left pretty much up to the individual shopkeeper.

HOLIDAYS

There's not a day in the entire year that a holiday is not being celebrated somewhere on Sardinia. The tourist information centre ESIT publishes a brochure listing 1,000 festivals. Often festivities are held in honour of a particular town's patron saint or are island-wide religious celebrations.

Carnival on the island is certainly a high point on the Sardinian holiday calendar. Especially worth mentioning is the *Sartiglia*, a horse-riding tournament performed in historical costume, held in Oristano. The archaic ceremonies which take place during the mask parades in Mamoiada and Ottana also present a fascinating spectacle and the lively carnival in Bosa attracts more and more enthusiasts each year.

Easter marks another high point on the calendar and is celebrated in many places with processions and brotherhood parades. The *lunissanti* in Castelsardo and Good Friday in Alghero are particularly interesting, but impressive processions take place as well in Sassari, Cagliari, Nuoro and Oliena.

In May, the event of the year in Cagliari is the *sagra di Sant'Efisio*, dedicated to the city's own patron saint. Trying to get a room on 1 May in Cagliari is impossible. People dressed in ethnic and historical costumes come from all corners of the country to participate in the procession beginning in Cagliari and finishing in Nora.

The *cavalcata sarda* in Sassari is a parade of people in ethnic dress or other outfits held solely for the purpose and pleasure of displaying old and valuable costumes. This festivity was resurrected in 1951 by the Rotary Club.

On 6 and 7 July the *s'ardia* takes place in Sedilo, a daring horse race with the finishing line in front of the pilgrimage church of San Costantino. The *s'ardia* is just as dangerous as it looks and during the race even Sardinian blood begins to boil.

On the first Sunday of August on the Temo River in Bosa, there's a boat procession called the *Santa Maria del mare*. August is a month full of holidays. Two more to be noted for the large number of participants wearing folk costumes are the candle festival *i candelieri* in Sassari (14 August) and the procession *l'assunta* in Orgosolo (15 August).

The best known festival in September is the *sagra di San Salvatore*, held in Cabras. A huge throng of young men carry the holy statue at a trot from the Church of San Salvatore into Cabras.

LANGUAGE

Italian is the official language on Sardinia. French and English are only occasionally spoken, primarily in places well-visited by tourists. In addition to Italian, there are also a number of original dialects, for example Sardu, the Sardinian dialect, which is in turn divided into specific regional dialects.

COMMUNICATIONS

MEDIA

In addition to the three national radio and television broadcasting stations of the RAI, there are many privately-owned stations. You can watch news broadcasts by the national television networks on Rai-Uno at 1, 8 and 10.30 p.m., on Rai-Due at 1.30, 7.45 and 10.30 p.m. and on Rai-Tre at 7 and 10.10 p.m.

The RAI runs a local station for Sardinia with headquarters located in Cagliari. At 2 p.m. on medium waveband Radio-Uno broadcasts a quadruple language programme with practical tips and information for tourists.

Some of the newspapers circulated on Sardinia include the left-wing oriented *La Nuova Sardegna*, published in Sassari, and the even more left-wing *l'Unione Sarda*, published in Cagliari. Major daily newspapers from the Italian mainland can be bought just about anywhere on the island.

In summer you can find foreign daily newspapers – usually a day late – nearly everywhere in the larger tourist centres. In Cagliari and Sassari, they can often be purchased on the same day they were printed. Outside the busy summer months, current foreign newspapers can generally only be found in big cities.

POSTAL SERVICES

Smaller post offices are open Mondays–Fridays from 8 a.m.–1 p.m, larger, main post offices from 8.30 a.m.–6.30 p.m. and from 8 a.m.–12.30 p.m. on Saturdays.

It is sometimes possible to purchase stamps in tobacco shops bearing a blue sign which reads *valori e bollati*.

In Italy, post and telephone offices are usually separated. The following is a list of main post office (*Posta Centrale*) locations:

Cagliari (also telegrams)
Piazza del Carmine
Mon–Fri: 8 a.m.–7.30 p.m.
Sat: 8 a.m.–1 p.m.

Iglésias
Via Centrale
Mon–Fri: 8 a.m.–7.30 p.m.
Sat: 8 a.m.–1 p.m.

Nuoro
Main Post Office (also telegrams)
Piazza Crispi
Mon–Fri: 8 a.m.–7.30 p.m.
Sat: 8 a.m.–1 p.m.

Olbia
Main Post Office (also telegrams)
Via Acquedotto
Mon–Fri: 8 a.m.–7.30 p.m.
Sat: 8 a.m.–1 p.m.

Oristano
Main Post Office (also telegrams)
Via Mariano IV d'Arborea
Mon–Fri: 8 a.m.–7.30 p.m.
Sat: 8 a.m.–1 p.m.

Sassari
Main Post Office (also telegrams)
Via Brigatta Sassari 13
Mon–Fri: 8 a.m.–7.30 p.m.
Sat: 8 a.m.–1 p.m.

TELEPHONE

Increasingly common throughout Sardinia are SIP telephone booths, operated with phone cards in denominations of 5,000 and 10,000 Lit. Their introduction should eventually replace inconvenient *gettoni* and the pocketfuls of change it can take to make a call. The only disadvantage of this new system is that it's not always easy to find phone cards.

EMERGENCIES

The following emergency numbers apply throughout Sardinia:

Carabinieri (**Police**) 112
Soccorso Pubblico di Emergenza (**Accident Rescue**) 113
Soccorso Stradale (**Automobile Breakdown Service ACI**) 116

Apart from a few local exceptions, **Chemists' Shops** are generally open between 8.30 a.m.–12 noon, and then again from 4.30 p.m.–7.30 p.m. By calling 192 in Cagliari you can find out which chemist is open for night duty that particular day.

Telephone numbers of important medical services:

Cagliari
Medical standby service, tel: 663237
First Aid/Red Cross, tel: 606979
First Aid, tel: 6018

Nuoro
Medical standby service, tel: 37333
First Aid, tel: 36302
Hospital San Francesco, tel: 36616

Olbia
Medical standby service, tel: 22394
First Aid, tel: 22707

Oristano
Medical standby service, tel: 74333
First Aid, tel: 74261
Hospital San Martino, tel: 74261

Sassari
Medical standby service, tel: 217346
First Aid/Red Cross, tel: 234522
First Aid, tel: 275131
First Aid, tel: 241113

Important medical terminology:
laxatives: *lassativo*
stomachache: *mal di pancia*
diarrhoea: *diarrea*
fever: *febbre*
flu: *influenza*
headache: *mal di testa*
upset stomach: *mal di stomaco*
emergency room, first aid: *pronto soccorso*
band aid: *cerotto*
pain medicine: *calmante, analgesico*
toothache: *mal di denti*

GETTING AROUND

By Bus: For people in a hurry or those who don't have much time to travel, public transport is probably not the optimal way to get around as it is usually quite time-consuming. However, there is an extensive and efficient bus network spread out over the entire island whereby you can reach even the smallest villages in the most remote areas at least once a day. The most important bus lines are **ARST** (Azienda Regionale Sarda Trasporti), **FCA** (Ferrovie Complementari Sarde), **SFS** (Strade Ferrate Sarde) and **FMS** (Ferrovie Meridionale Sardegna).

In addition to these, the bus company **PANI** offers an express bus service *torpedoni*, which connects the most important cities with each other. Routes served in this network (the bus stops at various towns along the way) lie between Nuoro–Cagliari (3.5 hrs), Sassari–Cagliari (4 hrs), and Nuoro–Sassari (2.5 hrs). There's also a direct bus service without any stops at all between Cagliari–Sassari (3 hrs).

By Train: The *Ferrovie dello Stato,* the national railway system, operates along the following routes: Cagliari–Sassari (4 hrs), Cagliari–Olbia (4 hrs), Cagliari–Oristano (1 hr), Oristano–Macomer (2.5 hrs) and Cagliari–Iglesias (1 hr).

A journey on the narrow-gauge railway from Cagliari to Arbatax is both romantic and lengthy. The steam-hauled *Ferrovie Complementari Sarde* needs about eight hours to complete this trip. You must change trains in Mandas. It is one of the best ways of exploring the Gennargentu Region.

Additional local trains running between Nuoro–Macomer, Sassari–Alghero and Sassari–Palau supplement the network.

In the mining area of Iglesiente you'll most likely come across long-abandoned tracks once used by the freight trains. Today, use them to guide you on a hike through the *macchia*.

DRIVING

Several different local and international car rental agencies have their offices at various airports. During a temporary stopover in Rome, or in any other European airport, it is easily possible to pick up a telephone and reserve a car in advance.

AVIS

Alghero
Fertilia Airport. Tel: 070 935064;
Piazza Sulis 7. Tel: 070 979577

Baia
Via Tre Monti. Tel: 0789 99139
(open 1 June–31 October)

Cagliari
Elmas Airport. Tel: 070 240081;
Stazione Marittima Via Roma. Tel: 070 668128

Olbia
Olbia Airport. Tel: 0789 22420
(open 1 April–30 September);
Via Genova 69. Tel: 0789 22420

Porto Cervo
Piazza Clipper. Tel: 0789 91244
(open 1 June–31 October)

Sassari
Via Mazzini. Tel: 079 235547

Stintino
Via Sassari 34. Tel: 079 523175

EURORENT

Cagliari
Via Roma 9, c/o Sardamondial. Tel: 070 668094

Olbia
Via Principe Umberto 3. Tel: 0789 22163
Olbia Zona Industriale. Tel: 0789 51694

Porto Cervo
Sottopiazza. Tel: 0789 94263
(open 1 June–31 October)

Porto Rotondo
Via R. Belli. Tel: 0789 34600

HERTZ
As is the case in all its other agencies in Italy, Hertz does not accept cash payments.

Alghero
Aeroporto Fertilia. Tel: 079 935054

Cagliari
Aeroporto Elmas. Tel: 070 240037;
Piazza Matteotti 8. Tel: 070 663457

Sassari
Via 4 Novembre. Tel: 079 280083

DRIVER'S LICENCES

Members of the EC in possession of a national driver's licence should have no trouble renting a car. Travellers not falling into this category must have an International Driver's Licence.

If you enter the country in a private vehicle, you'll need to have a Green International Insurance Card.

Petrol coupons, which enable you to buy petrol at reduced prices, may be purchased at national motoring organisations or at Italian borders; exchange them later for what are referred to as "Sardinia Packets", which allow the same discount on the island.

ON FOOT

The mountainous regions of Sardinia are wonderfully suited for hiking and excursions on foot. Over the past few years the term "trekking" – usually thought of in conjunction with Nepal – has been introduced here.

In step with this development, various hotels offer hiking trips lasting several days, either on foot or on horseback. The tourist agency Pro Loco in Nuoro, Ente Provinciale per il Tourismo, Nuoro, Piazza Italia 19, publishes a brochure suggesting nine routes for "trekking nella Provincia Nuoro". Detailed descriptions of routes together with a hiking map make decision-making much easier.

WHERE TO STAY

Hotels and other lodgings on Sardinia are usually a problem. Either everything has already been booked up the week before, or, especially during the off-season, everything is closed. Therefore, you would be wise to call and reserve accommodation in advance, rather than subject yourself to the often frustrating search for a place to stay.

Strung out along the coast are countless holiday villages, the majority of which are only inhabited for a few weeks during the high season. For the rest of the time these holiday houses and apartments are rented out by their owners through various agencies. If you rent these places in the off-season, their rates are frequently only a fraction of what they are during the high season. Holiday houses can either be rented through agencies with offices in other countries, or directly on the spot. Further information is available at **ESIT** in Cagliari, or in any other tourist agency.

The following list of hotels is organised by province; the dialling code is given in parentheses. Some areas have been combined.

CAGLIARI PROVINCE

CAGLIARI (070)

Regina Margherita ☆☆☆☆
Viale Regina Margherita, 44. Tel: 670342

Al Solemar ☆☆☆
Viale Diaz, 146. Tel: 301360

Capo S. Elia ☆☆☆
Località Calamosca. Tel: 371628

Italia ☆☆☆
Via Sardegna n. 31. Tel: 655772

Mediterraneo ☆☆☆
Lungomare Colombo, 46. Tel: 301271

Moderno ☆☆☆
Via Roma, 159. Tel: 653971

Motel Agip ☆☆☆
Circonvallazione Pirri. Tel: 521376

Panorama ☆☆☆
Viale Diaz, 231. Tel: 307691

Sardegna ☆☆☆
Via Lunigiana, 50/52. Tel: 286245

Quattro Mori ☆☆
Via G. Angioy, 27. Tel: 668535

Residence Ulivi E Palme ☆☆
Via Bembo, 25. Tel: 485861

Alla Pensione Vittoria ☆
Via Roma, 75. Tel: 657970

Centrale ☆
Via Sardegna, 4. Tel: 654783

Firenze Loc. ☆
Corso Vitt. Eman., 50. Tel: 653678

Flora ☆
Via Sassari, 45. Tel: 658219

La Perla ☆
Via Sardegna, 16/B. Tel: 669446

La Sirenetta ☆
Viale Poetto, 192. Tel: 370332

Melis ☆
Via S. Marghenta, 21. Tel: 668652

Miramarae ☆
Via Roma, 57. Tel: 664021

Olimpo Loc. ☆
Corso Vitt. Eman., 145. Tel: 658915

S. Anna ☆
Via S. Restituta, 4. Tel: 665712

ARBUS (070)

La Caletta ☆☆☆
Loc. Torre dei Corsari. Tel: 962104

ASSEMINI (070)

Il Grillo ☆☆☆
Tel: 941147

Argentina ☆☆
Tel: 941228

BARUMINI (070)

Santa Lucia ☆☆
Tel: 9368064

CALASETTA (0781)

Stella Del Sud ☆☆☆
Località Spiaggia Grande. Tel: 88488

FJBY ☆☆
Tel: 88444

Bellavista ☆
Località Sottotorre. Tel: 88211

CARBÓNIA (0781)

Centrale ☆☆☆
Tel: 62202

Sardegna ☆
Tel: 674004

CARLOFORTE (0781)

Hieracon ☆☆☆
Tel: 854028

Riviera ☆☆☆
Tel: 854004

Paola ☆☆
Località Tacca Rossa. Tel: 850898

GIBA (0781)

Rosella ☆☆
Tel: 964029

IGLÉSIAS (0781)

Artu ☆☆☆
Tel: 22492

Pan Di Zucchero ☆☆
Tel: 47114

MURAVERA (070)

Colostrai ☆☆
Località Colostrai. Tel: 9930496

Corallo ☆☆
Tel: 9930502

Free Beach Club ☆☆
Località Costa Rei (20 May–1 October). Tel: 991041

Stella D'Oro ☆
Tel: 9930445

Torre Salina ☆
Località Torre Salina (15 June–15 September). Tel: 9930658

PORTOSCUSO (0781)

Panorama ☆☆☆
Tel: 508077

Costa Del Sole ☆☆
Tel: 508123

Mistral ☆☆
Tel: 509230

S'Alegusta ☆☆
Tel: 509017

PULA (070)

Abamar ☆☆☆☆
Località S. Margherita (15 May–30 September). Tel: 921555

Castello ☆☆☆☆
Località S. Margherita (15 April–25 October). Tel: 92171

Flamingo ☆☆☆☆
Località S. Margherita (6 May–15 October).
Tel: 9208361

Is Morus ☆☆☆☆
Località S. Margherita (25 March–23 October). Tel: 921424

Is Molas Golf Hotel ☆☆☆
Località Is Molas. Tel: 9209457

Forte Viliage ☆☆☆
 Tel: 92171

Mare E Pineta ☆☆☆
Località S. Margherita (6 May–15 October).
Tel: 9209407

Sandalyon ☆☆
Tel: 9209151

Eleonora ☆
Tel: 9209691

Quattro Mori ☆
Tel: 9209124

Su Guventeddu ☆
Località Nora. Tel: 9209092

Costa Degli Angeli Park Hotel ☆☆☆☆
Località Santa Lucia. Tel: 805445

Califfo ☆☆☆
Località Foxi. Tel: 890131

Diran ☆☆☆
Tel: 815271

Setar ☆☆
Località S'Oru e Mari. Tel: 890001

SANLURI (070)

Mirage ☆☆
Tel: 9307100

Motel Ichnusa ☆☆
S.S. 131, Km. 42, 4. Tel: 9370404

ISOLA SANT'ANTIOCO (0781)

I Ciclopi ☆☆☆
Località Mercury (15 May–20 September).
Tel: 800087

La Fazenda ☆☆
Località Capo Sperone. Tel: 83477

Maladroxia ☆☆
Località Maladroxia (June–September). Tel:
82611

Moderno ☆☆
Tel: 83105

Firenze ☆
Tel: 83010

Scala Longa ☆
Tel: 99626

Elisabeth ☆☆
Tel: 99626

SARDARA (070)

Delle Terme ☆☆☆
Località S. Maria (7 May–26 November).
Tel: 9387200

SINNAI (070)

Residence Abbablu ☆☆☆
Località Solanas (29 May–September). Tel:
750662

VILLASIMIUS (070)

Capo Boi ☆☆☆☆
Località Capo Boi (13 May–September).
Tel: 791515

Altura ☆☆☆
(April–October). Tel: 791168

Cormoran
Località Foxi (20 May–l October). Tel:
791401

L'Oleandro ☆☆☆
Località Minnai. Tel: 791539

Simius Playa ☆☆☆
(30 March–October), Tel: 791227

Le Dune ☆☆☆
Località Simius. Tel: 791681

Tanka ☆☆☆
(27 May–29 September). Tel: 797002

Aldebaran Yachting Club
Località Cala Caterina. Tel: 791272

Stella D'Oro ☆
Tel: 791255

ORISTANO PROVINCE

ORISTANO (0783)

Mistral ☆☆☆☆
Via Martiri di Belfiore, l. Tel: 212505

Amsycora ☆☆☆
Via S. Martino, 3. Tel: 72503

Ca-Ma ☆☆☆
Via Veneto, 119. Tel: 74374

I.S.A. ☆☆☆
Piazza Mariano, 50. Tel: 78040

Piccolo Hotel ☆☆
Via Martignano, 19. Tel: 71500

ORIST. MARINA TORRE GRANDE (0783)

Del Sole ☆☆☆
Tel: 22000

ARBOREA (0783)

Ala Birdi Vacanze ☆☆☆
Strada n. 24. Tel: 8801083

Il Cannetto ☆☆
Strada n. 26. Tel: 800561

Il Pavone
Strada n. 14. Tel: 800358

Gallo Bianco ☆
Tel: 800241

CABRAS (0783)

El Sombrero ☆☆
Tel: 290659

Summertime ☆☆
Tel: 290837

Casas ☆
Tel: 290871

CUGLIERI (0785)

Desogos ☆☆
Tel: 39660

ESIT La Scogliera ☆☆
Tel: 38231

La Baja ☆☆☆
Tel: 38105

Columbaris ☆
Tel: 38092

GHILARZA (0785)

Su Cantaru ☆☆
Tel: 54523

TRESNURAGHES (0785)

Piccolo Hotel Alabe ☆☆☆
Tel: 35056

I Cedri ☆
Tel: 35125

NUORO PROVINCE

NUORO (0784)

Grazia Deledda ☆☆☆☆
Via Lamarmora. Tel: 31257

Fratelli Sacchi ☆☆☆
Loc. Monte Ortobene. Tel: 31200

Grillo ☆☆☆
Via Mons. Melas, 14. Tel: 38678

Motel Agip ☆☆☆
Viale Trieste. Tel: 34071

Paradiso ☆☆☆
Via Aosta. Tel: 835585

Sandalia ☆☆☆
Via Einaudi. Tel: 38353

Da Giovanni ☆☆
Via IV Novembre, 7. Tel: 30562

Il Portico ☆☆
Via Mannu. Tel: 37535

Mini Hotel ☆☆
Via Brofferio. Tel: 33159

ARITZO (0784)

Sa Muvara ☆☆☆
Via funtana Rubia. Tel: 629336

Castello ☆☆
Corso Umberto, 169. Tel: 629266

La Capannina ☆☆
Via Kennedy. Tel: 629121

BARISARDO (0782)

Il Cantuccio ☆☆☆
Via Mare. Tel: 29653

La Torre ☆☆
Via Mare. Tel: 29577

Nuraghe Kortiakas ☆☆
Via Mare. Tel: 29658

Il Fico ☆
Via Mare (15 May–15 Ocotber). Tel: 29377

Mirella ☆
Corso Vitt. Emanuele, 129. Tel: 29638

BAUNEI (0782)

Santa Maria ☆☆
Via Plammas. Tel: 615026

Agugliastra ☆
Via Lungomare, 28. Tel: 615005

BOSA (0785)

Al Gabbiano ☆☆☆
Viale Mediterraneo. Tel: 374123

Perry Clan ☆☆
Via Alghero. Tel: 373074

Pirino ☆☆
Viale Colombo, 13. Tel: 373586

Turas ☆☆
Loc. Turas. Tel: 373473

Bassu ☆
Via G. Deledda 15. Tel: 373456

Fiori ☆
Viale Marconi. Tel: 373011

Miramare ☆
Via Colombo. Tel: 373400

Sa Pischedda ☆
Via Roma. Tel: 373065

BUDONI (0784)

Agrustos ☆☆☆
Fraz. Agrustos. Tel: 846005

Club Don Hotels ☆☆☆
S.S. 125 Orientale Sarda. Tel: 837013

Eurovillage ☆☆☆
Fraz. Agrustos. Tel: 846020

Isabella ☆☆☆
Via Nazionale. Tel: 844048

Li Cucutti ☆☆☆
Fraz. Agrustos. Tel: 846001

Malamuri ☆☆☆
RTA. Tel: 846007

Marina Seada ☆☆☆
S.S. 125 Orient. S. (15 May–15 October).
Tel: 844165

Porto Ainu ☆☆☆
Loc. Tanaunella 8. Tel: 837059

La Conciglia ☆☆
Loc. Ottiolu (30 March–30 October). Tel:
846187

Pedra Niedda ☆☆
Via Porto Ainu. Tel: 83716

Solemar ☆☆
Via Nazionale. Tel: 844081

Da Giovanni ☆
Via Nazionale. Tel: 844037

DESULO (0784)

Gennargentu ☆☆☆
Via Kennedy. Tel: 61270

Lamarmora ☆☆☆
Via Lamarmora c. Tel: 61126

DORGALI (0784)

S'Adde ☆☆☆
Via Concordia. Tel: 94412

Querceto ☆☆
Via Lamarmora. Tel: 96509

San Pietro ☆
Via Lamarmora. Tel: 96142

DORGALI-CALA GONONE (0784)

Costa Dorada ☆☆☆
Via Lungomare. Tel: 93333

Nettuno ☆☆☆
Via Vasco Da Gama (15 April–30 October).
Tel: 93310

Pop ☆☆☆
Via M. Polo. Tel: 93185

Villaggio Palmasera ☆☆☆
Viale Bue Marino. Tel: 93191

Mastino "Delle Grazie" ☆☆☆
Via Colombo (20 March–10 October). Tel:
93150

Cala Luna ☆☆
Via Lungomare. Tel: 93133

La Favorita ☆☆
Via Lungomare (l March–30 October). Tel:
93169

La Playa ☆☆
Via Collodi. Tel: 93106

L'Oasi ☆☆
Via G. Lorca (15 April–5 October). Tel:
93111

Miramare ☆☆
Piazza Nettuno. Tel: 93140

Bue Marino ☆
Via Vespucci. Tel: 93130

Gabbiano ☆
Piazza Porto. Tel: 93021

La Ginestra ☆
Via Gustui. Tel: 93127

Piccolo Hotel ☆
Via Colombo. Tel: 93232

GAVOI (0784)

Taloro ☆☆☆
Loc. Ponte Aratu. Tel: 57174

Gusana ☆☆
Loc. Gusana. Tel: 53000

Sa Valasa ☆☆
Loc. Sa Valasa. Tel: 53423

LACONI (0782)

Sardegna ☆☆
Corso Garibaldi. Tel: 869033

LANUSEI (0782)

Villa Selene ☆☆☆
Loc. Coroddis. Tel: 42471

Belvedere ☆
Corso Umberto. Tel: 42184

LOTZORAI (0782)

Venezia ☆☆
Via Dante. Tel: 669459

Mediterraneo ☆☆
Lungomare. Tel: 669544

Stella Del Mare ☆☆
Lungomare. Tel: 669510

MACOMER (0785)

Motel Agip ☆☆☆
Corso Umberto. Tel: 71066

Su Talleri ☆☆☆
Via Cavour. Tel: 71491

Marghine ☆☆
Via Vittorio Emanuele. Tel: 70737

Nuraghe ☆☆
Via Ariosto. Tel: 70139

OLIENA (0784)

C.K. ☆☆☆
Via Luther King. Tel: 288733

Su Gologone ☆☆☆
Km. 8 da Oliena. Tel: 287512

ORGOSOLO (0784)

Sa 'E Jana ☆☆
Via E. Lussu. Tel: 402437

Ai Monti Del Gennargentu ☆
Loc. Settiles. Tel: 402374

OROSEI (0784)

Maria Rosaria ☆☆☆
Via G. Deledda 8. Tel: 98657

Su Barchile ☆☆☆
Via Mannu. Tel: 98879

Tirreno ☆☆☆
Tel: 91007

Cala Ginepro ☆☆☆
Loc. Cala Ginepro. Tel: 91047

OTTANA (0784)

Funtana 'E Donne ☆☆
S.S. Carlo Felice Nord. Tel: 75432

POSADA (0782)

Sa Rocca ☆☆☆
Via E. d'Arborea. Tel: 8542139

Donatella ☆☆☆
Via Gramsci. Tel: 854145

Fior Di Sardegna ☆☆☆
Loc. S. Giovanni. Tel: 810389

SAN TEODORO (0782)

Due Lune ☆☆☆☆
Loc. Punta Aldia. Tel: 864075

Hotel Bungalow ☆☆☆
Loc. Cala d'Ambra. Tel: 865786

Clamys ☆☆☆
Via Sardegna. Tel: 865230

Le Mimose ☆☆☆
Via Nazionale. Tel: 865763

Onda Marina ☆☆☆
Via del Tirreno. Tel: 865788

Sandalion ☆☆☆
Via del Tirreno. Tel: 865753

San Teodoro ☆☆☆
Loc. Badualga. Tel: 865687

Scintilla ☆☆☆
Via del Tirreno. Tel: 865519

Al Faro ☆☆
Via del Tirreno. Tel: 865665

L'Esagono ☆☆
Loc. Cala d'Ambra. Tel: 865783

La Palma ☆☆
Via del Tirreno. Tel: 865962

SINISCOLA (0784)

L'Aragosta ☆☆☆
Via Monte Longu. Tel: 810129

La Caletta ☆☆☆
Via Cagliari. Tel: 810077

Villa Pozzi ☆☆☆
Via Cagliari (1 April–10 October). Tel: 810076

L'Ancora ☆☆
Via N. Sauro. Tel: 810172

Meloni Fresu ☆☆
Via N. Sauro. Tel: 810063

Montalbo ☆☆
Via Gramsci. Tel: 878548

TORTOLI (0782)

Victoria ☆☆☆
Via Mons. Virgilio. Tel: 623457

Il Giardino ☆☆
Viale Umberto. Tel: 623145

Splendor ☆☆
Viale Arbatax. Tel: 623037

Sole ☆
Via Mons. Virgilio. Tel: 623115

TORTOLÌ-ARBATAX (0782)

Cala Moresca ☆☆☆
Loc. Cala Moresca. Tel: 667366

La Bitta ☆☆☆
Loc. Porto Frailis. Tel: 667080

Monte Turri ☆☆☆
Loc. Monte Turri. Tel: 667500

Villaggio Saraceno ☆☆☆
Loc. San Gemiliano. Tel: 667318

Villaggio Telis ☆☆☆
Loc. Porto Frailis. Tel: 667081

Speranza ☆
Via Napoli. Tel: 667248

Supersonic ☆
Loc. Porto Frailis. Tel: 623512

SASSARI PROVINCE

SASSARI (079)

Grazia Deledda ☆☆☆☆
Viale Dante, 47. Tel: 271235

Frank Hotel ☆☆☆
Via Diaz, 20. Tel: 276456

Leonardo Da Vinci ☆☆☆
Via Roma 79. Tel: 280744

Marini Due ☆☆☆
Via Chironi. Tel: 277282

Motel Agip ☆☆☆
Via Carlo Felice, 43. Tel: 271440

Giusy ☆☆
Piazza Sant'Antonio, 21. Tel: 233327

Gallura ☆
Vicolo S. Leonardo, 9. Tel: 238713

Famiglia ☆
Viale Umberto, 65. Tel: 239543

Rosita ☆
Via Pigliaru, 10. Tel: 241325

Hotel Marini ☆☆☆
Tel: 20716

ALGHERO (079)

Villa Las Tronas ☆☆☆☆
Lungomare Valencia. Tel: 975390

Calabona ☆☆☆
Località Calabona. Tel: 975728

Carlos V ☆☆☆
Lungomare Valencia, 24. Tel: 979501

Continental ☆☆☆
Via F.lli Kennedy, 66. Tel: 975250

El Balear ☆☆☆
Lungomare Dante, 32. Tel: 975229

Florida ☆☆☆
Via Lido, 15. Tel: 950500

Gran Catalunya ☆☆☆
Via Catalogna. Tel: 953172

Il Gabbiano ☆☆☆
Via Garibaldi, 97. Tel: 950407

La Margherita ☆☆☆
Via Sassari, 70. Tel: 979006

La Playa ☆☆☆
Via Pantelleria, 14. Tel: 950369

Mediterraneo ☆☆☆
Via F.lli Kennedy, 67. Tel: 979201

Mistral ☆☆☆
Via Liguria, 41. Tel: 951828

Oasis ☆☆☆
Viale 1° Maggio. Tel: 950518

Riviera ☆☆☆
Via F.lli Cervi, 6. Tel: 951230

San Marco ☆☆☆
Via Lido, 57. Tel: 951113

Soleado ☆☆☆
Via Lido, 17. Tel: 953399

Tarragona ☆☆☆
Via Gallura, 13. Tel: 952270

Villa Las Tronas (Dipendenza) ☆☆☆
Lungomare Valencia 1. Tel: 979227

Coral ☆☆
Via Kennedy, 64. Tel: 979345

Eleonora ☆☆
Piazzale Elrò, 14. Tel: 979236

Eliton ☆☆
Via Garibaldi. Tel: 952230

Internazionale ☆☆
Via don Minzoni, 126. Tel: 951208

Miramare ☆☆
Via Leopardi, 15. Tel: 979350

San Francesco ☆☆
Via Machin, 2. Tel: 979258

San Giuan ☆☆
Via Angioy, 2. Tel: 951222

Locanda Catalana
Via Catalogna, 5. Tel: 952440

ALGHERO-FERTILIA (079)

Bellavista ☆☆☆
Tel: 930124

Dei Pini ☆☆☆
Loc. Le Bombarde. Tel: 930157

Hotel Fertilla ☆☆☆
Tel: 930098

Punta Negra ☆☆☆
Tel: 930222

ALGHERO-PORTO CONTE (079)

Baja Di Conte ☆☆☆☆
Tel: 952003

El Faro ☆☆☆☆
Tel: 942010

Capo Caccia ☆☆☆
Tel: 946542

Corte Rosada ☆☆☆
Tel: 942038

Porto Conte ☆☆☆
Tel: 942036

ARZACHENA (0789)

Casa Mia ☆☆
Tel: 82790

Citti ☆☆
Tel: 82662

ARZACHENA-BAJA SARDINIA (0789)

Club Hotel ☆☆☆☆
Tel: 99006

Cormorano ☆☆☆
Tel: 99020

Delle Vigne ☆☆☆
Tel: 99411

La Bisaccia ☆☆☆ ,
Tel: 99002

La Bisaccia (Dipendenza) ☆☆☆
Tel: 99002

Mon Repos Hermitage ☆☆☆
Tel: 99011

RTA I Cormorani ☆☆☆
Tel: 99116

Olimpia ☆☆☆
Tel: 99176

Punta Est ☆☆☆
Tel: 99028

Residence Park ☆☆☆
Tel: 99016

Ringo ☆☆☆
Tel: 99024

RTA Pineta Uno ☆☆☆
Tel: 99235

Smeraldo Beach ☆☆☆
Tel: 99046

Tre Botti ☆☆☆
Tel: 99150

Villaggio Forte Cappellini ☆☆☆
Tel: 99051; 02/66981359

Villa Gemella ☆☆☆
Tel: 99303

ARZACHENA-CANNIGIONE (0789)

Baja ☆☆☆
Tel: 88010

Hotel Del Porto ☆☆☆
Tel: 88011

Laconia ☆☆☆
Tel: 86007

Li Capanni ☆☆☆
Tel: 86041

ARZACHENA-COSTA SMERALDA (0789)

Cala Di Volpe ☆☆☆☆☆ Luxe
Tel: 96083

Pitrizza ☆☆☆☆☆ Luxe
Tel: 91500

Romazzino ☆☆☆☆☆ Luxe
Tel: 96020

Cervo ☆☆☆☆☆
Tel: 92003

Cervo Tennis Club ☆☆☆☆
Tel: 92244

Le Ginestre ☆☆☆☆
Tel: 92030

Luci Di La Muntagna ☆☆☆☆
Tel: 92051

Balocco ☆☆☆
Tel: 91555

Capriccioli ☆☆☆
Tel: 96004

Le Magnolie ☆☆☆
Tel: 91723

Liscia Di Vacca ☆☆☆
Tel: 91560

Nibaru ☆☆☆
Tel: 96038

Valdiola ☆☆☆
Tel: 96215

Residenza Capriccioli ☆☆☆
Tel: 96016

ARZACHENA-TANCA MANNA (0789)

RTA Tanca Manna Service ☆☆☆
Tel: 86030

RTA Tanca Manna Vacanze ☆☆☆
Tel: 86043

ARZACHENA-TELZITTA (0789)

Grazia Deledda ☆☆☆☆
Tel: 98988

CASTELSARDO (079)

Baja Ostina ☆☆☆
Tel: 470223

Castello ☆☆☆
Tel: 470062

Hotel Costa Doria ☆☆☆
Tel: 474043

Pedra Ladda ☆☆☆
Tel: 470484

Riviera ☆☆☆
Tel: 470143

Ampurias ☆☆
Tel: 474008

Cinzia ☆☆
Tel: 47013

La Marina ☆☆
Tel: 470137

Pinna ☆☆
Tel: 470168

GOLFO ARANCI (079)

Baja Caddinas ☆☆☆
Tel: 46898

Castello ☆☆☆
Tel: 46073

Gabbiano Azzurro ☆☆☆
Tel: 46929

Margherita ☆☆☆
Tel: 46906

King's ☆☆
Tel: 46075

ISOLA LA MADDALENA (0789)

Cala Lunga ☆☆☆
Tel: 737389

Excelsior ☆☆☆
Tel: 737020

Giuseppe Garibaldi ☆☆☆
Tel: 737314

Nido O'Aquila ☆☆☆
Tel: 722130

Villa Marina ☆☆☆
Tel: 738340

Arcipelago ☆☆
Tel: 727328

Esit Il Gabbiano ☆☆
Tel: 737007

Hotel Villaggio Valtur S. Stefano ☆☆
Tel: 737061

Da Raffaele ☆
Tel: 738759

OLBIA (079)

President ☆☆☆☆
Via Principe Umberto, 9. Tel: 21551

Savoia ☆☆☆☆
Località Poltu Quadu. Tel: 69645

De Plam ☆☆☆
Via De Filippi, 43. Tel: 25777

Mediterraneo ☆☆☆
Via Montello, 3. Tel: 24173

Royal ☆☆☆
Via A. Moro. Tel: 50253

Centrale ☆☆
Corso Umberto, 85. Tel: 23017

Gallura ☆☆
Corso Umberto, 145. Tel: 24648

Minerva ☆☆
Via Mazzini, 6. Tel: 21 190

Motel Olbia ☆☆
Via A. Moro, 40. Tel: 51456

Mastino ☆
Via Vespucci, 5. Tel: 21320

Terranova ☆
Via Garibaldi, 3. Tel: 22395

OLBIA-PITTULONGU (0789)

Il Pellicano ☆☆☆
Tel: 39007

Mare Bleu ☆☆☆
Tel: 39001

Pozzo Sacro ☆☆☆
Tel: 21033

Sporting Hotel E Residence Palumbalza
☆☆☆
Tel: 32005

Abbaruia ☆☆
Tel: 39012

Tavolara ☆☆
Tel: 39044

OZIERI (079)

Mastino ☆☆☆
Tel: 787041

PALAU (0789)

Capo D'Orso ☆☆☆☆
Tel: 708100

Del Molo ☆☆☆
Tel: 708042

Excelsior Vanna ☆☆☆
Tel: 709589

La Roccia ☆☆☆
Tel: 709528

Piccada ☆☆☆
Tel: 709344

Villaggio Altura ☆☆☆
Tel: 709655

Serra ☆☆
Tel: 709519

PERFUGAS (079)

Domo De Janas ☆☆☆
Tel: 564007

PLATAMONA (079)

Bello Horizonte ☆☆☆
Tel: 367045

Del Golfo ☆☆☆
Tel: 310319

Pineta Beach ☆☆☆
Tel: 310224

Toluca ☆☆☆
Tel: 310234

RTA Pineta Beach (Bungalow) ☆☆
Tel: 310224

Maristella ☆
Tel: 310407

Tonnara ☆
Tel: 367001

PLOAGHE (079)

Da Nico E Lello ☆
Tel: 449803

PORTO ROTONDO (0789)

Relais Sporting ☆☆☆☆☆
Tel: 34005

San Marco ☆☆☆☆
Tel: 34108

Aldia Manna ☆☆☆
Tel: 35453

Nuraghe ☆☆☆
Tel: 34436

PORTO SAN PAOLO (079)

San Paolo ☆☆☆
Tel: 40001

Franciscu ☆☆
Tel: 40021

PORTO TORRES (079)

La Casa ☆☆☆
Tel: 14288

Libissonis ☆☆☆
Tel: 501613

Torres ☆☆☆
Tel: 501604

Da Elisa ☆☆
Tel: 514872

Royal ☆
Tel: 502278

S. TERESA DI GALLURA (0789)

Shardana ☆☆☆☆
Loc. S. Reparata. Tel: 754031

Bacchus ☆☆☆
Tel: 754556

Belvedere ☆☆☆
Tel: 754160

Capo Testa E Dei Due Mari ☆☆☆
Tel: 754333

Corallaro ☆☆☆
Tel: 754341

Esit Miramare ☆☆☆
Tel: 754103

Large Hotel Mirage ☆☆☆
Tel: 754207

Li Nibbari ☆☆☆
Tel: 754453

Moresco ☆☆☆
Tel: 754188

Sa Domo ☆☆☆
Tel: 754081

Tibula ☆☆☆
Tel: 754244

Al Porto ☆☆
Tel: 754154

Arduino ☆☆
Tel: 752002

Bellavista ☆☆
Tel: 754162

Canne Al Vento ☆☆
Tel: 754219

Conca Verde ☆☆
Tel: 750009

Da Cecco ☆☆
Tel: 754220

Hotel Villagio S. Teresa ☆☆
Tel: 751520

Marinaro ☆☆
Tel: 754112

Moderno ☆☆
Tel: 754233

Quattro Mori ☆☆
Tel: 754176

Sandalion ☆☆
Tel: 754541

Smeraldo ☆☆
Tel: 754175

Sole E Mare ☆☆
Tel: 754224

Bocche Di Bonifacio ☆
Tel: 754202

Da Colomba ☆
Tel: 754272

Esit Miramare (Dipendenza) ☆
Tel: 754103

Porto Pozzo ☆
Tel: 752124

Riva ☆
Tel: 754283

Scano ☆
Tel: 754447

SORSO (079)

Degli Ulivi ☆☆☆
Tel: 350479

Romangia ☆
Tel: 350236

STINTINO (079)

Ancora Residence ☆☆☆
Tel: 527085

Cala Reale ☆☆☆
Tel: 523127

Cala Regina ☆☆☆
Tel: 523126

Geranio Rosso ☆☆☆
Tel: 523292

Hotel Sporting ☆☆☆
Tel: 527187

La Pelosetta ☆☆☆
Tel: 527188

Rocca Ruja ☆☆☆
Tel: 527038

I Velici ☆☆
Tel: 523232

Lina ☆☆
Tel: 523071

Silvestrino ☆
Tel: 523007

TEMPIO PAUSANIA (079)

Delle Sorgenti ☆☆☆
Tel: 630033

Petit Hotel ☆☆☆
Tel: 631134

San Carlo ☆☆
Tel: 630697

Bassacutena ☆
Tel: 659621

COSTA PARADISO (079)

Li Rosi Marini ☆☆☆
Tel: 689731

Da Comita ☆☆
Tel: 689701

ISOLA ROSSA (079)

Corallo ☆☆☆
Tel: 694055

Vitty ☆☆☆
Tel: 694005

Meditterraneo ☆☆
Tel: 689801

Hermitage ☆☆
Tel: 681148

VALLEDORIA (079)

Cogas ☆☆
Tel: 582068

Sole E Mare ☆☆
Tel: 584031

La Vela ☆☆
Tel: 584097

Anglona ☆☆☆
Tel: 582143

Baja Verde ☆☆☆
Tel: 582290

FARM HOLIDAYS

Spending a week or two on a Sardinian farm is another holiday alternative. For information regarding **Agriturismo** in various provinces, contact:

Cooperativa Allevatrici Sarde
Località Sta. Lucia, 09070 Zeddiani (OR).
Tel: 0783 418066

In Gallura
Cooperativa Agrituristica Gallurese
Tenuta Valentino, 07023 Calangianus (SS).
Tel: 079 630181

In the area of Alghero
Cooperativa Dulcamara
Via Sassari, 07041 Alghero (SS). Tel: 079 979153 and 975092

CAMPING

Nearly all larger tourist and beach areas have camp sites, as a rule open from May until October. Further information is available in camping guides, purchased either in your own country or on Sardinia.

YOUTH HOSTELS

There are only three youth hostels on Sardinia. These are:

Alghero-Fertilia (SA)
Dei Guliani. Tel: 079 930015

Arzachena-Cannigione (NU)
Ostello di Giovanni. Tel: 0789 82585

Oristano-Torregrande (OR)
Eleonora d'Arborea. Tel: 0783 22097

FOOD DIGEST

CUISINE

Contrary to popular opinion, Sardinia is by no means a culinary backwater. Traditional Sardinian cuisine is usually simple and more strongly influenced by the sheep than fishing industry. In view of this, traditional dishes include a lot of roast meat. However, the pasta dishes usually associated with Italian cuisine, as well as first-class fish dishes, can now be found just about everywhere.

RESTAURANTS

If you want to take a culinary tour of Sardinia, the following restaurants are 10 of the best:

La Lepanto
Alghero (SS), Via Carlo Alberto. Tel: 079 979116
Closed on Mondays

Grazia Deledda
Baia Sardinia (SS), Loc. Tiltizza. Tel: 079 98988
Closed from 1 November–31 March

Lo Scoglio
Cagliari (CA), Capo S.Elia, Loc. Calamosca. Tel: 070 3911727
Closed on Sundays

Sa Cardiga E Su Schirioni
Capoterra (CA), Statale nach Pula (SS195) Km 11. Tel: 070 71652 and 71613
Closed on Mondays

Dal Corsaro
Cagliari (CA), Viale Regina Margherita, 28. Tel: 070 370295
Closed on Tuesdays

Mistral
Isola La Maddalena (SS), Via Santo Stefano, 16. Tel: 0789 738088
Closed from 1 November–31 December and on Fridays

Su Gologone
Oliena (NU), Loc. Su Gologone. Tel: 0784 287512
Closed in February

Il Faro
Oristano(OR), Via Bellini, 26. Tel: 0783 7002
Closed on Sunday evenings and Mondays

Nino'
Olbia (SS), Loc. Pittulongu. Tel: 079 39027
Closed on Wednesdays

Da Gianni E Amedeo
Sassari (SS), Via Alghero 69. Tel: 079 274598
Closed in August and on Sundays

Other restaurants that can be recommended on the island are named below. They are listed under the towns and regions in which they are located.

CAGLIARI

Antica Hostaria
Via Cavour, 60. Tel: 070 665870
Closed in August and on Sundays

Italia
Via Sardegna, 30. Tel: 070 657987
Closed on Sundays

St.Remy
Via Torino, 16. Tel: 070 657377
Closed on Sundays

CAGLIARI PROVINCE

Tanit
Carbonia (CA)
Località Sirai. Tel: 0781 763793
Closed on Mondays

Da Nicolo
Carloforte (CA), Corso Cavour, 32. Tel: 0781 854048
Closed from 15 November–15 February and on Mondays

La Stella D'Oro
Villasimius (CA)
Tel: 791255

Il Gardino
Vico Mariano, 2. Tel: 0783 71309
Closed on Sundays

Il Pavino
Arborea (OR). Tel: 0783 800358
Closed on Mondays

Da Giovanni
Torre Grande (OR), Via Colombo, 8. Tel:
0783 22051
Closed on Mondays

NUORO PROVINCE

Il Trattore
Bosa (NU)

Fratelli Sacchi
Nuoro (NU), Loc. Monte Ortobene. Tel:
0784 312000

Sant'Elene
Dorgali (NU), Loc. Sant'Elene. Tel: 0784
95224
Closed on Fridays

SASSARI PROVINCE

L'Assasino
Sassari (SA), Vico Ospizio Cappuccini, 1.
Tel: 079 235041
Closed in August and on Sundays

Gallura
Olbia (SA), Corso Umberto. Tel: 0789 24648

Riviera da Fofo
Castelsardo (SA), Lungomare Angrone, 1.
Tel: 079 490143

SPECIALITIES

Cheese: One of the most important products on Sardinia is cheese. It is always worth the effort to go a bit out of your way in order to make a side trip to visit one of the cheese factories, for example in Dorgali or Macomer. If you think you can manage to consume an entire *pecorino*, go ahead and buy a slab from one of the shepherds standing by the side of the road. They often position themselves here to sell their wares directly to the consumer.

Bread: Among the various types of bread, *pane carasau* – also frequently referred to as *carta della musica* – is probably the best known. These round, paper-thin loaves traditionally eaten by shepherds can now be found in just about any restaurant. In addition to this particular kind of bread, there are allegedly over 300 other types produced on Sardinia, many of which are still baked privately by families today. The well-known "acorn bread", only baked on special occasions, is a speciality in many regions.

Dolci Sardi: Almonds or other nuts are the basic ingredient of the deliciously sweet and varied Sardinian confections you can find everywhere you go. The preparation of these sweet treats are usually the pride and joy of their respective bakeries. Nougat *torrone*, from Gennargentu is especially worth trying.

VINEYARDS

Over the past years the quality of different wines produced on Sardinia has improved so considerably that a visit to one or another of the *fattoria* is certainly well worth the effort. Included on the list of what are referred to as D.O.C. wines (wines that are produced with grapes grown in controlled areas of cultivation), are the following white wines:

Malvasia di Bosa, Malvasia di Cagliari, Moscato di Cagliari, Moscato di Sorso-Sennori, Moscato di Sardegna Spumante, Nasco di Cagliari, Trebbiano di Arborea, Nuragus di Cagliari, Vermentino di Gallura, Vernaccia di Oristano, Vermentino di Sardegna Spumante.

Included among the generally hearty and simple red D.O.C. wines are:

Campidano di Terralba, Cannonau di Sardegna, Carignano del Sulcis, Giro di Cagliari, Mandrolisai, Monica di Cagliari, Monica di Sardegna, Sangiovese di Arborea.

Wine cooperatives, for example the *Cantine Sociale Cooperative*, are located at the following places: Berchidda (SS), Dolianova (CA), Dorgali (NU), Ierzu (NU), Mogoro (OR), Monzi (SS), Oristano (OR), S. Antioco (CA), Sanluri (CA), Santadi (CA), Senorbo (CA), Sorso (SS), Tempio Pausania (SS), Terralba (OR), Cabras (OR), San Vero Milis (OR) and Aggius (SS). Each of these cooperatives produces D.O.C. wines.

Also worth the visit is a trip to the Cantina Golfo degli Angeli, Via Gallus, 79 Selargius (CA), to Sella & Mosca in Alghero, on the SS 291, across from Anghelu Ruju, and a quick peek at the smaller *fattorias* in Bosa and the surrounding area.

CULTURE PLUS

MUSEUMS

Sardinia is home to a number of interesting museums and exhibits, of which here only the most important are mentioned. Emphasis is naturally on the history of the island. There are often small museums displaying local finds situated at archaeological excavation sites.

Museo Archeologico Nazionale
Cagliari, Piazza Indipendenza

Cittadella dei Musei
Collezione d'Arte Orientale
Cagliari, Piazza Arsenale

Galleria Comunale d'Arte
Cagliari, Giardini Publici, Viale regina Elena

Museo Archeologico Sanna
Sassari, Via Roma, 64

Compendio Garibaldino
Isola Caprera

Museo Etnografico della vita e delle tradizioni popolari
Nuoro, Via Mereu, 56

Museo Dellediano
Nuoro, Via Grazia Deledda

Raccolta di instrumenti musicali di sardi
Tadasuni (OR), Via Adua, 7

Museo Archeologico navale "Nino Lamboglia"
Isola La Maddalena

SHOPPING

Giving good shopping tips with regards to Sardinia is difficult as it is almost impossible to escape the abundance of tacky "folk art" made from cork and wool. If you're looking for something really special, or for handicrafts of excellent quality, your best bet is lace from Bosa, or perhaps a shepherd's knife. As is the case everywhere, quality has its price and in this respect Italy never has been a country for great bargains.

Be careful to look closely when purchasing basketry, ceramics and carpets and make sure that these articles really do come from Sardinia, and not from Yugoslavia or Korea. Even when you're looking at coral from the coral city itself, Alghero, you can pretty much assume that it has been brought in from everywhere, not just from the coast a few hundred yards away. Examine what you're buying so you don't end up with some cheap, plastic imitation manufactured in the Far East! If you want to acquire merchandise without having to be quite so vigilant, go to ISOLA (Instituto Sardo Organizzazione Lavoro Artigano) shops, where you'll not only find prices fair, but also a commitment to high artistic quality. The main office of this organisation is located in Cagliari.

ISOLA

Cagliari
Via Baccaredda 176–78

Sassari
Padiglione dell'artigianato

Nuoro
Via Monsignor Bua 10

Alghero
Via Catalogna 54–56

Porto Cervo
Sottopiazzza

Oristano
Via Tirso.

SPORTS

PARTICIPANT SPORTS

Sardinia offers the visitor a wide range of athletic activities. Many hotels, holiday villages and campgrounds have their own private tennis courts or if not that, then at least tennis courts in parks in the vicinity. During the main tourist season you can participate in a wind-surfing course just about anywhere along the coast. Surfboards, smaller sailboats and motorboats are available for rent. Waters around the off-shore islands and the rocky segments of the coast offer snorkellers and scuba divers ideal conditions. All information pertaining to sports activities is easily obtainable locally, so just ask around.

GOLF

Sardinia is home to two of the most beautiful 18-hole golf courses in the world:

Pevero Golf Club
Porto Cervo (SS). Tel: 0789 96210

Is Molas Golf Club
Pula (CA). Tel: 070 9209165

HORSE-RIDING

Exploring Sardinia on horseback is becoming an increasingly popular way to see the island. Programmes encompass everything from half-day excursions to expeditions lasting several days to traversing the entire island. Information is available at local tourist agencies, at ESIT in Cagliari, or directly from the Riders' Association:

ANTE Sardegna
Cagliari, Via Pasteur 4. Tel: 070 305816

The following hotel specialises in horseback riding excursions:

Hotel Ala Birdi
Arborea (OR), Strada Mare, 24. Tel: 0783 800268

HIKING

Nuoro is a good point of departure for hiking in the Barbagia. The tourist agency E.P.T. (*Enti Provinciali per il Turismo*) has a map which describes 10 hiking routes in this area. Hikes through the heart of the Barbagia and in the Sopramonte regions are arranged in Oliena by :

Cooperativa Enis
Oliena (NU), Via Aspromonte, 8. Tel: 0784 287460

PHOTOGRAPHY

Sardinia is full of attractive subjects for photographers, especially in the spring, when the island is in full bloom and the usually parched fields are a luminous green. To be on the safe side, camera and film buffs should bring necessary materials with them. Professional photographers or amateurs with high standards are advised to develop colour print or slide films at home.

USEFUL ADDRESSES

TOURIST INFORMATION

You can get more explicit information when you arrive in Sardinia, or prior to your visit via post from any of the many flourishing tourist agencies. In addition to the ESIT (Ente Sardo Industrie Turistiche) tourist agency, which is responsible for all of Sardinia, information can be obtained from the EPT (Ente Provinciale per il Turismo) as well as from various local agencies (Azienda Autonoma Soggiorno E Turismo).

ESIT

Cagliari
09100 Via Mamelli, 97. Tel: 070 60231. Tlx: 790134

EPT

Cagliari
09100 – Piazza Deffenu, 9. Tel: 070 663207;

Ufficio Aeroporto Elmas. Tel: 070 240200;
Ufficio Stazione Marittima. Tel: 070 668352

Nuoro
08100 Piazza Italia, 19. Tel: 0784 30083

Oristano
09170 Via Cagliari, 276. Tel: 0783 74191

Sassari
07100 Piazza Italia, 19. Tel: 079 275395/ 230129

Azienda Autonoma Soggiorno E Turismo:

Alghero
07041 Piazza Portaterra 9. Tel: 079 97054

Arzachena
07021 Via Risorgimento. Tel: 0789 82624

Cagliari
09100 Via Mamelli 97. Tel: 070 664195;
Piazza Matteotti 9. Tel: 070 669255

La Maddalena – Palau
07024 Via XX Settembre 24. Tel: 0789 736321 (Maddalena);
07020 Via Nazionale 94. Tel: 0789 709570 (Palau)

Muravera
09043 Piazza Europa 5. Tel: 070 993760

Olbia
07026 Via Catello Piro 1. Tel: 0789 21453

S. Teresa
07028 Piazza Vittorio Emanuele 24. Tel: 0789 754127

Sassari
07100 Via Brigata Sassari 19. Tel: 079 233534

TOURIST OFFICES OVERSEAS

The Italian State Tourist Board has offices in most major capitals:

London
1 Princes Street, London W1R 8AY. Tel: (71) 4081254. Fax: (71) 4936695

Dublin
47 Merrion Square, Dublin 2. Tel: (1) 766397

Brussels
176 Av. Louise, Brussels 1050. Tel: (2) 6471154. Fax: (2) 6405603

Paris
23 Rue de la Paix, 75002 Paris. Tel: (1) 42660396. Fax: (1) 47421974

New York
630 Fifth Avenue, Suite 1565, New York, NY 10111. Tel: (212) 2454822. Fax: (212) 5869249

Montreal
1 Place Ville Marie, Montreal, Quebec. Tel: (514) 8667557. Fax: (514) 3921429

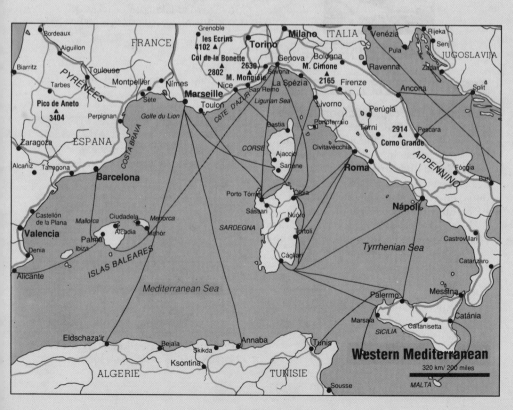

Western Mediterranean

320 km/ 200 miles

ART/PHOTO CREDITS

INDEX

D

E

F

G – H